A MARÉCHAL READER

JOSEPH MARÉCHAL, S.J.

A MARÉCHAL READER

Edited and Translated by
Joseph Donceel, S.J.

HERDER AND HERDER

1970
HERDER AND HERDER NEW YORK
232 Madison Avenue, New York, N.Y., 10016

ACKNOWLEDGMENTS

The following original editions of *Le Point de Départ de la Métaphysique* have been used in the preparation of this book: *Cahier I, De l'Antiquité à la fin du Moyen Age: La Critique Ancienne de la Connaissance,* second edition, 1927; *Cahier II, Le Conflit du Rationalisme et de l'Empirisme dans la Philosophie Moderne avant Kant,* third edition, 1944; *Cahier III, La Critique de Kant,* third edition, 1944; *Cahier V, Le Thomisme devant la Philosophie Critique,* second edition, 1949. All five volumes are published by Desclee de Brouwer, Paris, and L'édition Universelle, Brussels.

Extracts XLII-XLIII are excerpted from *Mélanges Joseph Maréchal,* volume 1, published by Desclee de Brouwer, Paris, 1950.

Acknowledgment is also made to: Benziger for its translation, by the Fathers of the English Dominican Province, of the *Summa Theologica,* New York, 1912-1917; Burns and Oates for its translation, by the Fathers of the English Dominican Province, of the *Summa contra Gentiles,* London, 1924-1929; and Regnery for its translation, by R. W. Mulligan, S.J., of *De Veritate,* Chicago, 1952-1953.

Contents

Introduction by Joseph Donceel, S.J.

THE STARTING POINT OF METAPHYSICS: LESSONS
ON THE HISTORICAL AND THEORETICAL
DEVELOPMENT OF THE PROBLEM OF KNOWLEDGE

CAHIER ONE
From Antiquity to the End of the Middle Ages:
The Critique of Knowledge

I.	Introduction: Object and Method (3–5)*	3
II.	The Necessity of Affirmation (32–36)	6
III.	The Aristotelian Solution: A Lessening of the Realism of the Understanding (66–68)	10
IV.	The Double Source of Antinomies Passed on to Modern Philosophy by Ockhamism (198–202)	12
V.	General Conclusions (203–208)	17

CAHIER TWO
The Conflict of Rationalism and Empiricism
in Modern Philosophy Before Kant

VI.	Introduction (9–11)	25
VII.	Descartes: Summary and Conclusions (75–78)	27
VIII.	Spinoza: Conclusions (123–128)	30
IX.	Leibniz: A Few Philosophical Consequences of His Dogmatism (144–149)	34

*The numbers in parentheses refer to pages in the original editions.

v

X. Hume: General Conclusion—Absolute Pheno-
    menalism and Scepticism. The Indirect Revenge
    of Metaphysics (239–242)   41
XI. General Conclusions (243–250)   44

CAHIER THREE
The Critique of Kant

XII. Introduction (9–11)   55
XIII. General Conclusions (305–308)   57

CAHIER FIVE
Thomism Confronting Critical Philosophy

XIV. Foreword (15–16)   65
XV. The Two Ways of the Critique of Knowledge
    (47–71)   66
XVI. Comparison of the Doubt of Aquinas with That
    of Descartes (83–84)   88
XVII. The Critical Problem: The Existence of Truth
    (86–87)   89
XVIII. The Absolute Posed in Every Application of
    the "First Principle" (92–99)   92
XIX. Analysis of Objective Knowledge (101–102)   97
XX. The Notion of Logical Truth (105–126)   98
XXI. The Elements of the Judgment (132–133)   115
XXII. The Object of Sense Knowledge (143–146)   116
XXIII. Formal Object and *A Priori* (156–158)   117
XXIV. Spatiality and Temporality as the Laws or
    Universal Rules of Sensation (170–178)   119
XXV. Relation of Agent Intellect to Phantasm in
    Terms of Formal and Efficient Causality
    (197–223)   125
XXVI. The Analogy of Intelligible Being (257–259)   144
XXVII. Abstraction (260–261)   146
XXVIII. Abstraction of the Transcendental Concepts
    (276–278)   147
XXIX. The Nature of Affirmation (310–315)   149
XXX. Deduction of the Ontological Affirmation
    (317–318)   153

XXXI.	The Actuality of the Object as the Measure of Affirmation (344–355)	154
XXXII.	Delimiting the Problem (357–361)	161
XXXIII.	The Dynamism of the Intellect (377–380)	163
XXXIV.	Reciprocal Relation of the First Acts of the Intellect and the Will (399–405)	166
XXXV.	Intellectual Dynamism and Supernatural End (412–424)	172
XXXVI.	Thomistic Exemplarism (432–437)	175
XXXVII.	Objectivation in Finality: Deduction of the Ontological Affirmation (439–468)	177
XXXVIII.	The Evidence of Form and the Evidence of Act (472–479)	198
XXXIX.	Synthesis and Consciousness (479–484)	203
XL.	Subjective or Objective Necessity (492–504)	207
XLI.	Thomistic Critique of Knowledge Transposed into the "Transcendental" Mode (515–561)	217

MÉLANGES JOSEPH MARÉCHAL

XLII.	Abstraction or Intuition (102–180)	235
XLIII.	On Intellectual Dynamism (75–101)	244

Introduction

Joseph Maréchal was born July 1, 1878, in Charleroi, an industrial town in southern Belgium. Upon finishing high school at the local Jesuit Collège du Sacré Coeur he was admitted into the Society of Jesus, on September 24, 1895. After two years of novitiate, he started his literary studies in the juniorate. At this time there was some doubt whether his recurrent headaches would ever allow him to complete the lengthy curriculum of the Jesuit order. He carried on nonetheless and made his first acquaintance with philosophy at the Louvain scholasticate in 1898. His three years of philosophical studies were spent under the uninspired guidance of a group of Jesuit teachers who indoctrinated him in the secondhand textbook Thomism prevailing in the Catholic seminaries of the day.

Having been informed by his superiors that he was destined to teach philosophy, he asked to spend, instead of the fourth year of philosophical studies planned for him, one year at Louvain University studying biology. This one year eventually turned into a four-year stretch, at the end of which he earned, brilliantly, a Ph.D. in biology. He retained the highest esteem for the sciences and in later life he would frequently advise future philosophy teachers to spend some time in the thorough study of one of them, so as to avoid, as he put it himself, the danger of " metaphysical autosuggestion."

Maréchal was ordained in 1908. He started teaching biology and experimental psychology at the Louvain scholasticate of the Society of Jesus in the fall of 1910. He spent the fall semester of 1911 doing graduate research in experimental psychology in various German universities, where he visited, among other pioneers, Wilhelm Wundt and Wolfgang Köhler. At the 1914 outbreak of World War I, his superior sent him, with a group of his Jesuit students, as a refugee to England. By then he was

teaching philosophy to his younger confrères, on whose behalf
he began to compose the *Cahiers*[1] of his *Le Point de Départ de
la Métaphysique*. After his return to German-occupied Belgium in the fall of 1915, he continued to work on the *Cahiers*
and on *Studies in the Psychology of the Mystics. Cahiers I, II*
and *III* were published in 1922-1923, and the famous *Cahier V*
appeared in 1926; *Cahier IV* was published posthumously.

   Cahier III was one of the first fair evaluations of the philosophy of Kant ever published by a Catholic author. It provoked
the suspicion and ire of some fellow Catholics, who began to
accuse Maréchal of being a Kantian. In order to show where he
agreed and where he disagreed with Kant, Maréchal decided to
put off the publication of *Cahier IV,* which was to treat the great
post-Kantian idealistic philosophers, and to bring out his *Cahier
V,* which was devoted to a comparison of Thomistic and Critical
Philosophy.

   These were hard and difficult years for original and creative
thinkers in the Catholic Church. Although the worst excesses of
" integrism " and the antimodernistic phobia were over, censorship remained harsh and new insights were discouraged,
especially in philosophy and theology. It took the Belgian
Jesuit sixteen long months of rewriting before *Cahier V* was
allowed to come out. Maréchal was heard to complain that
Cahier V had become bulky and involved because everyone
wanted to " contribute his stone to the monument." It was not
the book the author had wanted to write; it was the book he
had to write in order to squeeze through the narrow-minded
censorship of his time.

   Meanwhile he kept teaching various courses, reviewing many
books, reading and correcting manuscripts submitted to his
approval. His precarious health continued to deteriorate. After
the publication of *Cahier V* he resumed work on *Cahier IV.*
Many new publications had to be read and evaluated. With an
increasing workload, and failing health, Maréchal had a hard
time catching up with the steadily growing new literature on the
broad topic he intended to treat in this volume. At the start of

----

[1] *Cahier* is the French word for a " student's notebook." Maréchal,
who was modest to a fault, considered it a fitting name for the various
volumes of his great work.

World War II (1939) a fire destroyed the house where he was living and with it most of the notes he had accumulated during years of research. Although he bravely resumed work, he was unable to finish *Cahier IV* and *Cahier VI*, which was to study Contemporary Philosophy, remained a mere project. Maréchal died in Louvain on December 11, 1944, at the age of 66.

During his life, Maréchal's influence and reputation never quite matched the originality and depth of his thought. This imbalance can be explained quite simply. Failing health slowed down his work and cut him off from many useful contacts; stifling censorship forced him to show in endless detail that he was only saying with new words what the scholastic tradition had been saying before him. Finally, this great philosopher, recipient of the 1938 decennial *Prix de Philosophie* conferred by the Royal Academy of Belgium, spent his whole professional career teaching Jesuit undergraduate students. The neighboring Catholic University of Louvain, which boasted of a world-famous philosophy department, never thought it fitting to appoint him one of its professors. Maréchal himself considered this one of the most severe handicaps of his philosophical career.

Apart from his scientific interests and philosophic creativity, Father Maréchal was a master stylist of French prose and a keen connoisseur of the arts of painting and engraving. His impeccable courtesy and sharp sense of humor made conversation with him a delight. The man was also a saintly priest for whom the Absolute (of whom he wrote so profoundly in his books) was no mere abstraction, but rather a living and inspiring presence.

The purpose of this book is to give the English reading public a sample of Maréchal's work. Maréchal was one of the great pioneers of the neo-Thomistic revival at the beginning of our century. Recently, neo-Thomism has come upon hard times. The number of its adherents keeps shrinking, and even in the philosophy departments of Catholic universities and colleges it is steadily retreating before phenomenology, existentialism, linguistic analysis or a purely historical study of philosophy. One may bewail this demise of St. Thomas' philosophy as a typical feature of the universal breakdown of most real values, not only in the world at large, but also within the Church. Or one may—with more reason, it seems to me—consider the present decline of perennial philosophy as a stage in its own dialectical development, as the unavoidable enriching *antithesis* which had to follow upon its triumphal, possibly triumphalistic, *thesis* of the 1920's and 1930's.

Even many of its faithful followers are now willing to admit that neo-Thomism had serious shortcomings. To mention only the most important ones: insufficient attention to history and development, overlooking of the importance of the subject or Ego in philosophy and neglect of intersubjectivity.

A growing awareness of these undeniable weaknesses has turned some of St. Thomas' disciples, and many thinkers who started their philosophical career in his school, away from neo-Thomism. They are looking for greener pastures, deriving their inspiration from other modern or contemporary philosophical schools.

Might not these understandable reactions represent an *antithetical* stage in the dialectical development of the perennial philosophy? Should we not expect, in a not too far away future, a return to a richer, wider, more comprehensive Thomism, which will have dropped much useless ballast, and have grown more vividly aware of the far reaching implications of its own assumptions? To believe that perennial or Christian philosophy is definitely on the wane is to show little historical awareness. Every great philosophical system knows its ups and downs, its times of stability, expansion and popularity, and its periods of inner struggle, transformation and relative obscurity.

When—after the thesis of the early twentieth century and the present antithesis—the new synthesis of Thomism will come, it will not be the work of Maréchal alone; but it will owe him a great debt. By introducing the transcendental method into Thomistic philosophy, Maréchal saved it from the increasing danger of turning into some kind of dogmatic empiricism, and he made it more capable of holding its own before the philosophies of Kant and his many successors.

That is why the thinkers who wish or hope for a renascence of Christian philosophy, the theologians who begin again to feel the need for a real metaphysics and the philosophers who would like to contribute to the revival of Thomism may find it useful to become acquainted with some of the writings of this great

Belgian philosopher, the acknowledged leader of what is sometimes called *Transcendental Thomism.*

For more biographical details about Maréchal, the reader is
referred to the *Mélanges Joseph Maréchal,* vol. I, Part I. He
will also find there a complete bibliography of Maréchal's
publications, and of books, articles and reviews that treat of
Maréchal's philosophy.

The following books, published after 1950, may also be
consulted: Otto Muck, *The Transcendental Method* (New York,
1968); Sister Helen James John, *The Thomist Spectrum* (New
York, 1966); E. Dirven, *De La Forme à l'Acte* (Paris, 1965).
The latter has a bibliography of the later research on Maréchal.

Since Maréchal's *Studies in the Psychology of the Mystics* is
again available in English (Albany, 1964), the *Maréchal Reader*
will not include any of his publications in the field of Christian
mysticism or asceticism. Our choice will be restricted to four of
the five *Cahiers*; we will not consider the posthumous *Cahier IV,*
which contains writings from different periods of the author's
life. We include in the *Reader* a selection from the lectures
which were published in the *Mélanges Joseph Maréchal.*

The notes have been translated only as required for the
understanding of the main text. Maréchal quoted St. Thomas
extensively, especially in the second book of *Cahier V.* Some of
these quotations have here been replaced by mere references to
the work of Aquinas. The author frequently added emphasis to
these quotations without mentioning that the italics came not
from St. Thomas, but from himself. He also made frequent use
of capitals, which we have often replaced with lower case letters
in the translation.

The translator wishes to mention his indebtedness to Father
Léopold Malevez, S.J., for much useful advice.

Joseph Donceel, S.J.

CAHIER ONE

FROM ANTIQUITY
TO THE END OF THE MIDDLE AGES:

THE CRITIQUE OF KNOWLEDGE

We begin with a translation of an excerpt from the introduction to Cahier I. *The general title of the* Cahiers *is* Le Point de Départ de la Métaphysique—The Starting Point of Metaphysics. *Extract I explains the meaning of this title and the purpose of the* Cahiers.

I. INTRODUCTION: OBJECT AND METHOD

The General title of our *Cahiers* indicates their precise object.

We do not intend to examine the theory of knowledge in all its details, but to concentrate our effort upon the fundamental problem, whose solution prepares and even anticipates that of most secondary problems usually treated in epistemology and logic.

We might for the time being formulate this fundamental problem as follows: if metaphysics is possible, it must possess as its starting point an absolute, objective affirmation. Do we meet in our consciousness such an affirmation, surrounded by all the guarantees demanded by the most exacting critique?

Philosophers who do not profess scholasticism admit without difficulty that the metaphysical affirmation must be critically justified. They might even exaggerate the rights of such a critique.

On the other hand, among scholastic philosophers there are, even nowadays, some who reject the problem of knowledge formulated in such a radical way. We might say that they are both wrong and right.

On the one hand, their distrust derives from a misunderstanding of the real nature of the desired "critical justification." On the other hand, their rejection is ultimately based upon a principle whose truth we must admit. They take for granted—wrongly—that a critical demonstration consists in first shutting knowledge up within the circle of one's own subjective modifications, in order to proceed thence, if possible, to the knowledge of objects in themselves; they remark—rightly—that every inference from a pure representation, from a subjective form or phenomenon to a "thing in itself," external to the subject, is wholly illusory. For, even if we discover in ourselves an invincible tendency to project our immanent representations into the absolute of the object, such a tendency would, by itself

alone, provide in behalf of the " object in itself " nothing but a
" subjective and blind evidence." This is not enough as the basis
of a metaphysical affirmation. Hence, if our direct knowledge
does not at once reach the " object in itself," we remain strictly
confined within the subject as such, we are walled in within the
" relative," and no artifice of demonstration will enable us to
" throw a bridge " towards the outside and the absolute.

Hence we do not intend to reopen the misleading *quaestio de
ponte* (the problem of the bridge) which is dutifully rejected by
all the textbooks of scholastic logic. If we allow this question to
arise, we must also admit that we cannot answer it. If we reach
metaphysical truth, it will ultimately be in the light of an
immediate objective evidence.

But this does not settle the problem. Descartes, Spinoza and
Wolff admitted the criterion of immediate objective evidence.
Spinoza stated that, when I know a thing, I do not know it
through some previous knowledge of the idea of this thing;
objective knowledge is a direct knowledge of the object.

Yet the Cartesian criterion for evidence is quite different from
the one proposed by the majority of scholastics. The evidence
of the Cartesians falls apart under Kant's critique; the evidence
of the scholastics can—we will show—withstand the test. Hence
we must at least define more precisely what we mean by
" objective evidence " and by " immediate grasping of the
object."

On the other hand, there are quite a number of philosophers—
relativists and phenomenalists, leaning more or less towards
pragmatism—who would willingly give up the " absolute objective affirmation "; or at least, like Kant, they attribute to it,
within the domain of speculative reason, only the function of
coordinating the phenomenal objects: creation of an " ideal,"
and not, strictly speaking, revelation of a metempirical " object."
What is the use of denying before them the right of a critique
by waving before their eyes, like a scarecrow, their own banner:
the (speculative) inanity of the metaphysical object? They are
quite willing to become totally agnostic. Our weapon of objective
evidence is blunted against their agnostic epistemology.

Shall we then have to yield before phenomenalist relativism as
before an error which cannot be refuted in strict reason?

No scholastic philosopher will admit such a quasi-defeat. And every one of them will agree that, in order to refute phenomenalist agnosticism radically, it is not enough to oppose it to the instinctive tendency, to the " practical necessity " which forces us to make absolute affirmations. An error can be overcome only when we manage to show that it includes a contradiction; in other words, we can say that the metaphysical affirmation will victoriously maintain itself against relativism only if it can show that not only is it " morally " or " practically " necessary, but that it is also " theoretically " necessary.

But if we endeavor to establish such a necessity, that is, to show that rejecting or abstaining from the absolute affirmation of the object implies a logical contradiction, we are in fact accepting the critical problem in all its intensity.

Hence we do not see how scholastic philosophy itself could reject this subtle task, unless it is willing to lock itself up within the ivory tower of narrow dogmatism. Thus the following two questions should interest scholastics as much as they interest the philosophers from other schools:

(1) Since the absolute affirmation of the object, that is, the metaphysical affirmation, represents the natural attitude of the human mind, how did some philosophers reach the point where they demanded a critical justification of this primordial affirmation? In other words, how could the critical problem of knowledge originate?

(2) To what extent is such a justification possible? In other words, is there a solution to the critical problem of knowledge?
We will try to answer this double question.

The first two parts of Cahier I *are devoted to a study of the origins of philosophical thought in ancient Greece. Maréchal recalls for us the manner in which Greek philosophy proceeded from the old poetical cosmogonies to the first " cosmologies," how it met and was staggered by the basic antinomy of the One (Parmenides) and the Many (Heraclitus), how this antinomy led some thinkers to various forms of scepticism (the Sophists) and how Socrates, Plato and Aristotle reacted against this scepticism. He pays special attention to*

Aristotle's insistence on the necessity of the affirmation (Extract II), and ends the second part with a summary of the Aristotelian critique of knowledge (Extract III).

The third part of Cahier I *is devoted to a study of the antinomy of the One and the Many in medieval philosophy. Maréchal tries to show how the old problem was revived in the early Middle Ages, how it was solved through a wide and comprehensive synthesis in the philosophy of St. Thomas Aquinas and how the Thomistic synthesis was gradually undermined, if not by Duns Scotus himself, then at least by his followers.*

The fourth part tries to show how the decadence of Thomistic philosophy slowly led towards the modern conflict of rationalism and empiricism. It contains an exposé of Ockham's agnostic fideism and ends with a short study of the double source of antinomies which were passed on to modern philosophy by Ockham (Extract IV).

Extract V contains the general conclusions of Cahier I.

II. THE NECESSITY OF AFFIRMATION

What is the underlying weakness of every kind of real scepticism? . . . Aristotle has pointed it out with great accuracy: it is the sceptic's doubt about the " first principle," with its practical consequence, the *epochè.* In other words, it is the rejection of every affirmation.

If we take into account the latent or formal realism of ancient philosophy, that is, the identification which it practically admitted of the absolute nature of the affirmation with the absolute nature of the object, we understand without difficulty why the ancient refutations of scepticism are invariably restricted to two types:

(1) An effort is made to solve the apparent antinomies or contradictions which seemed to destroy the affirmation. Such was the method of Socrates: after having publicly humiliated the presumptuous " sophist " under the blows of his irony, he endeavors to heal the " sceptic " in the sophist by helping him correct his own generic and specific concepts. For, as a rule, contradiction will vanish when reason is brought back to the sober use of well defined concepts. Such was the method of

Plato and Aristotle; through a complete and coherent systematization of the great rational points of view, their metaphysics
tried to remove from human intelligence the very temptation of
capitulating before antinomies which had already been overcome.
Did they reach their purpose, *de facto* or even only *de jure*? At
least a way had been discovered for solving the critical problem :
the complete and systematic inventory of the formal object of
our intelligence. The question will come up whether this way is
adequate to the problem.

(2) The second kind of refutation tried to catch the sceptic in
open contradiction with himself. On one hand, he professes the
epochè and the ensuing suspension of volition. On the other
hand, he wills and fears a great number of things; but every
willing and striving on the rational level is an explicit or an
implicit affirmation. In other words, one shows that the sceptic
affirms, whatever he may say.

How valid is this way of reasoning? It certainly might have
good results in particular instances. If you solve all my reasons
for doubting, I shall succeed in getting rid of my doubt,
especially if you provide me with a comprehensive and indubitable system which protects me in advance against the scandal
of contradiction. But even if the coherence of my thought is
guaranteed, does this take away all possibility of doubting? I
have no reasons for doubting; but do I have any reasons for
affirming? May I not shut myself up in a negative doubt? We
have to admit that non-contradiction is by itself not sufficient to
overcome the initial inertia which would consist in a universal
negative doubt. But are these the terms of the problem? Do we
really encounter, at the starting point of metaphysics, an intelligence that is wholly passive, wholly indifferent to YES or NO,
some kind of reflecting surface whose only function is to notice
the right order of the images gliding over it? This basic question
will be answered only at the end of our critical investigation.

There remains a second way: ruthlessly to uncover the
affirmation in the sceptic himself. For the sceptic " wills," and
the affirmation cannot be avoided in the domain of willing, since
every volition implicitly or explicitly posits an end and a series of
means towards this end. True, this manner of refutation may
work when it shows me in a number of instances the practical

emptiness of my scepticism. But what if I apologize and if I withdraw one after the other all these partial volitions which had eluded my absentmindedness? As long as my opponent argues from particular ends, I may get away by giving up successively all these secondary ends in order to reach the safety of the *epochè*. I shall have to withdraw my doubt only if I am shown that my attitudes imply an end which is so universal, so inherent to myself, that I cannot deny it. But I really cling to no attitude, I commit myself to no determinable end. *I simply abstain.*

You will convince me only when you show me that to abstain from willing is to will, that "*nolle est velle.*" The typical sceptic of antiquity will be wholly refuted when we can show that he wills, hence that he affirms, not *although* he is a sceptic, but *because* he is a sceptic. For it can be shown that the sceptical attitude is essentially one of affirmation.

For that purpose it would be sufficient to bear in mind a simple fact of internal experience: abstaining from every judgment and from every volition, if indeed possible, would not be an attitude easy to assume or to sustain. It would imply a continuous repression of emerging velleities, a stiffening against steady solicitations. There is no gainsaying that our mind naturally tends to affirm, our will to translate affirmation into action. To withstand this inner and permanent impulsion is not the same as to yield to complete passivity, to an absolute lack of activity; it implies, rather, a strong reaction against oneself, deriving from a precise and firm decision: it means breaking the affirmative mood of the intellect by means of an affirmation which is even more basic and more ruthless. One wills to will nothing, and one affirms to oneself not only that one wills nothing, but even that it is better to will nothing. Concerning dilettantism and sceptical estheticism Maurice Blondel writes: " to know that one wills nothing means to will nothing. And ' I do not will to will, *nolo velle,*' may be immediately translated in the language of reflection, into these two words: ' *volo nolle, I* will not to will '. Unless we totally overlook the laws of consciousness, and conceal the true state of affairs under mere verbal subtleties, the very feeling of an absence of volition implies the idea of a will which does not will and which abdicates " (*L'Action,* Paris, 1893, p. 12).

Nature gives us our faculties in spontaneous exercise, in action. The *epochè* represents a violent holding in check which requires reflective and concentrated effort. This effort must be voluntary; hence it is the pursuit of an " end " which we adopt. What end? When we suspend our judgment in particular cases, it is not difficult to define the more universal and more attractive end in behalf of which we give up secondary or less attractive ends: all our rational cautions, prudence in affirming, hesitation in concluding, even partial scepticisms simply decrease the number of ends acknowledged by us. The *epoché* of universal scepticism is a monstrous attempt at suppressing finality itself. But this voluntary attempt needs a fulcrum and that is where reality takes its revenge: this fulcrum is necessarily one more " end," *any kind* of end which is set up not only as final end but as exclusive end. In its very claim of avoiding all dogmatism scepticism stands forth as the most shocking and most narrow dogmatism conceivable.

The sceptic affirms and wills. What does he will? Blondel has shown it in a very profound way: the sceptic who uses life and is unwilling to yield his intellect and his will has discovered the only manner of being wholly selfish—for every action, even the most selfish one, still implies some risk and a partial gift of oneself. " When the dilettante glides between the stone fingers of all idols, he does so because he accepts some other worship, self-worship: as he looks down on everything from the height of Sirius, everything seems so narrow and petty to him, every-thing except the love of one being, of *himself*. . . . Thus the very fact of not willing conceals a subjective end. Not to will anything means to refuse oneself to every object in order to keep oneself entirely to oneself, in order to reject every gift, every devotion and abnegation " (*L'Action,* p. 16).

Since we are not interested here in the moral aspect of scepticism, we shall rest satisfied with a more restricted conclu-sion, which seems to be abundantly justified: *the supreme effort of the human mind to keep away from affirming is one more affirmation. Hence affirmation is unavoidable.* This will do as a refutation of ancient scepticism, within the realism that it accepts.

III. THE ARISTOTELIAN SOLUTION:
A LESSENING OF THE REALISM
OF THE UNDERSTANDING

The whole Aristotelian critique of knowledge might be summarized as follows:

(1) *Every content of consciousness, by the very fact that it is ruled by the first principle, is referred to the absolute order of being :* a mere relativity of the contents of consciousness would contradict the first principle.

As for the first principle itself, it cannot be demonstrated objectively *in itself,* but its necessity can be solidly demonstrated *for every knowing subject* (whatever this subject's attitude may be towards the principle in question: acceptance, denial or doubt): " about such matters there is no proof in the full sense, though there is proof *ad hominem* " (*Metaphysics,* K, 1062 a, 2 and 30).[1] If we had not decided to avoid, at every stage, anticipating the later stages of philosophical evolution, we might translate this remark of Aristotle into the language of modern philosophy: " In its absolute sense the first principle cannot be demonstrated analytically, but it can be *demonstrated transcendentally.*" For it is really an attempt at a *transcendental proof* of the absolute affirmation which the Philosopher delineates in the passage that we have quoted.

(2) If every content of consciousness *is,* absolutely, to the extent it is identified with itself, that is, to the exact extent of its essence with all the relations implied by it, *the science of existence and the science of the essence are identical;* in other words, the logical or ideal order expresses the ontological order: hence " it belongs to the same kind of thinking to show what it is and that it is " (*Metaphysics,* E, 1025 b, 17; McKeon, p. 778). But this should be well understood.

(3) The *essences* (that is, the objective contents of thought), all of which we refer to the absolute order of *being,* and which we designate by the common name *beings (entia, onta), are multiple and varied, not only in their representative notes, but also in*

---

[1] R. McKeon, ed. and tr., *The Basic Works of Aristotle* (New York, The Modern Library, n.d.), p. 856. Further translations from this book will be cited as McKeon.

their relation to concrete existence; each one of them exists only according to the respective conditions belonging to it: although every one of them is connected in some way to a " subsistence," not every one of them is by itself and according to its representative notes, a " subsistence," an *" ousia."* Their degree of proximity to existence in itself, to " subsistence," may be gathered from the peculiar mode of their essence itself as it stands before our thought: thus one object of our thought assumes the reality of a substance, another of an accident, a third of a potency, still another of an act, or of a relation or of a becoming. In these objects our power of abstraction allows us to distinguish different aspects, each of which will really share *being* to the very extent to which it shares the totality from which we have abstracted it. This aspect will have the reality of an objective abstraction, of an " absolute nature," that one the purely relative reality which belongs to the " intentional mode," another one the reality which goes with a subjective activity and so on. In general, the task of determining this relation of the essences to the absolute order of being might be said to belong to logic; in the Aristotelian conception it belongs primarily and strictly speaking to metaphysics, to the " First Philosophy," as it organizes the various modes of being under the norm of the first principle.

Here are a few examples of Aristotle's application of this " metaphysical sorting " to the problem of existence. Let us suppose a simple essence which is fully in act. If as such it is present to my thought, I cannot err about it, I necessarily affirm its subsistence. For it can only possess one way of being thought and of being referred to the real order: "About the things, then, which are essences and actualities it is not possible to be in error, but only to know them or not to know them " (*Metaphysics,* TH, 1051 b; McKeon, p. 834). On the other hand, an essence which contains in any way whatsoever some indetermination, a certain amount of " potency," will be affirmed only according to the nature of this " potency "; if this potency is precisely an indetermination with respect to subsistence, it is evident that this essence will not be given the attribute of actual subsistence. This happens with the abstract universal and with the " second substances." This is the case especially with abstract

unity, with abstract being or entity (*to on*) and with everything
which, in the real objects, functions merely as an element or a
principle: " Evidently neither unity nor being can be the substance of things, just as being an element or a principle cannot
be the substance " (*Metaphysics*, Z, 1040 b, 18; McKeon, p. 809).

In short, reality in general belongs to all essences, but in
various ways and for various reasons, not necessarily by way of
proper subsistence; *being,* the formal object of our affirming
reason, has many meanings: ". . . the unqualified term ' being '
has several meanings, of which one was seen to be the accidental,
and another the true (' non-being ' being the false), while besides
these there are the figures of predication (for example, the
' what,' quality, quantity, place, time, and any similar meanings
which ' being ' may have), and again besides all these there is
that which ' is ' potentially or actually . . ." (*Metaphysics,* E,
1026 a, 33; McKeon, p. 779).

Therefore in Aristotle the problem of objective knowledge
does not consist in passing somehow from the logical or ideal to
the ontological order: the whole logical order itself is ontological. The problem is rather to discover the intelligible relation
of each particular essence to the actual subsistence, whether
subjective or objective, mediate or immediate, postulated by it.
This problem belongs to the critique of knowledge, but to a
critique formulated from the start in metaphysical terms.

IV. THE DOUBLE SOURCE OF ANTINOMIES PASSED ON TO MODERN PHILOSOPHY BY OCKHAMISM

First Source of Antinomies: The Relation Between Senses and Understanding

We remember that the philosophy of St. Thomas admits a
synthetic unity in the concept deriving from the fact that the
" phantasm "—the product of a sensory and quantitative elaboration—is animated by the formal objective unity of the intellect,
in other words, by the intelligible unity of " being." The intellect

as such has no immediate contact with its outside object. Neither does it contemplate the phantasm as if it were an object. But, of its very nature, it refers its own internal unity to the qualitative diversity of the phantasm (*convertit naturaliter se ad phantasma*). The fact that the intellect conforms itself actively to the phantasm is due only to the ontological identity of the soul from the sensory to the intellectual level, in other words, to the " substantial unity of the human composite." Hence a concept necessarily supposes : (1) in the senses a quantitative representation, a " phantasm " to which it may be referred; (2) in the intellect, a non-quantitative unity, which is particularized, " specified," by its very relation to the qualitative content of the phantasm. The " direct universal," the primary object of our intelligence according to the Thomists, realizes the synthesis of this double condition.

It follows that, despite its essential relativity, the sensory representation possesses not only a practical or kinetic, but also an *objective* function : in its material reality the phantasm is indispensable for the internal and specific diversification of the concept. Thus we see that the unity of senses and understanding is extremely strong, since it is the only thing which makes possible man's primary intellectual activity.

With Ockham, on the other hand, as a logical consequence of principles borrowed from Duns Scotus and the whole anti-Thomistic tradition, the synthetic unity, in the direct concept, of the senses and the understanding, is replaced by a mere extrinsic coordination of sensation and concept : the senses express, in their manner, the contingent events; the intellect, on the other hand, perceives them intuitively in its own way.[1] Gone is the theory which holds that the understanding and the senses are both united and distinct through their intimate co-operation in the synthetic unity of the concept, to which the former provides the form, the latter the matter. Instead, Ockham juxtaposes in us two faculties which ultimately seem to have

[1] We should note that this disjunction of senses and understanding—with its corollary, the intellectualization of matter—led philosophers to overlook the strict unity of the human composite. Thus the way was open for Cartesian dualism; and the problem of the relations between body and soul was presented to modern philosophy in terms which precluded every solution.

the same formal object. He insists that the senses are material, the understanding immaterial; but on closer examination the difference vanishes. Hence either faculty becomes superfluous. Which one shall we give up?

Centuries elapsed before the sacrifice was made, but it was finally made. Empiricism, free from all ontologistic prejudices and spiritualistic concerns, finally gave up the immaterial understanding, which was reduced to the function of an "internal sense." Elsewhere, in the Cartesian school, the immaterial understanding was kept and sensation was given up. The latter was reduced to the understanding; it became a confused intellection. It follows that the diversity of the content of our concepts could no longer be explained through the material passivity of the senses. Inborn ideas (Descartes, Leibniz) or ontologistic intuitionism (Malebranche) are the only solutions which were not *a priori* rejected by the Cartesian conception of the origin of our ideas. Moreover, to top it all, it soon became evident that the understanding, which had thus taken over the function of the senses, had kept remnants of bodily quantity. These material remnants would stealthily penetrate into the intellect itself and make possible Spinoza's monism, according to which extension clings as a constitutive "attribute" to the supremely intelligible, the absolute Being.

But this brings us to the threshold of transcendent reason.

Second Source of Antinomies: The Relation Between Understanding and Reason

The second alternative in which pre-Kantian modern philosophy was caught is that of understanding and reason. We use the word "reason" in the modern sense of the "faculty of transcendent being."

Here again we should remember the kind of unity which St. Thomas, in virtue of his thesis on the proper object of the human understanding, had to admit between these two forms of intellectual activity. In the direct concept which derives from sense experience, the intellect endows the quantitative phantasm with its own non-quantitative unity. But we know that the intellect's own unity, which has thus become the objective unity of the concept, is a unity, of itself illimited, and which is fully expressed only by the word being (*ens*). The very act which refers the intellect to the phantasm refers the latter's quantitative content to the illimited unity of being, that is, to absolute unity.

Hence the particular unity which the qualitative content of the phantasm thus receives in the concept is not the *absolute* unity of being—which extends beyond the phantasm as it extends beyond every finite content—but a " relation to," a " participation in " this absolute unity.

Moreover, our human intelligence, left to its own devices, never reaches objectively and in itself the absolute unity of being which would correspond to the total capacity of the intellect. This unity is only " posited " in every act of the intellect as the absolute principle of the partial, conceptual unities and as their infinite " beyond." Our reason does not directly reach its transcendent object, but affirms it implicitly in the very exercise of the understanding. Reflective analysis must render this " implicit " explicit.

Hence, for a Thomist, the activity of the understanding virtually embraces the whole field of reason. In other, more objective terms: the analogical opposition of contingent participated being and transcendent being is dimly " given " to us in every object of experience. Or again: the intellect is a faculty which universalizes the sense data only because it is a transcendental faculty of being. These three statements affirm the same thing. No contradiction is possible between understanding and reason—between experience and metaphysics—because the former is defined in function of the latter.

Is this true also in the nominalistic (terministic) philosophies? Let us first note that here nominalism is especially burdened by a few anti-Thomistic principles coming from previous philosophies. *Ockham's* position is very simple: since the rational operation is but an analytical operation on symbols, it lacks all objective validity. In the alternative " understanding or reason," reason, as the understanding's quintessence, as a higher abstraction, cannot claim higher validity than the lower abstractions, which are still near experience and can to some

extent be checked. The agnosticism of Ockham is quite logical
and derives from his nominalism. One might escape it only
by admitting, besides understanding and analytic reason, a
higher reason which penetrates directly into the mystery of being.
This would lead to intuitionistic ontologism (Malebranche) or,
if we admit inborn principles of metempirical knowledge, to
innatistic ontologism (Descartes, Leibniz).

But a conflict is bound to arise between such a higher reason
and the understanding. Once more either term is virtually given
up. For if we allow the operation of these two faculties to go
on separately, we notice that the products of these operations
stand in irreducible logical contradiction to each other. We
will soon become aware of this contradiction (with Nicholas of
Cusa) not only between higher reason and understanding, but
even within discursive understanding. And we shall meet it
again, formulated and codified in the Kantian antinomies.
Facing the alternative of reason and an understanding teeming
with antinomies, some philosophers will, after the undecided
semi-empiricism of Locke, proceed to the most radical agnostic
phenomenism (Hume). Together with reason, the faculty of the
transcendent, they will give up the understanding itself. Others
will set up the understanding, that is, purely analytic reason,
as the faculty of the absolute (rationalism). Spinoza and Wolff
went all the way in this direction, the former in monistic, the
latter in pluralistic rationalism. Still others, finally, will give up
the understanding on behalf of higher reason and will end
up in mysticism, like Nicholas of Cusa, or in intuitionistic
ontologism, like Malebranche.

Yet there was one, and only one, middle term for the alternative of senses and understanding, as well as for the alternative
of understanding and reason: the synthetic unity of these three
great domains of knowledge, as expressed in the proper object of
our human thought—the "direct universal," the "abstract
quiddity of material things." But the universal acceptance of a
few anti-Thomistic positions led very logically and unhappily to
a rejection of this solution. With this false start modern philosophy would slowly start its brilliant progress . . . into dead
alleys.

V. GENERAL CONCLUSIONS

The *Lectures* reproduced in this first *Cahier* constitute only a remote introduction to the modern problem of metaphysical knowledge. Yet they emphasize some points of view which should have been pointed out in order to situate the most recent critical philosophies in their exact perspective.

(1) Thus it was first necessary to define the meaning and the epistemological scope of ancient realism. It is easy to call Greek realism " dogmatism " in the Kantian sense of the word. But it would really be too simple to be satisfied with such a summary evaluation. The realism of the ancients rested on a rational basis, which they became aware of very early—from the time of Parmenides. In Aristotelian philosophy this basis has already been thoroughly mapped out. We do not claim that Kant was wrong and that we would be wrong if, with him, we brand as " dogmatic " the metaphysical systems of his time— the only ones which he knew well—that is, in fact, Leibnizian-Wolffian metaphysics. But Kant was wrong when he assimilated *every* metaphysics of " transcendent being " to the Cartesian type of metaphysics; the basically " dogmatic " feature of the latter was not its fundamental realistic principle, but its arbitrary claim to restrict realism purely and simply to the framework of the understanding. It is true that a critique of the understanding, not only as employed empirically, but especially as used transcendentally, is indispensable for every human metaphysics. But Kant seems not to have known of the existence of philosophies in which this critique had been completed in all essentials. In the following *Cahiers* we shall show how the realistic principle survived in Kant himself and even in the seemingly most extreme forms of modern relativism, including the methodological transcendentalism of the neo-Kantians of Marburg.

(2) In order to understand correctly the epistemology of the ancients and to discover in it the preparation of modern theories of knowledge, it was also required to emphasize the critical function which may be assumed by metaphysics itself.

We have noticed that the doctrine, whether latent or manifest, which we might call the " ancient critique of knowledge," essentially comprises two aspects: (1) a general critique of affirmation as an absolute positing of " being "; (2) an ontological critique of the content of the absolute affirmation.

The former aspect corresponds rather well, for all essentials, to what might be called in Kantian terms a " transcendental proof " of the absolute affirmation; it goes beyond the Kantian " transcendental proof " only by extending to the absolute domain of the " object." We might summarize this first aspect of the ancient critique in a few statements, whose main content might be found in Aristotle as well as in St. Thomas. The need for action imposes itself *a priori,* since to refuse action is still to posit it. But the necessity of action logically implies the necessity of the objective affirmation (judgment). The necessity of the objective affirmation (judgment) entails a corresponding necessity in the affirmed object, as affirmed object. The necessity of the affirmed object, as affirmed, is, at least, to be identical with itself (" first principle "): pure variability is not an object of affirmation. But the necessity of being identical with itself has a meaning only if referred to the absolute necessity of " being." Therefore, since the absolute necessity of being is thus implied in human action as the ultimate condition of its possibility, to deny this absolute necessity of being would mean to try to deny *action* through *an action.* Hence the absolute affirmation: *being is,* forces itself upon me if I wish to avoid logical contradiction. Likewise, on account of the same necessity, both theoretical and practical, I cannot reject the following statement: " Every object of affirmation, by the very fact that it may be affirmed, is connected with the absolute domain of being; hence in one way or another, it *is.*"

If every affirmable object, that is, if every thought object, is being, in a real and absolute sense, metaphysics has a solid foundation; there only remains to organize it, that is, to distinguish and to classify the possible meanings of the unavoidable attribution of being: for this attribution of being which is absolutely true for every content of consciousness cannot, without contradiction, be true of them in only one meaning.

That is where the ancient metaphysicians faced the comprehensive problem of the One and the Many. They had to look for a privileged point of view from which the division of the object of thought in function of being might be seen to be both necessary and coherent. In other words, they had to try to reduce the multiplicity of the particular affirmations (at least insofar as they bore the stamp of necessity) to the unity of a rational system. Because of this the metaphysical system-atization already deserved to be called a " critique " of know-ledge, since it provides the necessary norms which rule the legitimate meanings of the absolute predication of " being."

(3) But the metaphysical construction becomes a " critique of knowledge " more deservedly as soon as, in its objective sifting of being, it includes the content of reflexive consciousness, that is, the very opposition and relation between the knowing subject and the known object. As this relation of knowledge enters our reflection as an " object " of consciousness, it too must find its place in the system of being. The ancients admitted this exigency in principle: being-as-object does not go without being-as-subject, and, the other way round: " Every being is true; what-ever is true, is a being." Hence a *metaphysics of knowledge* is required.

But, as it defines the necessary or possible ontological rela-tions of a subject and an object, a metaphysics of knowledge points out the contribution of the subject and that of the object in their psychological relationship; which amounts to saying that it sets forth the limits and the scope of knowledge itself. At this point of the metaphysical critique, we may speak not only of the diversity of the " objective categories " of being, but of the distinction of a *modus mentis* (the way things are in the mind) and a *modus rei* (the way things are in reality) within each objective predicate.

Later we shall have to employ these considerations in order to find the key which allows us to transpose, lawfully, in the theories of knowledge, the metaphysical " tone " into the critical " tone " and the other way round.

(4) We have just reminded the reader that, in order to con-stitute a real critique, the metaphysical construction had to constitute a comprehensive system of " being," comprising as one of its organic parts a metaphysics of knowledge. Hence there is a great *solidarity* between a general system of being and a metaphysics of knowledge. To modify the basic principles of the system of being entails at once a modification of the ontological

conception of knowledge; likewise, to change the metaphysical
type of knowledge means to bring about—logically—an alteration in the other parts of the general system of being. No
wonder then, if in the history of the ancient and medieval
doctrines—despite the part of contingency involved in every
historical development—whole groups of metaphysical theses
show a variation which runs parallel to the very variation of
the theory of the concept.

Moreover, history also shows that it is not so easy to bring
together into one coherent system the totality of the relations
which connect to being every content of consciousness without
exception. From only one point of view may this totality be
embraced in its full amplitude. Aristotle, among the Greeks, had
the good fortune—or the merit—of discovering it. And St.
Thomas, with more assurance and precision, brought medieval
philosophy back to this central and dominant position indicated
by the Stagyrite.

Outside the Aristotelian point of view, as worked out in
greater detail and precision by St. Thomas, there is always one
element of the content of consciousness which is overlooked, or
some antinomy which hides under the insufficiently criticized
postulates. We have discovered this hidden weakness and
these hidden contradictions both in pre-Aristotelian Greek
philosophy and in medieval philosophy after St. Thomas.
Whether in a rational synthesis which is still insufficiently
worked out or in a finished synthesis which starts to disinte-
grate, the logical consequences are essentially the same.

(5) We noted these consequences in more detail in the
philosophies of Duns Scotus and Ockham, wherein they already
prefigure the various lines of evolution in modern philosophy.
Scotism and Ockhamism represent the two finished forms—one
dogmatic, the other critical—of the non-Thomistic scholasticism
which claimed to be Aristotelian, and which borrowed many
formulas from Aristotle, without, however, penetrating into the
deeper unity of peripatetic metaphysics.

It may be worthwhile to recall here the kind of philosophical
solutions which Duns Scotus and especially Ockham, by rejecting the characteristic theses of Thomism, banished for a long
time from the horizon of modern philosophy. In a few words:

they gave up the *synthetic unity* of our primitive concepts, wherein that which is intelligible meets matter within the universal; as a result they broke up *the rigorous substantial unity of the human composite,* without which the synthetic unity of the concept becomes unintelligible. And why were both these unities overlooked by them? Undoubtedly because, having too much confidence in our imperfect understanding, which cuts up and isolates after the manner of quantitative division, they were unable to appreciate the value of the Thomistic idea of the essential complementarity of matter and form under the unity of being, or, more generally, the idea of a " reciprocal causality " which opposes relatively, not entitatively, the terms united by it.

To the extent in which they gave up the double synthetic unity of our immediate concepts and of our human nature, Duns Scotus and Ockham condemned by anticipation the philosophers who would succeed them to a frustrating oscillation between extreme positions: in epistemology, ontologism or narrow empiricism with its agnostic consequences; in psychology, exclusive spiritualism, coarse materialism or irreducible dualism. The middle way was barred; it took Kantian philosophy to reopen it, and this only in part.

In the following *Cahier* (*Cahier II*) we shall outline the great stages of the unconscious progression which the philosophers from the fifteenth to the eighteenth centuries will make, in two divergent columns, towards the ultimate consequences of decadent scholasticism.

(6) One more remark. We have shown that the inability (evident in and admitted by Ockham) to demonstrate rationally the absolute transcendence of God derived ultimately from an erroneous theory of the concept. And we affirmed that only the Thomistic theory of the concept was capable of establishing a real analogical knowledge of the transcendent, that is, a knowledge which transcends the limitation of the understanding and discovers in our objective thought a " meaning " which infinitely surpasses the direct conceptual " representation."

We are quite willing to acknowledge that this really bold Thomistic thesis of metaphysical analogy calls for a critical justification which we have not yet furnished. For, if we claim that we know the transcendental relation of analogy, if we feel entitled to raise the "meaning" of some privileged concepts above that which they directly "represent," then the Thomistic theory of knowledge demands that the higher term of the analogy (the *analogatum princeps*)—the transcendent object, which is "meant" although not "represented" in its own form—be somehow present in us. If it is not represented in us according to its own form, how is it present in us? How does our thought get hold of it?

Although this problem has been glimpsed by the author of the *Theoremata* and by Ockham in their critiques of the argument from causality, we deem it preferable to postpone its complete solution until the time when, taught by the experiences of modern philosophy, we will be able to resume the examination of the foundations of Thomistic metaphysics in greater depth. We will only repeat that which we have already insinuated occasionally in the preceding pages: in order to reach a critical solution which is entirely satisfactory, this problem supposes a complete theory of the strict unity and reciprocal causality of intellect and will. Such a theory existed in St. Thomas, although, on account of the main trends of his time, its epistemological value was not clearly realized. Unfortunately, this theory vanished after him. Outside Thomistic schools, from Duns Scotus until our contemporary critical philosophers, the clear and neat formula of Aristotle and St. Thomas—*Voluntas in ratione est* ("The will is in the reason")—has lost its original emphasis. The too radical separation between the intellectual and the appetitive function, which Ockham even pushed all the way into irrationalism of the will, induced philosophers to forget that our intelligence is, in its nature, an appetite for "being," and in its exercise, conquest of "being."

We shall expose in the following *Cahiers* how this schism of the intellect and the will, of speculation and action, after having caused the metaphysical impotency of the rationalisms, decreased the usefulness of the Kantian critique by rendering it unduly negative and destructive.

CAHIER TWO

THE CONFLICT OF RATIONALISM
AND EMPIRICISM IN MODERN
PHILOSOPHY BEFORE KANT

After a short introduction (part of which is translated in Extract VI), Maréchal describes the philosophical system of Nicholas of Cusa and the philosophical milieu of the Renaissance (Part I). He then studies successively the development of pre-Kantian philosophy in the line of rationalism, with chapters devoted to Descartes, Malebranche, Spinoza, Leibniz and Wolff (Part II); and the development of the same philosophy in the line of empiricism, with chapters devoted to the logical derivation of empiricism, the historical development of empiricism, the semi-empiricism of Locke, the system of Berkeley and the pheno-menalistic empiricism of Hume. Extract VII contains Maréchal's conclusions about the philosophy of Descartes; Extract VIII, his overall judgment of the system of Spinoza; Extract IX, " a few philosophical consequences of the dogmatism of Leibniz"; and Extract X, the conclusions of Maréchal's study of Hume. Finally, Extract XI is a translation of the general conclusions of Cahier II.

VI. INTRODUCTION

We have tried, in a first series of Lectures (*Cahier I*), to make evident the compenetration in the ancient philosophies of metaphysics and epistemology. With the Greek and medieval philosophers the general problem of realism is necessarily followed by the special problem of the definition of the " essences " or forms of being. In order to fulfill its epistemological function this defining of " essences " must be rigorously coherent and must cover the whole domain of reality; it must be systematic and comprehensive; otherwise the affirmation of the metaphysical absolute—although unavoidable—would founder in contradiction or go down in uncertainty.

Have we succeeded in showing that this double condition was realized, during the Middle Ages, in—and only in—authentic

Thomism? It seems to us that the validity of the ancient critique and the inner equilibrium of every realistic metaphysics are tied to a noetic presupposition, which constituted precisely the central thesis of the Aristotelianism of St. Thomas. We may call it what we like: the " synthetic " theory of the concept, as opposed to an intuitive and analytical theory; or the theory of the " direct universal," produced by a total abstraction performed on sense knowledge; or the theory of the " proper object of human intelligence " identified with the " abstract quiddity of the material things "; or, finally, the theory of " the essential participation of sensibility in our intellections, owing to the substantial unity of soul and body." Whatever formula we choose, it will amount to saying that that which is *first* given to us, through the natural exercise of our knowledge, is not, as some believed, antinomical terms facing each other in an original hostility and confronting us with the impossible task of reconciling them without changing them. It is rather a synthetic unity, experienced by us in its essential undividedness, and yielding only *afterwards* the relative opposition of its constitutive principles. The problem of the One and the Many considered in its full range, up to the very meeting of pure Unity (pure Intelligibility) and pure Multiplicity (pure Materiality), is from the start presented to us as " solved " in a vital synthesis which is both subjective and objective. If we misinterpret this primitive and basic synthesis, we shall never fully overcome the metaphysical antinomies. The reason for this incapacity will become more and more manifest throughout our Lessons.

The schoolmen of the late Middle Ages ignored this Thomistic point of view. We have noted in some detail what resulted from this neglect, especially in Duns Scotus and Ockham. Born under the patronage of Ockham's nominalism, modern philosophy inherited from it, as an undiscussed appanage, the intuitive and analytical theory of the concept—a burden which, at first unnoticed, would, during three centuries, slow down the development of the systems and be, likewise, a source of many antinomies that would emerge one after another under the gropings of the philosophers, to flock together ultimately into two clearly divergent systems: *rationalistic dogmatism* and *phenomenalistic empiricism.* It is in this supreme antinomy, in this alternative without exit, that pre-Kantian philosophy, with all its brilliance, originality and love for precision, but too oblivious of its origins, would be stopped in its tracks and rendered powerless.

VII. DESCARTES:
SUMMARY AND CONCLUSIONS

If we should be allowed to summarize in a few words the pages which precede, we would say:

(1) That the originality of Cartesian philosophy consisted less in the theses which it professed than *in the spirit which animated it* and in the point of view which it opened up. For if Descartes depended more than is generally held—and than he himself held—on the philosophical milieu of his time, in his turn he thoroughly modified this milieu: the radical nature of his reforming intentions powerfully stimulated the critical tendencies which, long emerged but not yet fully developed, would lie at the base of modern philosophy. From this viewpoint one can—as several historians have done—date modern philosophy from Descartes. Moreover, by awakening the critical endeavor Descartes proposed to philosophy an ideal of sober exactness and lucid clearness, the mathematical ideal. Although incomplete, it is a most precious ideal, one that preserved modern thought from exaggerated subtleties and brought back the practice of precision. It seems to us that the real contribution of Cartesian philosophy is this " spirit " of boldness and solidity. We do not overlook the fact that Descartes may claim the credit for a few specific theses which have been more universally taken into consideration because of him. But this other contribution to philosophical progress seems to be less important and even questionable.

(2) Despite the originality of the effort from which it derived, Cartesian epistemology has contributed no really new constructive principles. Descartes deserves credit for having tried to find for philosophy a starting point which might be wholly certain, but he has not instituted the integral critique of the

presupposita of knowledge. Before the great antinomies of ancient philosophy his position does not differ much from that of Duns Scotus and of Ockham. Like them, he does not discover the privileged point where (infra-intelligible) *prime matter* as well as (supra-intelligible) *transcendent Being* manifests itself sidewise within our human " intelligible objects," namely the " abstract quiddity of the material things." The nominalistic contamination renders Descartes inhospitable to the Thomistic idea (of which in his time so many Thomists themselves were so little aware) of a synthesis of material quantity with the absolute unity in the universal concept.

That is why, despite his attempts at a renovation, he will be caught unawares and carried along by the latent logic of his starting points. In spite of himself he falls back into the ruts of decadent scholasticism. Absolutely speaking, he might have advanced in the direction of a phenomenalistic agnosticism. But, since by temperament he was neither an empiricist nor a sceptic, he instinctively chose metaphysical idealism among the roads which opened up before him. Once he had started upon this road he could remain consistent with himself only by adopting some kind of intuitionistic ontologism. In fact we have seen that his rather ambiguous epistemology advances in this direction. But in this development—which will be completed in the successors of Descartes—there is, in spite of some contingent episodes, nothing basically new, nothing which interrupts the logical development of the principles already posited at the end of the Middle Ages.

(3) Yet Descartes had, as it were, a premonition of the importance which, in the modern solutions of the critical problem, would be assumed by the consideration of the *knowing Subject*. This does not imply that Cartesian philosophy ever suspected the critical notion of a " transcendental subject "; it starts and remains on the objective and realistic viewpoint of the Ego as *substance,* as the *ontological* Subject, taking as solved, rather than solving integrally, the problem of metaphysical knowledge. Yet it is certain that the " I think " of Descartes will haunt Kant's mind in the most decisive passages of the *Critique of Pure Reason* and will to a great extent explain the importance

assumed later by the idea of the "transcendental unity of consciousness."

(4) Like Duns Scotus and Ockham, and for the same reasons, Descartes *separates too radically the domain of speculation and the domain of striving,* that is, the intelligence and the will. We have shown that his metaphysics avoids Ockham's agnosticism exactly to the extent made possible by a wider use of intellectual intuition among the principles of knowledge. At the heart of Cartesianism, as at the heart of every ontologistic philosophy, there lurks some higher empiricism whose providers are only *direct intuition* and *analysis.* Intuition provides contents of consciousness and ontological relations of objects, analysis dissociates and classifies. But the intuitive understanding is conceived by Descartes not as spontaneity which creates its own object—this would obviously go beyond the power of human understanding—nor as an inquiring and assimilating activity, but as a transcendent receptivity, as the locus of latent ideas, which are received ready-made and which have only to pass from the "virtual" to the "actual," from the "confused" state to the "clear" state. Since knowledge is serenely passive and analytical, confined within the domain of form, implying essentially neither productive nor creative nor assimilating activity, unavoidably every form of active and conquering finality discovered in man will have to be attributed to another faculty, to an autonomous and independent will. Thus even the assent in judgment, as an active attitude, turns into a voluntary and free act. In a word, speculation in man, instead of being an enriching activity, striving towards the ultimate end of the intellectual subject, is only a motionless and disinterested reflection; speculation is cut off from action and, on the other hand, finality is no longer "intelligible." Against a reason which is confined to the analysis of static intuitions stands a liberty lacking all real intellectual control.

In this embarrassing situation several theories remained possible: to maintain liberty and to profess an absolute voluntarism—such was the solution of Descartes, who followed therein the dominant tradition of the early Middle Ages; or to give up liberty in behalf of analytical reason—such was the monistic

solution of Spinoza. The former solution conflicts with rationalism; the latter pushes it to its ultimate consequences. Between
these two the optimism of Leibniz, as a pluralistic rationalism,
travels a middle road which leads back to Nicholas of Cusa.

VIII. SPINOZA: CONCLUSIONS

Spinoza's metaphysics is a marvelously finished example of the
perfection which may be reached and of the limits which cannot
be exceeded by a *metaphysics of the understanding.*

Such a metaphysics is based entirely on the analytical relations of our objective concepts, accepted as such, readymade, as
a direct representation of ontological reality without any other
critique of their validity than the mere logical coherence of the
deductive connections by which they derive one from another.

But no metaphysics can yield more than is contained in its
constitutive elements and in the *form* which organizes them into
a system.

It is obvious that in the *Ethica,* the *systematic form* of connection is simply the principle of identity or of non-contradiction,
the basis of every analytic and substitutive operation. It is true
that Spinoza speaks of *causes.* But these causes are not understood in a dynamic sense, which would imply a synthetic extension of our reason, but only in the sense of constitutive and
immanent rational elements discovered by analysis. *Cause* comes
down to *substance;* it coincides with *logical reason,* which enters
into the definition of the essence. Hence Spinoza's way of reasoning remains strictly analytical.

But such a way of reasoning adds nothing to the data elaborated by it. It reaches the end of its tether as soon as it has
uncovered the most general attributes precontained in these
data. Spinoza's metaphysics will discover only that which was
implicitly contained in its *first elements.* But when such concepts
—whether inborn or coming from the senses—are considered
only, as happens with Spinoza, at the stage where they express
well determined objects, they will never yield more than components whose objective " signification," according to the basic
postulate of Cartesian realism, will possess the same amplitude

as their formal " representation."[1] Signification and representation go together; the essential condition of the latter will necessarily cling to all analytic components which may be known as objects.

But what are these essential conditions of the " representative element " of our concepts? One of them is absolutely basic and undeniable for internal observations: virtual extensivity, the relation to extension, to quantity, to number. The direct object of our concepts, however much we may reduce their " comprehension," up to the *ratio entis* (being) inclusively, is always and necessarily seen to refer to extension. It is true that the objective concept represents more than mere extension. It gives an extension unified by a unity which transcends it. Yet this unity remains strictly commensurate with extension. It is unity in extension.

What shall we conclude from this? The only kind of metaphysics which can be derived from premises which affirm a complete identity of " representation " and " ontological signification " in the " clear and distinct concepts " is the monistic metaphysics of the *Ethica*.

If one clings to the concepts of the understanding as the exclusive starting point and if, on the other hand, one is, like Spinoza, heroically logical, disregarding all prejudices, one has to drive the extensivity of the " representation " all the way up to the primary principle, to the supreme unity which rules the totality of all objects. In other words, since extension is indissolubly attached to intelligible unity in our concepts, one will define God not only as *thought,* but, for the same reason, also as *extension.* But whoever says of God that the two attributes by which he manifests himself to us are thought and extension—both pushed to an infinite degree and both unable to be multiplied, since they are the *a priori* principles of the multiple modes—says that in God unity continues to be the unity of a multiplicity *which is created by this unity while still*

---

[1] The difference between *signification* and *representation* is that which exists between something we can *mean* or intend and something we can *picture* or represent before the mind's eyes. Thus a Thomist holds that, although man cannot represent or picture God, he can mean or intend him. All our concepts of God are deficient in representation, but not necessarily in signification. (Tr.)

measuring it. This multiplicity is, of course, an infinite one. Spinoza's God represents to the eyes of our reason the subsisting integration of the infinite number.

The quantitative principle has thus become intelligible in itself; it turns up as a divine " attribute." This is the logical conclusion of every metaphysics of the pure understanding. Among the Cartesians only Spinoza had the courage to go that far in his conclusions. He did even more.

Later we will show in more detail how, according to St. Thomas, the extensivity which affects our understanding in its union with matter determines the structure of our basic concepts, their " concretion ": every concept " represents " a unified diversity, an " informed " matter, more technically, " the synthetic unity of an undetermined *suppositum* and of formal determinations." And since, according to his Cartesian philosophy, absolute Reality must have the same structure as our objective concepts, Spinoza conceives of it in fact, and despite artificial qualifications which are supposed to hide the brutality of this conclusion, as a *suppositum* which is undifferentiated in itself and which carries eternally the totality of all representable forms, in other words, " as a unique substantial principle which is the immanent cause of the infinity of all attributes and modes." Thus the monism of the substance is seen to be nothing but the transposition into the absolute of the concretive mode of our concepts. . . .

(2) Although it is elaborated by a powerful dialectics, the Spinozian solution of the metaphysical problem looks very strange. In a perfectly logical way it multiplies the antinomical conclusions, thus making it quite evident that there is a contradiction hidden in its starting point, the absolute realism of our concepts.

There is the antinomy of thought and extension—of the radical principle of unity and the radical principle of multiplicity—within the divine essence itself.

There is the antinomy of the unity of the divine substance and the infinite sum of the attributes. This is undeniably an antinomy. How shall we understand the " attributes "? Substantively? Then subsistent multiplicity would define subsistent unity. Adjectively? Then these attributes become real " modes."

Moreover, we do not see how adjectival properties would not imply the "potentiality" of their substratum. As "external denominations" of God, as mere "ideal aspects" projected in him by our imperfect thought? But what becomes then of the absolute realism of the understanding, the only epistemological support of immanent monism? Besides, Spinoza's text does not allow of this interpretation.

Finally, the antinomy between the sole divine substance, demanding the purity of Act, and the multiplicity of the "modes," the variability of the inadequate ideas: this multiplicity and variability suppose a "passive potency" in God. Here again we cannot escape the antinomy by attributing to the imperfection of our concepts, not to reality itself, the limitation of the modes and the variability of the ideas. This would suppose that we locate the limitation and the mobility in an intellect which is extrinsic to the system of being, an absurd hypothesis which never crossed Spinoza's mind.

We understand without too much difficulty why Spinoza, and with him so many realistic pantheists, carried away by a dialectic which they considered irresistible, overlooked these antinomies. But we do not see at all how they would try to solve them.

We should not look for the original *source* of these antinomies in Spinoza, nor in Descartes, nor even in the Middle Ages, in the anti- or pre-Thomistic Platonic schools. We find it among the Greeks, at the dim dawn of metaphysical realism before the Eleatics. This source was even then the insufficiently critical realism of the understanding. Time and again, in systems of unequal value, the extreme consequences of this realism became visible—thus in Eleatic monism, in Alexandrian immanentistic emanatism and in its medieval re-editions by John Scotus Eriugena or by the school of Chartres, in the pantheistic naturalism of Giordano Bruno and, finally, in Spinozism. These successive philosophies possessed one common thesis: the basic identity or (which amounts to the same) the essential and reciprocal relation between God and the world.

(3) We have shown how post-Thomistic metaphysics had lost the idea of the dynamism of the intellect, in other words, the idea of a synthesis of "tendency" and "form" in knowledge

itself. Unless one be willing to overlook in man every kind of conquering activity, a merely static conception of thought will not work without the juxtaposition of radical voluntarism and extreme rationalism. Ockham and Descartes tried to some extent this mixture of water and fire. Spinoza, whose mind craved unity, was unable to accept it, and gave up without further ado the voluntarism of Descartes. But what could he do, then, with those psychological states which we call " tendencies," " desires," " volitions "? Inflexibly faithful to the rationalist prejudice, the Dutch philosopher, despite the richly elegant terminology in which he envelops what, like everybody else, he calls " affec- tions," " moral progress," " destiny," " liberty," succeeds in emptying these notions of all real dynamism. The metaphysics of Spinoza not only leaves no room for true freedom, it also absorbs the will in the reason, and it reduces every subordination of ends to a hierarchy of logical conditions. Finality has been banished, and of the will there only remains the name.

IX. LEIBNIZ: A FEW PHILOSOPHICAL CONSEQUENCES OF HIS DOGMATISM

All the typical theses of the philosophy of Leibniz, as opposed to Cartesianism and Spinozism, derive from the special dog- matism which we have mentioned, and which we might designate either as the dynamism of reason or the plurality of substances. Let us briefly examine a few of the more characteristic theses.

Dualism of the Human Composite

We have several times remarked above that the Thomistic conception of act and potency, in the strictest metaphysical sense of these terms, safeguards better than any other conception the unity of the human composite. As soon as the theory of act and potency is directly or indirectly weakened, the sub- stantial unity of man is weakened, too. Matter becomes an " entity " in itself, and the one form splits up in superposited forms; in short, it becomes more and more difficult to define the unity of the human substance.

Things get even worse when the notions of act and potency, form and matter, are given up altogether, as happened in the Cartesian schools. In that event the substantial unity of man turns necessarily into a substantial duality or plurality. The bond between the substance, " soul," and the group of sub-stances, " body," is reduced to a constant parallelism, whose cause is difficult to establish. Although opposed to the idea of a simple mutual interaction between spirit and extension, Descartes settled for some kind of interaction. This was a weakness, and an illogical one, which his followers noticed and tried to correct. The unity which Descartes still hoped to find in a direct relation between body and soul was located by them directly in God, in God as the only agent for Malebranche, as the only substance for Spinoza. Leibniz, being a dynamist and a pluralist, felt unable to accept these solutions. Neither could he admit an interaction from one monad to another, and he repeatedly criticized Descartes on this point. On the other hand, his pre-suppositions, like those of Descartes, made him unable to avoid dualism. In order to explain the parallelism of body and soul he too had to recur to the very unity of divine action. Hence his theory of " pre-established harmony."

It is obvious that the substantial unity of the human composite constitutes a great difficulty in the metaphysics of Leibniz as well as in that of Descartes. Even if we adopt Leibniz' point of view, we must admit that the " pre-established harmony " between the monad, " soul," and the monads, " body," is only a particular instance of the one which obtains between all monads without distinction. Since the harmonic connections are universal, the harmony between body and soul differs from all other harmonies only quantitatively. It represents a maximum of parallelism. Is this enough to express rationally the real unity of the Ego to which we objectively refer all " our " material and other phenomena? Is it enough for the constitution of an essential unity, an *unum per se* according to the classical termi-nology, adopted by Leibniz himself, because the strict unity of the Ego forces itself upon our spontaneous knowledge? (See *Lettre à Rém. de Montmort,* 1715, III, IV; ed. Erdmann II,

p. 736, cols. 1 and 2.) Or is it the case that what Leibniz calls the
" metaphysical union of soul and body, which causes them to
constitute an *unum per se*, an animal, a living being," contains in
itself and by itself something which is quantitatively different
from the usual correspondence between monads? What is this
special feature? Other than reciprocal efficient causality, metaphysics possesses no other notion which is applicable in the
present case, except the complementary causality of matter and
form. But like efficient causality between finite substances, this
complementary causality is incompatible with Leibniz' monad-
ology. Moreover, its acceptance implies a synthetic theory of
the concept and would force Leibniz to re-examine the very
principle of Cartesian ontologism.

Definition of the Intellect through Formal and Functional Features

With Duns Scotus and Ockham the exaggerated dualism between
body and soul corresponded to a functional dualism which
endangered the synergic unity of the faculties of knowledge. Let
us not speak, for the time being, of the " higher reason " which
was, at least theoretically, either contained within the confines
of the understanding or totally reserved for mystical illumina-
tions. The understanding itself, the faculty of concepts, which
perceives directly (*per speciem specialissimam*, or intuitively)
the concrete existences and their contingent differences, performed the same function as the senses, whose work it took over,
thus becoming independent of them. At the utmost, the understanding might still depend on the senses as on an extrinsic
occasion of their activity.

However, if the human understanding can perform the function of material sensibility, why should we keep the latter as a
distinct faculty, wedged in without any specific purpose between
the understanding and the merely physical modification of the
sense organs?

Descartes proceeded logically when he equated the conscious
with the intelligible, and considered sensation a spiritual
modality originating, without any psychophysiological inter-

mediary, on the occasion of some modification of the material sensorium. The bodily power of sensation, having become useless, has quietly and spontaneously disintegrated. What remained was, on the one hand, the bodily " automaton " and, on the other, the spirit with its inborn and adventitious ideas, composed of sensations. Sensation or the sensorial idea differed from the other ideas only through its " occasional " origin and the " confused " state of its content, not through its intimate nature. For Descartes the whole psychological gamut was composed of modalities of the spiritual soul.

For Leibniz, likewise, the monad " soul " is the only subject of all the cognitive phenomena, from " the small non-apperceived perceptions " up to the most elaborate ideas. As they become clearer, they increase in consciousness. Since the monad possesses neither doors nor windows, the whole content of the mind must be inborn. For Leibniz innatism is total. It was only partial for Descartes, who admitted " adventitious ideas," and who restricted the power of possessing inborn representations to the spiritual soul. Leibniz, on the other hand, held that every monad, even the bodily one, has " perceptions," that is, virtual representations, although the clarity of " apperception " belongs exclusively to the spiritual soul or intellect. Therefore, for Leibniz, that which characterizes the spiritual soul in contrast with the other monads, derives less from the contents it receives or possesses than from the *active manner in which it reacts* upon these contents by referring them to some *principle*. He claims that the human soul reacts upon its perception in two ways which are found only in it—through analysis, that is, through a conscious application of the " norm of contradiction," and through transcendence, that is, through the absolute affirmation of the " sufficient reason." These two modes of action, a formal and a dynamic one, express that which is essential to the monad " human soul " and distinguishes it from the lower monads.

Leibniz seems here to have progressed beyond Descartes. When he defines human intelligence by means of functional features, he seems to have started a still rudimentary " critique of the cognitive faculty." For the " critique of a cognitive faculty " defines the latter's " formal object." But a faculty

which elaborates the whole content whatsoever of the " perceptions " according to the rule of identity and the dynamism of
sufficient reason, operates like the faculty of " being " under the
latter's two logically irreducible aspects—being as the identical
measure of the perceptions and being as their cause or intelligible reason. Leibniz notes that under the first aspect the mind
is capable of constructing an analytically developed mathematics;
under the second aspect it may also study physics and metaphysics (see, for example, *Seconde réplique de Leibniz à Clarke,*
I; ed. Erdmann, II, p. 748, cols. 1 and 2).

Thus the totality of knowledge is justified by two aspects which
express the deeper nature of the intellect, the original capacity
which it possesses on account of its special participation in
creative wisdom.

Yet throughout all this Leibniz remains a dogmatist. If his
dogmatism is not as vague as that of Descartes, he owes this
more clearly defined position to the dynamistic idea which he
borrowed from Aristotelian and scholastic philosophy. This
explains why ultimately Leibnizian dogmatism stands much
nearer to scholasticism than Cartesian dogmatism.

The reason is that the idea of an internal dynamism nearly
coincides with that of " immanent finality," of " entelechy "; and
the idea of " immanent finality " implies that of " formal
causality." But according to the Thomistic scholastics, the
human soul is the " subsistent form of the human composite ";
that is, while exerting its own activity even beyond the power
of matter, it is united to matter as the latter's formal principle.
Thomistic ideology is based on this strange condition : an intelligence whose internal dynamism is partially restricted to
material limitations. For the scholastic, therefore, human knowledge will have two levels : one which corresponds to the activities of the soul inasmuch as it informs matter—this is sensation,
an " act of the composite "; another which corresponds to the
activities of the soul inasmuch as it transcends informed matter
—this is the proper operation of the understanding and reason
as they immaterially elaborate the sensations.

These two levels or zones correspond to something analogous
in Leibniz : the former zone to the " small perceptions " of the
monad; the latter to their elaboration into concepts or ideas

under the influence of the double principle in which the nature of the intellect is expressed. It is true that a scholastic sees, in the pure " sensations," knowledge *acquired* by the substantial composite; for Leibniz, the perceptions are *inborn* in the monad. This constitutes, of course, a considerable difference. Yet both sides attribute to the sensations or " perceptions " the function of a " matter " in intellectual knowledge; a matter which is grasped by a regulating and transcendent activity for Leibniz, a matter which is informed by a unity which is wider than it for the scholastics. The intellectual " dynamism " of the former is not far from the spontaneity of the agent intellect of the latter, and both agree at least on this, that they deny the existence of the ambiguous function of containing *a priori* an ideal multiplicity, whether formal or virtual, in the intellect *as such*. This simplification of the intellectual *function* will prepare the point of view of Kant, who will base his critique upon the purely functional value of the understanding.

The Rationalism of the Will: Fatalism or Optimism (Controversy with Clarke)

Cartesian rationalism could lead to the necessity of creation and the determinism of human action. We have seen how Spinoza boldly drew these conclusions from the principle of intelligibility; but Descartes himself did not drive logic to that extreme. Since he considered the freedom of indifference a positive perfection, immediately given in internal experience, he attributed it to God in the highest degree and was thus induced to profess some kind of absolute voluntarism, analogous to that of Ockham. This voluntarism very aptly corrected his rationalism.

Because of his dynamic conception of the monads, Leibniz did not need this indifferentistic voluntarism in order to escape the powerful clutches of Spinozian reason. That is why, somewhat like Spinoza, he defined freedom as the absence of all external constraint which would prevent one from choosing according to reason. God is absolutely free because nothing can force him to act. Yet, as God is the supreme Reason, his action

cannot be arbitrary nor lack a " sufficient reason ": this reason
must be decisive, infallibly decisive, or else it would not be
sufficient. Hence God will choose " the better "; it would have
been morally impossible for him, under pain of imperfection, to
have acted in any other way than he did. Therefore the world is
the best of all possible worlds and it is even inconceivable that
God would not have created. Thus the thesis of optimism is
based on the principle of sufficient reason, interpreted in the
wider sense of a principle of entire " rationality."

But this optimism is not tantamount to setting up divine
Reason as some kind of Fatality, endowed with the attributes of
the ancient *Anankè*. It is true that with Leibniz, as formerly
with Nicholas of Cusa, the *Fatum* remains within God and is
not a blind "fatality." But does this take away that it is a
necessity imposed upon the divine activity, a restriction of God's
omnipotence? Among Leibniz' opponents, Clarke, the New-
tonian philosopher, kept pushing this difficulty with British
tenacity. In the exchange of " answers " and " replies " between
the two of them (*Lettres entre Leibniz et Clarke,* 1715-1716;
ed. Erdmann, II, pp. 747-780), we see the irreconcilable conflict
of two conceptions of freedom.

Clarke, who derives his notion of freedom from experience,
finds in it only active indifference. He admits that " nothing
exists without a sufficient reason. . . . But this sufficient reason
often is merely the will of God " (*ibid.,* 1, p. 750; second reply
of Clarke). A faculty is free insofar as it is for itself the sufficient
reason of its acts. Freedom means autodetermination.

Leibniz, who wishes above all to safeguard the rights of
rational causality, denies this: the act of the will itself must " be
determined " by a " sufficient reason," and likewise the manner
in which it is carried out, otherwise it would be irrational.
Accepting Clarke's thesis " would mean to fall back again into
vague indifference, which I have exposed as absolutely chimerical, even in the creatures, and contrary to God's wisdom, as if
he could operate without acting out of reason." What we must
avoid is not this rational necessity, " but a brute fatality or
necessity . . . in which there is neither wisdom nor choice "
(*ibid.,* p. 752; second reply of Leibniz, 7, 8).

It is easy to recognize under the opposed arguments of the

two adversaries the basic antinomy of freedom and causality, extended here to the higher activity of the spirit. Later we shall find it formulated by Kant within the framework of "cosmology" and solved according to the principles of critical philosophy. That is where we shall look more deeply into the causes of the antinomy and discuss its solution.

Let us not forget, however, that as long ago as the thirteenth century, a healthy critique of the transcendent use of concepts had been achieved for all essential points, which would have made it possible to avoid the antinomy. Unfortunately, until the advent of Kantian philosophy, post-medieval rationalism had forgotten the real meaning and did not know the critical basis of the scholastic theory of "analogy." It was up to Kantianism to expose systematically a thesis which Thomism had already posited in principle and elaborated in part—namely, that there are limits to some of our bolder ways of using concepts. Possibly Kant made these limits too stringent. But by attributing the "antinomies" into which every dogmatism leads to the unlawful use of concepts, he unknowingly repeated the great thinkers of the thirteenth century. Besides, in his new critique of the concept, Kant himself had been preceded by the last representatives of a trend which we must now examine: pre-Kantian empiricism.

X. HUME: GENERAL CONCLUSION— ABSOLUTE PHENOMENALISM AND SCEPTICISM. THE INDIRECT REVENGE OF METAPHYSICS

With Hume the only speculative values which remain are the immediate data of experience, that is, "perception" as such (as a "Kantian phenomenon"). This may be either the simple perception which provides us with the elements of our knowledge, or the differential perception which discovers also a few of their elementary relations.

Hence the empiricist critique of Hume leads to an *absolute phenomenalism.*

This explains the meaning of the sceptical remark which

terminates Hume's *Enquiry Concerning Human Understanding*:
" When we run over libraries persuaded of these principles, what
havoc must we make? If we take in our hand any volume; of
divinity or school metaphysics, for instance; let us ask, *Does it
contain any abstract reasoning concerning quantity or number?*
No. *Does it contain any experimental reasoning concerning matter of fact and existence?* No. Commit it then to the flames; for
it can contain nothing but sophistry and illusion."[1] Except for
one abstract science, mathematics, the empiricist recognizes as
valid only the experimental sciences. Such are the limits of the
field of human knowledge. Yet even within these limits the
understanding possesses no legitimate means to distinguish the
" objective " from the " subjective," reality from appearance,
ideal from external existence; every perception affirms only itself
and that which depends on it; everything for man is mere
" phenomenon."

It will have been noticed that the critical reasonings which
lead Hume into phenomenalism are ultimately always based
upon the fundamental postulates of empiricism—immediate experience and analysis. One might possibly question the logical
value of some of these reasonings; yet, as a rule, they hit the
mark if one admits their premises. It seems to us that we have
a right to repeat that Hume is but an empiricist who proceeds
logically to the very end of his system.

Does it follow that, provided one accept the empiricistic
principle, the phenomenalism of Hume provides a solution for
all the problems which human reason cannot help bringing up?
By no means. And the British philosopher himself frequently
admits that he is puzzled. He feels confronted with an antinomy
which comes up time and again and which faces him on many
sides.

In virtue of the empiricist principle, the isolated perceptions
do not need any further justification: they are the primitive
elements, the psychological atoms to which all the rest must be
reduced. Yet, on the other hand, these perceptions become
associated, necessarily and regularly. They are associated in
objective wholes and in the unity of consciousness. What is this

---

[1] Chicago, 1965, p. 173.

mysterious connection which is not justified by the sole elements which are thus connected and which forces itself nonetheless upon the understanding's activity? I may notice this connection in me like an unavoidable process, " but all my hopes vanish when I come to explain the principles that unite our successive perceptions in our thought or consciousness. I cannot discover any theory, which gives me satisfaction on this head."[1]

Hence I undergo a unifying necessity which I feel unable to define in itself and to explain; I shall simply have to describe its effects and to examine its analogies. Especially since the empiricist principle forces me to accept two conclusions which are incompatible with any reasonable explanation of my associating tendencies: " In short, there are two principles, which I cannot render consistent; nor is it in my power to renounce either of them, namely *that all our distinct perceptions are distinct existences, and that the mind never perceives any real connexion among distinct existences.*"[2] Everything would become clear if I could admit the inherence of several distinct perceptions in a simple and existing subject, or the direct perception of a real connection between the impressions whose respective existences are given to me. But this would mean giving up the empiricist principle of analysis, the first foundation of my critique. What then shall I do? " For my part, I must plead the privilege of a sceptic, and confess, that this difficulty is too hard for my understanding."[3]

It is easy to see what antinomy Hume tries to avoid by this sceptical pirouette: it is the old and primitive antinomy of *multiplicity* and *unity*. Empiricism pulverizes human knowledge; as a result it feels quite embarrassed before the manifestations of unity which mischievous nature continually throws before it as so many obnoxious and insoluble problems.

As a matter of fact, empiricism is even unable to take cognizance of the ancient antinomy. It is aware of the multiplicity, because experience is multiple. As for the unity of this multiplicity, empiricism does not deny it, it ignores it. It must ignore it, for it cannot discover its ultimate explanation.

[1]*Treatise of Human Nature,* Oxford, 1896, pp. 635-636.
[2]*Ibid.,* p. 636.
[3]*Ibid.*

But metempirical unity takes its revenge. It clings to every movement of the phenomenalistic philosopher. It is driven from the luminous stage of knowledge, but it hides under the floor amidst the machinery which mysteriously but efficiently controls the settings of the stage. Hume feels unable to expel it thence; he has to admit its deep and inexplicable influence. Thus for the abstract unity of the general ideas; it is absent from clear consciousness but it takes shape in the specific features of the *evocating tendency.* Thus again, between the successive impressions and ideas, *active habit* will throw as a connecting link the dynamic bond of causality. Finally, the discontinuities and the eclipses of a too short experience will be made up in some way by the encroachments of that *belief* which creates among the variegated diversity of the ideas the stability of a "value in itself." The terms which Hume repeats so frequently—*custom, habit, belief* or *assent*—are indirect homages to metaphysical unity by which pure empiricism acknowledges its own impotence. It would not take great effort to point out in them the metaphysical notions of *specification, formal causality, finality* and *being.*

XI. GENERAL CONCLUSIONS

(1) The history of modern philosophy before Kant has allowed us to check, in fact and in detail, the theoretical prediction which we made at the beginning of this *Cahier,* namely that pre-Kantian philosophy, rationalism as well as empiricism, *develops the very consequences of the general theory of concepts which prevailed at the end of the Middle Ages.*

Would another development have been possible on the same foundation? Most probably not. If the *direct* conceptual knowledge of material objects is not synthetic and universalizing as explained by St. Thomas, it can only be intuitive and singular, whether by merely reproducing sense perception so as not to differ essentially from it—such was the position of the empiricists, who were willing to admit the most radical agnosticism— or because it derives from a direct intellectual intuition of the essences without the real intervention of a passive sensibility, as admitted by the various ontologists with their exaggerated metaphysical realism. On the road to empiricism, mere logic led to Hume's phenomenalism. On the road to ontologistic dogmatism or to rationalism, the same ruthless logic led to Spinoza's monism. The sceptical philosophy of Hume and the realistic philosophy of Spinoza represent, each in its own way, complete systems, terminal points for human thought. We might even say, blind alleys whence one escapes only by retrogressing. Both of them also reveal the exact scope of the remote presuppositions which control them.

(2) It will have been noticed that the double development—rationalist and empiricist—of pre-Kantian philosophy happens along divergent lines. Their terminal stages show an irreducible opposition, the opposition of pure reason and sense experience, of intelligible unity and material multiplicity. Moreover, beneath the general antinomy of rationalism and empiricism which shows up the original error of pre-Kantian philosophy taken as a whole, we discover plenty of secondary antinomies. They are more numerous in rationalism, which affirms more easily. There are fewer of them in phenomenalistic empiricism, which minimizes affirmation. . . . Their proximate cause derived from the fact that both philosophical trends omitted to distinguish in the concept the " representation " from the " signification," thus being unable to extend the " signification " of the concepts beyond the objects whose specific form they directly " represent." Thence resulted, in rationalism, the unnoticed intrusion of quantitative multiplicity into the intelligible. In empiricism the result was the unconscious attribution of *intelligible value* to the phenomenon as such, which is tantamount to confusing, to some extent, metaphysical unity with inconsistent multiplicity, the absolute with the relative, the necessary with the contingent.

In the final analysis, pre-Kantian philosophy, deriving from Ockham's nominalism, or at least from a thesis which was the basis of Ockhamism, was *imprisoned in a fundamental alternative, the two terms of which in their turn gave rise to antinomies.* But " from a true premise only follow true conclusions." It is evident that the starting point was wrong since the terminal philosophies—Spinozism and Wolffianism on one hand, empiricist phenomenalism on the other—both contain their share of errors.

(3) However, there are no total errors. Every error contains a partial truth. Kant will take upon himself precisely the task of rediscovering the partial truth of empiricism and rationalist metaphysics, of going back beyond their logical point of divergence and reconciling them by correcting the causes of their deviation, that is, rationalist dogmatism and empiricist exclusivism. For simplicity's sake we shall call this an attempt at a *synthesis of rationalism and empiricism.* Before describing and evaluating this attempt (*Cahier III*), we must here draw the reader's attention to a few important points which Kant had to consider.

(4) First, some may wonder why a study which takes historical connections into account presents the monism of Spinoza as a complete example of pre-Kantian rationalism, when it was not Spinozism but Leibnizian-Wolffian rationalism which influenced the beginning of critical philosophy.

It is indeed not Spinoza but Wolff whom Kant tried to reconcile with Hume. But this hardly matters, for the precise point which interests critical philosophy is common to both rationalistic metaphysicians. Moreover, it is really Spinoza who, from the doctrinal point of view, constitutes the most advanced form of pre-Kantian rationalism. It might even be of some interest to remark that, logically speaking, Wolff had no other defense against monism than the strange bit of reasoning by which he tried to deduce from the formal principle of identity the ontological principle of sufficient reason.

Now this reasoning not only clearly begs the question, it also conceals a real contradiction. Kant pointed this out when, in the pre-critical stage of his personal evolution, he realized that it was impossible to demonstrate analytically any kind of ontological " cause," that is, to discover the " logical reason " of an effect in some reality distinct from it. It followed that, for Kant, the opposition between cause and effect was not rationally justifiable. A rational justification could reach in the objects only their immanent principle, the foundation of their necessary identity. If Kant had stopped here instead of advancing along the road of the critique, and had tried to build a system of speculative metaphysics, he would have been unable, without proceeding illogically or at least arbitrarily, to avoid Spinozian pantheism. As soon as the shaky barrier of Wolff's paralogism is overthrown, the principles of rationalism lead quite naturally to monism. We will meet another confirmation of this logical affinity when we later study the great transcendental systems derived from Kant which are almost identical with a Spinozism transposed in the key of critical idealism.

Hence we might say that, if in the history of ideas Wolffianism is the " real " starting point for Kantian philosophy, Spinozism is its " virtual " starting point.

(5) Kant not only had behind him (as an aid or possibly as a brake) the rationalistic systems of metaphysics, but he was also able to use the attempts made by his predecessors in building *a critical epistemology.* We shall reduce to three main points the conclusions reached in these attempts.

The Epistemological Function of the Subject

Modern philosophy is sometimes credited with having introduced the subject into the problem of knowledge. Let us not insist on the exaggerated nature of this claim, whose exclusiveness is not quite fair to those ancient philosophers who emphasized the subject's spontaneity and the object's immanence in intellectual knowledge. Furthermore, every system which reaches a metaphysics of knowledge must emphasize the consideration of the subject. For the relation of knowledge necessarily enters into an ontological system as an immanent synthesis of subject and object.

It is true, however, that modern philosophy has more explicitly used the notion of the Ego or subject in epistemology. And theoretically speaking, rightly so. The general validity of ancient realism had been questioned. A critique of our basic certitudes had become necessary. Where could we find a better foundation for it than in this peculiar point where subject and object meet and coincide, that is, in the Ego?

By making " I think, therefore I am " the cornerstone of his whole philosophy, Descartes inaugurated the unavoidable subjectivism of the modern critique. Yet he did not discover the special point of view from which the Ego might really serve as the basis of a rigorous critique. The Cartesian Ego remains the Ego as substance, a part of the ontological object. Moreover, the direct epistemological function of the Cartesian *cogito* consists merely in providing, in a specially clear instance, the criterion of undoubtable evidence which was then analogically extended by Descartes to other objects. Hence, all in all, the precedence of the Ego is only that of an object privileged among all others. Although it aimed at absolute independence, Cartesian epistemology evolved within the framework of the objectivist realism of ancient philosophy.

Empiricism also appeals to the subject, but only to a " psychological subject "—the place where and the agent by which the sense representations are put together. Although the activities of a " psychological ego " might explain the mechanism of knowledge, they cannot establish its objective value. Hume himself admitted this with the smiling nonchalance of the sceptic.

On the other hand, the Leibniz of the *Nouveaux Essais* almost succeeded when he defined the intellect as an objective (apperceptive) function which is both formal and active. But he was unable to justify critically his dynamic point of view.

Will we then have to give up, in epistemology if not in metaphysics, every consideration of the thinking subject? Not necessarily. The very failure of the attempts mentioned above suggests, by way of exclusion, the condition under which the thinking subject might lawfully be used in the critique of the object. This condition is that in our critique we do not consider the subject either as an object (Descartes) or as a mere psychological faculty extrinsic to the object (Hume). The subject can define the value of the object only insofar as, identified with the object, it remains opposed to it. In other words, insofar as that which actually knows becomes identically that which is actually known. This new conception of the subject, considered as *a function which is intrinsic to and constitutive of knowledge* (as a " transcendental subject ") will impose itself upon every critical philosophy, beginning with the philosophy of Kant.

The Notion of Phenomenon

To bring up the problem of metaphysical realism means to separate, for purposes of investigation, the content of consciousness and the ontological affirmation which embraces it; hence it means to define the phenomenon as a " precisive " object of investigation. Every time the ancients tried to justify their realism, they used—at least implicitly—the notion of phenomenon. Yet we must admit that this notion received its full critical meaning only in modern philosophy, when for the first time metaphysical reality was not only questioned but was totally and systematically relegated to the hypothetical domain of the unknowable. Then the notion of phenomenon ceased to represent a merely methodical and temporary viewpoint of the mind and was used to delimit a privileged domain of knowledge and to designate a philosophy. When we remember the critique of the ideas of Ego, substance and existence in Hume's empiricism, we realize that here the rejection of metaphysical realism corresponds explicitly to the adoption of the phenomenon as the formal object of knowledge. Here the phenomenon acquires a clear technical meaning; it is the pure content of consciousness deprived of every ontological property; or again, it is the representation insofar as it posits only itself.

Kant utilized Hume's pioneering attempts. He again took up the notion of phenomenon, which had by now become the obligatory starting point of every critical investigation. But he first had to get rid of an ambiguity which remained in Hume's system and which we have already pointed out. It is worth our while to insist upon it once more before studying Kant's philosophy. Hume makes no theoretical distinction between the " phenomenon " and the " phenomenal object." For him the " phenomenon " is the representation as given in clear consciousness, as entering into associative connections, and as symbolized in language; in short, as possessing all the features of an " object " of thought. But the conditions which explain the presence of a mere representation in our knowing faculties, that is, of some diversified content, might not be sufficient to explain how this representation assumes for us the value of an " object," how it opposes itself within our mind to our knowing subjectivity. The " objectivation " of the empirical diversity presents a problem which Hume seems not to have suspected and which will become the central problem of the *Critique of Pure Reason*: how can simple representations refer to objects, that is, assume the value of objects in our thought?

We shall see how Kant differentiated between the problem of metaphysical realism (studied by Hume) and the new problem of the " objectivation " as such.

Space, Identity and Cause

From the beginning of his philosophical career, Kant faced these three notions (space, identity and cause) which would play an important part in the slow elaboration of the critical point of view. They had been provided with interpretations which not only contradicted each other, but which, as he slowly found out, were also unacceptable in themselves.

Space—in which most scholastics acknowledged an irrational element deriving from matter—had been " intellectualized " by the Cartesians. In the Leibnizian-Wolffian philosophy, it even became the mere indistinct stage of an idea of objective coexistence. On the other hand, with the empiricists space was connected with the sense representation, not as its universal and previous condition, but as a secondary elaboration of visual, tactile and kinesthetic sensations.

Identity—for the empiricists it had turned into the mere factual coincidence of the representation with itself. For the rationalists, the basic relation of identity had a character of strict necessity, both logical and ontological.

Wolffianism was anxious to rationalize causality by basing it upon an analytic necessity; it discovered strange analogies between the relation of identity and *causality*. The " intelligible reason " or the " logical reason " (*Grund*) was equated with the " ontological reason " or with the " cause " (*Ursache*). Thus the notion of cause tended to be identified with that of essence. On the other hand, under Hume's analysis the idea of ontological cause disintegrated into a plurality of phenomenal relations.

It took Kant long and painstaking efforts to discover in these three difficult and much debated notions a meaning which would force him logically neither into sceptical impotence nor into antinomical dogmatism, and to discover a way which would lead to a general synthesis of rationalism and empiricism.

CAHIER THREE

THE CRITIQUE OF KANT

Maréchal's Cahier III *contains five parts : (1) the stages of Kant's philosophy—from Wolffianism to the* Critique; *(2) the object and method of the* Critique of Pure Reason; *(3) the unity of the senses and the understanding in experience; (4) the "regulating" function of pure reason; (5) the ideas of reason as postulated by the moral will and presupposed by sentiment.*

Maréchal's interpretation of Kant was well received by the experts. It was one of the first and most influential commentaries written by a scholastic philosopher, in a scholarly spirit of fairness, on the great philosopher of Königsberg. It remains one of the best introductions to Kant, and perhaps deserves to be translated in its entirety.

Here, however, we are limited to two extracts. The first one, Extract XII, is the introduction to Cahier III. *It repeats some of the ideas mentioned in Extract XI, and carries on from there. The second passage, excerpted from* Cahier III, *is the general conclusion of Maréchal's study of Kant (Extract XIII).*

XII. INTRODUCTION

In the history of western philosophy there have occurred a small number of decisive moments when the influence of a philosophical genius imposed itself irresistibly upon human thought, either to accelerate its evolution or, at least, to overcome a partial crisis. We are thinking of Parmenides, who recovered the unity of being from the initial chaos of cosmological speculation; of Plato and Aristotle, who dominated the turmoil stirred up by the sophists and rebuilt metaphysics; of St. Thomas, who rediscovered the full meaning of Aristotelianism and reconciled it with Christian supernaturalism; of Descartes, who boldly re-established the uncompromising leadership of reason and in this way hastened the maturation of the problem of knowledge.

Kant assumed a role which is at least as important as that of his great predecessors when he took upon himself the job of instituting the definitive critique of rational thinking. Whatever may have been the theoretical, moral or religious value of his intervention, it has been singularly efficacious. The Kantian critique has deeply modified modern philosophy. In this sense all our contemporaries acknowledge their indebtedness to Kant: some of them because they formally take over some of his teachings; others because they are indirectly influenced by him; others, finally, because they have at least been forced to consider new problems and to organize on new bases the defense of old positions.

Moreover, like Cartesianism, Kantianism is not an absolute beginning in the history of philosophy. Kant had his precursors. Elsewhere we have studied the attempts at a critical epistemology undertaken by rationalists like Descartes and Leibniz, or by empiricists like Locke and Hume (*Cahier II*). Their solutions were incomplete and unilateral, but they at least had the advan-
what stumbling blocks must be avoided. Each one of these
tage of clearing the ground and of showing by their very failure
attempts made a lasting contribution. Descartes called our attention to the possible epistemological function of the Ego; Leibniz emphasized the dynamism of the intellect in the constitution of the intelligible object; Locke and Hume showed how inadmissible was the opinion that man possessed inborn ideas and what serious difficulties derived from every kind of onto-logistic realism.

Moreover, Kant's critique was to some extent predetermined by the concrete terms of the problem he faced. We have shown in the previous *Cahier* how the natural development of modern philosophy starting from Ockhamism had driven this philosophy into two extreme positions, two blind alleys: on the one hand, *phenomenalistic empiricism* (Hume), on the other hand, *rationalistic dogmatism* of the monistic (Spinoza) or the pluralistic kind (Wolff). On both sides no further development was possible. Empiricism landed in sceptical impotence; rationalism disintegrated in internal contradictions. Kant will need many years of laborious reflection to keep out of the former and to take stock of the latter. Kant's critique is so important historically and so interesting for us because it slowly emerged from the direct and continued confrontation of the two great tendencies which divided the philosophy of his time. The century-long conflict between dogmatic rationalism and empiricism was finally resolved, after thirty years, in the head of an honest, patient, rigorous and systematic thinker. The upshot was at least a partial solution to the fundamental antinomy of rationalism and empiricism. Since the two opposing tendencies had by then developed their most extreme consequences, Kant was able to reconcile them only by returning unconsciously to a synthetic viewpoint which had been overlooked by the ancestors of modern philosophy. In fact, by dint of patient, personal reflection, Kant forced philosophy to travel backwards towards the crossroads whence empiricism and dogmatic rationalism had started on their diverging ways. From this viewpoint, the founder of the modern critique should, despite the insufficiencies of his solution, be counted among the restorers of the necessary unity of the One and the Many which had been compromised ever since the end of the Middle Ages.

We said that the Kantian restoration of unity was incomplete. We shall try to indicate exactly where it is lacking, and why. Here again we will see that Kant is with the mainstream of the general philosophical environment; hence he depends on remote historical antecedents. Despite some velleities which show up in the *Critique of Judgment,* he is afraid of going beyond a prudent agnosticism, of proceeding in the direction of a finalistic metaphysics or absolute idealism. The obstacle, of which he himself was not aware, is a prejudice which he shares with the whole of pre-Kantian philosophy (from the time medieval Thomism went out of style). Once we have spotted this obstacle it will not be too difficult for us in the following *Cahiers* to consider the possibility of a position which lies " beyond " Kant, strange as it may seem to speak of a "beyond " in relation to a doctrine whose most typical feature seems to be to impose upon reason limits beyond which it can never venture.

XIII. GENERAL CONCLUSIONS

We should not forget that Kant, despite strong reservations deriving from his meticulous critique, admits that the trans-

cendental ideas, which for theoretical reason are only subjective exigencies, receive a strong backing from man's will and
feelings. A real convergence of his knowing and striving faculties induces man in many ways to affirm the same problematic
objects. First *God,* either as absolute Being, or at least as the
" supreme architect of the universe "; next the Ego, as a moral,
free and subsistent subject, or as an active finality which reacts
upon the objects; finally, *Nature,* as a cosmic unity or as a
system of objective ends.

Thus these ideas enjoy strong support in the mind. What
would transform the subjective certitude which they possess into
the full " objective truth " of objects of *science?* Kant has
repeated countless times that this would happen only if they
were *constitutive of a theoretically necessary object.*

Kant admits that the *presupposita* of feeling are " constitutive " of our concrete action whenever we intend particular ends
(*praktisch-bestimmend;* see *Critique of Judgment,* para. 88). But
our concrete action is never in itself *absolutely* necessary. Likewise the postulates of practical reason are " constitutive " of our
action, more specifically, of our moral action as such, hence of
an action which is *absolutely* necessary because it is wholly
obligatory. Therefore, their practical value is absolute, but they
do not yet possess the *theoretical* necessity which characterizes
objective truth. Neither the *presupposita* of feeling nor the
postulates of practical reason are " theoretically constitutive "
(*theoretisch-bestimmend, ibid.*). This means, says Kant, that
although they seem to be the " only possible form of our
thought " either with respect to some given action, or even
" absolutely " and for every possible action, they do not appear
to be the " only form of possibility of the objects " (*ibid.*). Hence,
from the theoretical viewpoint they are only " regulating " principles of our thought, expressions of our reason's " subjective
need for unity " and nothing more.

Among the intellectual functions of knowledge only the categories are " constitutive " of a necessary theoretical object since
without their formal participation no object of thought is
possible for us. But the theoretical object which they render
intrinsically possible, thus sharing its objective necessity, is but
a relative " phenomenal object." Since they possess no " trans-

cendental content " the categories are of no " transcendental use," that is, they lack all immediate ontological meaning (see the conclusions of the *Transcendental Analytic*).

An absolute reality—not any vague " thing-in-itself," but a reality determined as absolute—might be known *objectively* by *theoretical reason* only if this reality were the *internal* condition of possibility of the very constitution of the necessary object of our understanding. In this event Kant would admit the metempirical function of the objectivity of our reason. But then he would also have to admit that in our human knowledge there is no purely phenomenal object. The noumenal object of reason, the metaphysical object, would be implicitly contained in the very object of understanding. Needless to add that Kant excluded any possible realization of this hypothesis. For him it was quite evident that speculative reason was unable to build a metaphysics[1] without a real *intellectual intuition* of the objects.

The question is then whether such an intellectual intuition is absolutely necessary for metaphysics. Is it not possible to think of some intermediary between the phenomenal object of the understanding and the noumenal object of an intellectual intuition? Kant himself has hinted at a third possibility. He wrote that from the " transcendental ideas," the postulates of practical reason, " we learn that they *have* objects, yet we cannot show *how* their concept refers to an object; and this is not yet a knowledge of *these objects.* . . . Yet in this way a problematical thought has for the first time acquired *objective reality* " (*Kritik der praktischen Vernunft,* 1788, p. 243). But as mentioned above, this indirect objectivity derives only from a *practical* necessity of reason. Let us proceed slightly further in this direction and consider a hypothesis, as is always permissible when we wish to get out of a pressing alternative. Let us suppose that we can show that the postulates of practical reason—at least the divine Absolute—are likewise " conditions of the possibility " of the most basic exercise of theoretical reason, that is, *of the very function through which theoretical reason gives itself an object in experience.* In that event we would have established the objective reality of these postulates upon a " necessity " which belongs

---

[1] We mean a metaphysics in the strict sense, that is, an objective knowledge of noumena.

to the speculative domain. They would, as it were, become "postulates of speculative reason." Yet, on the other hand, as they lack all metaphysical intuitive content, they would not provide us with the *proper and direct* concept of the transcendent objects, whose necessary existence they would nonetheless indirectly reveal to us.

One vaguely foresees very complicated problems, possibly contradictions, on this intermediary road. Yet it seems that if one wishes to escape the Kantian dilemma, it is the only possible road. It is also in this direction that one may rediscover, via the critique itself, the profound meaning which Thomism attached to *analogical knowledge.*

The objection might be raised that this way out, which transfers to theoretical reason the most essential prerogatives of practical reason, will in final analysis be based on the primordial necessity of action in the widest sense of the term—on the priority of act over form, on the dynamic nature of speculation. Are these points of view not wholly opposed to the spirit and method of the critique? It is true that in spite of the dynamistic expressions (function, synthetic activity, and so on) which Kant employs like all other philosophers, his demonstrations are totally based on the static interlocking of *a priori* conditions, upon a logically necessary hierarchy of " forms " and of " rules." In this respect the neo-Kantians were right: the *Critique of Pure Reason* is above all a nomology and a methodology of reason. Kant was unable to rid himself totally of the leaven of Wolffianism. He did not go beyond a static analysis; with him the transcendental consideration from which, according to Fichte, might emerge the conquering affirmation of the *act,* is restricted to the careful and definitive analysis of the *form.*

That is why the dynamistic conception of the understanding which we have in mind can get a foothold in the critique only if backed up by the strongest reasons, that is, by the most undeniable postulates and the most fundamental exigencies of this critique, notwithstanding the rationalistic spirit and even, to some extent, notwithstanding the method which rules it.

Is such a violent irruption into the solid and profound work we have analyzed at all possible? Will we be able to force Kant to go beyond himself, to give up in behalf of *the* critique, the agnostic conclusions of his critique? Everybody knows of the attempts of philosophers who, in various ways and with varying success, have undertaken this task. Less well known is the fact that medieval Aristotelianism contained, virtually and by anticipation, some epistemological principles overlooked since the first beginnings of modern philosophy which might enable us to widen the masterful but incomplete Kantian analysis.

CAHIER FIVE

THOMISM CONFRONTING CRITICAL
PHILOSOPHY

Maréchal's most important work is the famous Cinquième Cahier *of* Le Point de Départ de la Métaphysique. *This volume came out in 1926. We have explained in our Introduction why the author published it before* Cahier IV, *how much trouble he had with censorship and that this difficulty contributed towards making the book unwieldy and difficult to read.*

The work consists of a long Preambulum *and three Books, here called Parts. In the* Preambulum, *or Foreword, Maréchal endeavors to avoid all misunderstandings by very precisely defining his point of view. Part One has only one chapter; it explains the two main methods of instituting a critique of knowledge: the metaphysical critique of the object as practiced by the ancients and the transcendental critique of the object or the critique of the knowing faculty as practiced by Kant and his successors. Part Two studies the theory of knowledge within the framework of Thomistic metaphysics. Part Three presents the Thomistic critique of knowledge transposed into the transcendental mode.*

Extract XIV is taken from the Foreword.

Extract XV is a translation of Part One of Cahier V. *It compares the metaphysical critique of the ancients with the transcendental critique of the moderns.*

XIV. FOREWORD

When confronting the claims of modern criticism, there are two ways of upholding the rights of traditional intellectual realism: (1) to deny, partially or wholly, the legitimacy of the critical demands; (2) to show that metaphysical realism satisfies these demands, even though they are exaggerated or arbitrary. These two approaches do not exclude each other. We shall use both of them.

We have already devoted four volumes to showing to what great extent the starting points of Kant's critique have been historically and logically conditioned by the fateful loosening of the metaphysical synthesis which started in the fourteenth century. This was one way of calling into doubt, if not the relative opportunity, at least the absolute and universal validity of the methodological demands of Kant. In *Cahier V* we would like to show more directly, through the doctrines themselves, that a metaphysical realism based on the primary evidence of the ontological affirmation contains no internal contradiction and needs no artificial shoring. This is the second way of denying in fact the absolute validity of the critical exigencies formulated by Kant.

At the end of the present *Cahier* (Part III) we will use the second method mentioned above, that is, we will investigate whether the initial postulates of Kant (the *phenomenal object* and the *transcendental method of analysis*) might not conceal, no matter what Kant may have thought, the implicit affirmation of a real metaphysical *object*. Whatever the answer to this question may be, the permanent value of ancient realism remains solidly established in our eyes. Yet we do not consider this new inquiry wholly useless. It would be interesting to find out that metaphysical realism so thoroughly permeates human thought that it is already contained with logical necessity, in the mere " objective " representation of any datum whatsoever.

Hence this volume will suggest in behalf of metaphysical realism a double demonstration, one mainly doctrinal, the other mainly polemical. The first one, starting from the basic realism of direct and reflexive intellectual knowledge, will investigate knowledge itself as a totality of ontological relations between subject and object, and discover in these ontological relations the logical characteristics of our various faculties. The second will first go along with Kant in order to proceed beyond him. It will reach the same conclusion about the ontological value of the intellect, the conclusion which constituted the starting point of the first demonstration.

XV. THE TWO WAYS OF THE CRITIQUE OF KNOWLEDGE

The epistemology of the ancients did not totally overlook the critical problems; yet their theory of knowledge proceeds from a viewpoint which differs from the modern critique. It is time to compare these two points of view more directly so as to discover where they may agree and where they are incompatible.

If we consider only its main lines, the history of epistemology comprises a preliminary period and two main successive stages, namely, metaphysical and transcendental.

After some initial gropings, the triumph of the Socratic school over the sophists solidly established the unavoidable *necessity of affirmation,* insofar as the latter coincides with the absolute positing of the contents of consciousness according to the universal rule of the first principle (whatever is, is; considered from the same viewpoint, being and non-being exclude each other).

What was immediately at stake in the struggle against the sophists was not so much logical truth, but rather the emancipation of objective thought from the material inconsistencies of language. Henceforth the infinite versatility of verbal combinations, which was not even stopped by contradiction, was held in check by an elementary and universal regularity discovered in the combination of the concepts signified by the words. Account had to be taken of the insurmountable obstacle of an absolute norm: *being,* as always implicitly affirmed in its identity with itself.

Despite the many consequences of this first discovery, it was only a prelude to the real critical problem—the problem of truth. It meant especially that, notwithstanding the sophists, the problem made sense, and notwithstanding the later sceptics, it could not be avoided and did not tolerate any abstention, any ἐποχή.

But acknowledging that the critical problem forces itself upon the human mind was ultimately tantamount to acknowledging the existence of a *logical truth,* the existence of a *necessary content* of our affirmation. What kind of truth is this? Of what kind must this content be? It is precisely the task of a theory of knowledge to solve this double enigma.

The search for this solution occurred successively in two ways. The ancients led the critique of knowledge into the way of *metaphysics.* It did not take them long to discover that the mind's brute content contains contradictory elements which cannot become indistinctly the object of legitimate affirmations. Hence the problem consisted in introducing in the mind's content the distinctions and the gradations required to safeguard the normative " first principle " while acknowledging the absolute and universal necessity of affirmation. This objective critique of knowledge, which was almost brought to completion by the Greeks, reached its peak in the Aristotelianism of St. Thomas. This was the initial phase of the critique of knowledge.

Starting from this objectivist phase, the spreading neglect of a few fundamental principles of the Thomistic synthesis brought about by way of reaction a second stage of the critique. We have seen how after the attacks of Ockhamism modern philosophy, unable to re-establish the balance of theoretical thought by means of a metaphysical critique, was induced to give up all the past and to attempt the radical critique " of the very faculty of knowledge." This new undertaking, prepared by Locke and Hume on the one hand, by Descartes and Leibniz on the other, received its final organization from Kant.

Metaphysical critique of the object; *transcendental* critique of the object: we must compare more carefully these two possible ways of a critique of knowledge.

The "Metaphysical" Critique of the Object

The reader is invited to consult *Cahier I* for a detailed study of the foundations of ancient realism. We shall here present only an outline of every metaphysical (or realistic) critique of the object.

(1) It supposes, besides some data of consciousness (some matter or content of consciousness), the absolute value of the " first principle " in its application to these data. This means a universal, objective affirmation of being or the necessary synthesis of being and of the affirmable datum.

(2) It is developed through a progressive diversification of this affirmation of being under the constant guidance of the " first principle." Theoretically, an object comes under the general objective affirmation only to the extent that it can be integrated in a structured system of concepts. The logical coherence of

the concepts expresses the extent to which being must be necessarily attributed to the objects.

But as soon as we begin to affirm the most primitive data, logical coherence seems threatened. Unity goes together with multiplicity, being is weighed down by non-being. The ontological critique necessarily demands a synthetic viewpoint from which this primitive antinomy may be objectively overcome. Since a merely static synthesis appears sooner or later to be inconsistent, the dynamic synthesis by means of (the notion of) " beginning " looks like the only way to reconcile the opposed terms. But beginning itself is defined by an opposition of *act and potency*. The various proportions of act and potency, going all the way from pure act to pure potency, must supply the complete table of the objective categories of being and constitute the framework of a true first philosophy in the Aristotelian sense.

This objective classification of being extends to the totality of all the possible objects of knowledge. Hence it includes the object of *reflective* knowledge as well as that of direct knowledge. But as soon as we reflect on it, any content of consciousness whatsoever shows an opposition between object and subject, between I and not-I. Reflection, which reaches the *subject,* discovers in it a new level of objectivity—the subject turned into an object. We might say, in a rather clumsy terminology, that the objective determinations of the immediate content of consciousness in general are divided into *objectivo-objective* or cosmological, and *objectivo-subjective* or psychological determinations.

Hence in the light of reflection the content of consciousness is something which belongs ontologically both to the Ego and to the non-Ego, that is, a relation between a real Subject and a real Object.

Hence, with the exception of natural theology, which belongs to the domain of analogical knowledge, all the immediate problems of speculative philosophy consist in finding a logical form of equilibrium of the cosmological elements with each other, of the psychological elements with each other, and finally of these two groups in their mutual relationship. The steady combination of the first principle and the manifold

data will give rise to a metaphysics of the non-Ego, a metaphysics of the Ego, and finally to a theory of knowledge as
relation between the metaphysical Ego and non-Ego.

(3) Moreover, a " critique of the object " cannot be complete and lasting if it does not integrate *voluntary action* within
the system of reason. In other words, a metaphysical critique
must embrace both theoretical and practical reason. For among
the objects of internal experience we discover not only speculative possession, but also action in the real sense of the word—
action which intends the realization of conscious purposes.
Speculation and action are in continual interaction, each one
preparing the way for the other. How shall we reduce to logical
unity this alternation of knowing and willing in our inner
" becoming "?

Aristotle and St. Thomas have tackled this difficult problem.
They claimed that the analysis of the data of consciousness reveals the initial indigence of our speculative action, since it depends on outside data of knowledge for its exercise. On the
other hand, it shows how our practical activity is always busy
reaching out for and appropriating these outside data so as to
reduce the distance between potency and act in our faculty of
knowledge. In this way, by steadily expanding our knowledge,
it makes us strive in a groping fashion towards the fullness of
theoretical activity: *the intellectual intuition of being,* the contemplation of the supreme intelligible—*contemplatio optimi
intelligibilis,* as St. Thomas says after Aristotle (S.T., II^a-II^{ae},
180, art. 4, c).

Thus the unity which St. Thomas established between speculation and action is mainly the concrete unity of a speculative
and absolute ultimate end, which we discover in the *movement*
that drives us towards this end. Since the ultimate end of action
is contemplation, our voluntary action itself turns into an
Intelligible *in fieri;* it is the becoming of the Intelligible in us.

The "Transcendental" Critique of the Object or the Critique of the Faculty of Knowledge

Whereas the metaphysical critique, yielding to the mind's spontaneous impulse, affirms *at once* the absolute reality of the object

and only afterwards re-examines the latter, subdividing and organizing it in conformity with the strictest rules of analytic logic, the transcendental critique *first* stops the movement of the mind, holds the realistic affirmation in abeyance and concentrates on the apparent content of consciousness in order to consider it in itself. Its starting point is not an " ontological absolute " recognized at once behind the appearances, but an ordered diversity of contingent " phenomena," present to the mind, whose eventual relation to an ontological absolute must be evaluated.

In the transcendental critique the " first principle " (the principle of identity) remains beyond doubt as *the norm of thought;* in the metaphysical critique it also supplied at once the *key to* (ontological) *reality.*

Besides the logical norm of identity and the power of receiving phenomenal data (this alone would not lead beyond Hume's empiricism), a transcendental critique necessarily assumes something else—the legitimacy of a *transcendental method of analysis.* The importance of this assumption has been made clear in *Cahier III.*

This new critique intends to define the value of the conscious object by means of its transcendental composition, that is, by means of the relation of its constitutive elements to the " faculties " from which they derive. A " faculty " is precisely nothing but a *power of* a priori *determination* of the object. The transcendental method should allow us to discover the effects of such determination within the object.

Kant claims that our power of " reflecting " on our objective contents of consciousness is the tool required for this task. Underneath the unity of every represented object reflection discovers a gradation of complementary elements standing with respect to each other in the logical relation of determined to determining, matter to form, multiplicity to synthetic unity. We discover a group of *a priori* formal conditions affecting each other, and underlying all of them, matter as known by the senses. Matter looks like a restricting, an irrational condition, a primary and extrinsic diversity which connects the object to *this* part of space and *that* moment of time. On the other hand, all the formal conditions possess a certain degree of generality which extends their scope beyond the particular object and present moment. They are *a priori* unifying and universalizing conditions whose impact increases as they come nearer to a supreme condition, to pure apperceptive unity. The latter, which is the *a priori* condition of every possible "object" in consciousness, corresponds, in critical terms to the pure "knowing subject," whereas the subordinated *a priori* conditions define only the "faculties" of this subject, that is, its categorical understanding and sensibility.

If Kant's analysis is correct, to know *objectively*, that is, to become aware of anything whatsoever as an object, consists in the *a priori* determination, according to formal conditions which grow more and more general, of some material content imposed upon our sensibility from without. Hence the following fundamental critical conclusion: since in the critique we accept as unavoidable initial datum the "conscious phenomenon" or "the object in the mind," we accept by the same token all its conditions of possibility, all its necessary "constitutive conditions"; and we accept them exactly as they come to our knowledge in the analysis of the object. Should they imply the objective existence of some *absolute,* we would acknowledge this absolute; should they reveal that everything is relative and connected with the phenomenon, we would treat them as mere functions of the phenomenal object.

Hence in Kantianism the whole value of theoretical knowledge depends on the very value of the *transcendental analysis* of the object. How trustworthy is such an analysis?

We have noted previously (*Cahier III*) that for Kant the existence of "pure sciences" (such as mathematics and pure physics) or more generally, the existence of universal and necessary synthetic propositions (synthetic *a priori* judgments) constituted, as it were, a practical demonstration of the value of transcendental analysis. Rejecting the results of such an analysis (that is, rejecting the *a priori* character of some determinations of the object) would necessarily entail the denial of the apodictical value of the pure sciences and of all true universality and necessity.

All this is true; but an empiricist would be willing to deny it without denying theoretically that the apriorism of the form in the object of knowledge should be the foundation of every universal and necessary proposition—if there were such propositions.

Hence, in order to convince an empiricist of the value of transcendental analysis, we should first convince him of the existence of an objective apodictical knowledge. This is a difficult task which cannot succeed without a thorough analytical study of concepts and judgments. No wonder then that Salomon Maimon should have reproached Kant (although erroneously) that he had not refuted Hume.

Hence if we wish to build a critique which does not, previously to all investigation, presuppose the universal and necessary character of some categories of synthetic judgments, we shall have to show more directly than by appealing to the pure sciences that some *a priori* conditions are involved in the very constitution of every object.

After having appealed in the Prologue of the *Critique* to the fact of "*a priori* synthetic judgments" (considered by Kant as undeniable data in need only of an investigation of their logical presuppositions), Kant himself points out in the *Aesthetics* and the *Analytic* a more direct vindication of his transcendental method.

He used the principle that every unified diversity, and *a fortiori* every "synthesis" properly so-called, supposes a complementary duality of constitutive elements—an element of multiplicity and a unifying element. Thus, when we put three or four dots down on paper, this group of dots shows besides a multiplicity (each dot separately) some unity (their juxtaposition in space). Since the multiple as such precontains in no way the unity which holds it together, the unifying element (here space as making possible the juxtaposition of the dots) cannot derive from the multiplicity itself. It is originally independent of it; it is logically previous or *a priori* with respect to it. The same reasoning might be applied to every form and every matter on all levels of being.

But the object of our sense knowledge, that which is given in immediate experience, is undeniably synthetic: it offers us a unified diversity. A reflective analysis of this diversity does not allow us to break it down beyond the qualitative diversity of the *sensations*. Thus we notice that this basic diversity of the sense datum manifests in our objective consciousness a unification at several levels: *space and time—categories* and *apperceptive unity*. All these unifying determinations are necessarily *a priori* with respect to the diversity unified by them. Hence space and time are conditions of the immanent object which are not in themselves restricted to the boundaries of *this* presently given sense diversity; otherwise they would purely and simply coincide with *this* diversity. The categories represent objective (or objectivating) conditions whose scope, far from extending only to *this* given sense diversity, is not even restricted to any time or space determination. And apperceptive unity, of which the categories are the multiple expression, extends without any limit to the object of thought in general, to Kant's "transcendental object."

All this is evident; and it would seem that, with Kant, we have discovered this hierarchy of *a priori* conditions by means of simple analytic reasoning on the objectivated data. This analysis seems to imply nothing but the more attentive noticing of the opposition between unity and diversity as it is given to our consciousness in every apprehension of some object. We notice these "*a priori* functions" (objective conditions of being? or subjective conditions of knowing?) as soon as we admit that unity does not derive from diversity as such.

In fact, the manner in which this Kantian analysis proceeds implies something of that which we mentioned, but it is much more complex and difficult to justify. It is very important for our purpose to remove from it even the shadow of ambiguity.

When, with Kant, I claim that I am performing a transcendental analysis of the "objective data," do I consider in them only their static aspect as "representations," thus excluding every kind of "*fieri*," every real activity which might appear in them?

Let us suppose that this is the case. I may then distinguish two aspects in the representation: a material diversity and the passive, already achieved unification of this diversity; in other words, a matter and a form, both concretely presented. But this leads me nowhere; I am locked up in my present and concrete representation. I might perhaps, without giving up the static point of view, distinguish these two aspects more clearly from each other—the material diversity and the unity which holds it together. I might, for instance, imagine a similar way of putting things together embedded in another kind of material diversity. In this way I would reach a notion of unification which is wider than the one I derived from this specific unified whole and, through successive abstraction, reach formal notions which become more and more general.

But is this really a " transcendental " analysis? Certainly not, for if I proceed in this way, the increasing generality of my abstract notions remains extrinsic to the given object; it derives from my possibly arbitrary power of restricting the logical comprehension of the objects of my thought by neglecting a more or less large number of their determinations. I can find out the value of my gradually growing abstractions *as internal laws of the object* only through a study of the objective value of my power of abstracting, that is, by performing a transcendental analysis of the object itself. The problem remains unsolved.

When we consider his very expressions, Kant attributed another meaning and scope to the transcendental method of analytic reflection. Its purpose was not to abstract arbitrarily, but really to *discover* the structural elements within the object of consciousness. It was supposed to reveal within this object not a scale of more or less abstract notes, but a relation like that which exists between an " *a priori* condition " and " that which is conditioned, an information " (not simply a " form "), an " active synthesis " of phenomena, a " spontaneity " in action. All these expressions have a meaning only within the order of dynamism and causality. It is quite evident that a dynamic principle cannot rise from a lifeless, passive object, contemplated in itself, in its merely representative outline. When we discover in it the " conditioning " of one part by another, we discover more than a purely static representation; we perceive a real activity. In mechanics, when we represent an equilibrium by means of an opposition of forces which neutralize each other, we necessarily suppose that the system contains " virtual movements," hence some internal activity. Therefore the Kantian transcendental analytic supposes that the object is " dynami-

cally " present in our consciousness as a totality of " determinations " or " conditions " which actively affect some matter
coming from the senses and that it may be known as such.

It is obvious that without this dynamic point of view Kant,
employing a logical analysis of the object and not a psychological analysis of the subject, would have spoken neither
of a " subject," nor of " faculties." Even for Kant a " transcendental subject " is quite different from an abstract view
detached from the object. In the *Critique* the subject is a
functional reality, the *locus* of the totality of the *a priori*
determinations of the object; and for Kant the " faculties " too
are not abstract labels cut out of the object, but partial groups
of *a priori* determinations of the object. Once more these
definitions lack all foundation and become even unintelligible
if the formal apriorism in the object is not understood in an
active, dynamic sense.

But if we define the *a priori* as an " activity " within the
immanent object, as an activity which takes hold of the sense
datum and renders it " knowable in act," transcendental reflection which detaches the *a priori* from the object will consist in
discovering *the active share of the subject in the* (immanent)
object. As this share increases, the object of knowledge draws
nearer to perfect objectivity—to intellectual intuition in which
according to Kant the object would be totally constituted by
the activity of the subject.

In order to understand Kant correctly we must explain more
precisely the nature of this subjective activity which inserts
itself in the constitution of the object. Kant has frequently noted
that to some extent it corresponds to the notion of " formal
causality." The unity always stands to unified multiplicity in
the relation of a form to some matter. But this is perhaps not
enough: for in the usual terminology a " form " means only
the immobile wrapping around some matter, the motionless
bond of a diversity; the form of a statue appears frozen in the
lifelessness of the marble. But the " *a priori* " formal condition
discovered through transcendental analysis must continue to
carry a virtual universality and, as it were, an " expansive "
meaning. It is a " form," but only insofar as it imposes itself
actively upon matter, thus showing that it logically existed

before this matter and that it extends beyond it, by way of a permanent and dominating condition.

In scholastic language we might say that the " formal causality " of the *a priori* conditions in the immanent object of knowledge is not a lifeless remnant, a structure which we discover and describe, but the activity by which the matter of knowledge is actively informed by the *internal finality,* by the " natural becoming " of the subject. The matter of knowledge can become an " object " only if it is grasped by the torrent which carries the subject towards his natural end : strictly speaking, the object in our consciousness is this very grasping of some matter coming from the senses by the vital movement of our intellectual nature.

How can we discover in the immanent object the apriorism which has thus been defined? Let us remember that the transcendental method, as a critical method, should establish not only the *fact* (nor even only the particular necessity) of some *a priori* in the objects which happen to be present in our consciousness, but the *universal necessity* of this *a priori* as a condition of every possible object (of a non-intuitive understanding).

A mere " transcendental reflection," the discovery of an *a priori* in objects which happen to be represented, corresponds only to the first of these two requirements; the *a priori* which it uncovers is a condition of the possibility of this or that singular object, even though the series of such objects may go on indefinitely. At the utmost the necessity of a reflectively discovered *a priori* does not extend theoretically beyond the limits of an inductive generalization.

Kant intends more than this. The necessary relation between the *a priori* and the objects must be shown with a strictly analytical evidence to be a constitutive element of every possible object of our understanding. Hence this relation must be deduced from the very *concept* of " the object of the understanding as such " (the object of a non-intuitive understanding, the " object of experience " in the Kantian sense), whatever the secondary peculiarities may be under which this concept may appear in our psychological activity. We recognize the process of " transcendental deduction," the indispensable crowning of the transcendental method. Kant was performing a transcenden-

tal deduction when he demonstrated that our objective knowledge is not only *in fact* constituted in our judgments by our
grasping of concrete phenomena under an *a priori* function of
unity and universality, but that, absolutely speaking, an object
containing a phenomenal content (an object of the understanding) *is possible only* under such an *a priori* function of
unity and universality. Once this has been demonstrated, the
reflective experience of the *a priori,* being subsumed under a
principle of rational necessity, acquires a real *critical* scope
since it is evident that the transcendental fact expressed by it
contains a condition of objective value which does not depend
on any contingent psychological circumstance.

We cannot spend much time on these methodological questions, which have been studied in *Cahiers III* and *IV*. But we
had to indicate in a few words the opposition and the solidarity
of the two characteristic aspects of the transcendental deduction.
First, because, in view of our overall purpose, they will control
the whole framework of the present volume; secondly, because
we deemed it necessary to remind the reader that the *a priori*
whose rational connection with the object is demonstrated by
the transcendental deduction is, under new logical properties,
the same *a priori* which simple reflection discovers.

Hence, since every *a priori* in a formal condition implies a
dynamic character, the transcendental method will be applicable
to our knowledge only if we are capable of perceiving through
reflection the immanent activity of our thought at the precise
spot where this activity inserts itself into and activates the
material element of our representations; we must be able to
reach the intellect in act in its very identity with the intelligible
in act; in other words, the object of our thought must be given
to us in reflection immediately, not as a " lifeless thing," but
as " passing from potency to act," as the stage of a " movement "
or an intellectual " becoming."

Does " reflection " really reveal it to us in this way? Do we,
by means of reflection, directly perceive in the immanent object
the *act* which determines it *a priori,* which makes it into an
object of knowledge? We are, of course, not asking whether
the subject has an essential intuition of himself as a metaphysical principle of activity, as an ontological cause; for

Kantian transcendental analysis it would be enough that the immanent object should reveal itself to reflection as the exercise of some activity, and not merely as a lifeless form.

But it is precisely this property of reverting to the content of consciousness, not simply as an outside object nor as a mere representative form, but, at least to some extent, as *act* (of the subject), which differentiates direct from reflective knowledge. Contemplating some concrete or abstract object does not constitute reflection; keeping or bringing a representation back into the focus of consciousness is still nothing more than a secondary exercise of objective attention or memory; it does not constitute reflection. Reflection in the proper sense of this word brings the objective representation back to the Ego, that is, it puts the representation back in the stream of activity from which it detached itself as object.

Hence, a philosopher who admits a faculty of reflection in man capable of perceiving, in the object of thought, the subject in act, can have no theoretical objections (we do not speak here of the detailed applications) against the process of transcendental reflection as understood above. He would deny the existence of this power of reflection only if he claimed that the consciousness which we undoubtedly have of our intellectual acts does not go beyond the static and discontinuous awareness of their succeeding content, without any awareness of activity in this change. Whence would we then derive our illusory notion of internal activity?

In short, the transcendental method of analysis seems to presuppose this: that in reflection our objective concepts are given to us as active determinations of some assimilated matter, as the passing from an objective potency of determination to actual determinations, as the immanent " movement " of a knowing faculty as such. Besides, it is only on this condition that the transcendental critique of the object would really constitute, as Kant claims, a " critique of the power of knowledge," not simply an abstractive analysis of the object.

The reflective perception of the inner dynamism of knowledge is so essential for critical analysis that we are disappointed when we notice the apparent vagueness of Kant's doctrine on this

point. And we find the same vagueness again in the inter-
preters of his philosophy.

It is true that the dynamic relation between subject and
object did not wholly escape his attention. In the *Critique of
Pure Reason* he uses expressions such as *principle of* a priori
determination; function or *act* ("which goes over, collects and
binds an empirical diversity "); active or experienced *connecting*
previous to the *representation of the connection; synthesis*
(postulated as "foundation of the synthetic unity "); *action of
the understanding (Verstandeshandlung); act of the spontaneity*
(of the understanding). His imagination, if not his reflexive
thought, was filled with dynamism. Why did he not draw all the
conclusions from these premises? Why did he not try like
Fichte to unify speculative and practical Reason on the basis
of a pure activity of the Ego, of a *Sollen?* We have said elsewhere that the Kantian critique seemed to us to be vague and
incomplete in this respect, and that, despite Kant's protesta-
tions, Fichte was not wholly wrong when he believed that he
continued the critique by developing its implicit principles.

Kant has overlooked the essential role which the active
finality of the Subject performs in the very constitution of the
immanent object, and this fact made his transcendental method
partially impotent. It looks as if two influences were in conflict
during the unconscious maturation of his critical doctrine. On
the one hand, the very obviousness of inner evidence pushes him
towards a dynamic conception of knowledge: he compares our
whole intellectual knowledge with the unreachable ideal of an
intellectual intuition which would be wholly spontaneous and
produce the object of knowledge by itself. Here he stands on the
viewpoint of the " act,"—the perfect act of intelligible possession
and more or less distant approximations of this act. But, on the
other hand, when formulating his conclusions, he seems to fall
back into the static and abstract spirit of Cartesian-Wolffian
rationalism and shuts himself up again in the rigid viewpoint of
the " form." Then he seems to proceed as follows: taking as his
first datum the motionless representation, he finds a hierarchy
in it; he sees that it is coordinated with other notions, inserted
in *a priori* synthetic judgments, in higher abstract unities which
in their turn are unified into a pure apperception; and it is this

state of affairs which he tries to describe by means of symbols which express the positive scope and boundaries of our knowledge. In this way the highest synthetic principle, apperceptive unity, is no longer perceived in reflection as a determining activity; it turns into a merely abstract label of unity. Likewise, the categorial functions harden into a general framework, and the whole problem of knowledge is narrowed down to a simple problem of formal unity. But can the object—even Kant's phenomenal object—be explained as an object through its formal unity alone? This is very doubtful: for an object stands in our consciousness not only as a " formal essence " (a logical, ideal essence), but also—rightly or wrongly, it does not matter here—as referred to some " in itself " opposed to the subject. How shall we explain this feature by a simple hierarchical structure of unities? This is a difficult problem to which we shall devote serious attention.

According to whether we insist on these or those ways of speaking used by Kant, we shall reduce the *Critique* to rationalist ideology, to a dogmatism of formal essences, which are decreed objective (" possible ") by the sole consideration of their logical unity; or we shall lead it up to a theory of knowledge whose central idea would be the intuition of a " movement " or immanent " *fieri*," that is, of a dynamic state of the Object in the Subject.

Within the latter line of the Kantian critique's development we meet Fichte and Schelling, whose impressive systems yield still too much to abstraction, and nearer to us, without exclusive historical dependence, Bergson, whose supple analysis takes apart the mechanism of our intelligence and discovers under its abstractions the ceaseless progress of some Becoming, of a vital Becoming which we might perceive from within.

At this final stage the critique of knowledge would already be a metaphysics, whatever its nature and value.

The reader may discover by now the presuppositions which, to our mind, and whatever may have been the historical idea of Kant, should constitute the foundation of a *transcendental critique of the object,* or, which amounts to the same, of a *critique of the faculty of knowledge.* They are not only the objective data considered as phenomena and the " first prin-

ciple " used as the regulating norm of thought, but also the
power of grasping the data in the very act which objectivates
them in us, not merely in their representational outline. We
shall call this power " transcendental reflection," or the faculty
of " transcendental analysis." For lack of this " transcendental
analysis " it is possible to perform an ever more abstract
analysis of the data themselves, not, however, strictly speaking
a critique of the faculties.

Comparison of the Two Critiques, Metaphysical and Transcendental

This comparison has already been made to a great extent in
the two preceding outlines. We shall content ourselves with
emphasizing one feature which very well typifies the initial
attitude of both critiques.

The ancients were objectivists because they consciously or unconsciously adopted a *finalistic outlook*. By clinging to the " first
principle " as an ontological principle they refused to admit that
any datum of consciousness might remain totally undetermined
with respect to affirmation, which is after all the prelude to
action. You *act* since you discuss, Aristotle replies to the
sophist. Besides, what is human life but a continual action,
ruled by fears and wishes? To stop acting would mean to stop
being human. But when you act, that is, when you react to all
your thoughts, you unceasingly acknowledge that you *affirm;* and
when you affirm you posit each time a stable relationship
between what you affirm and *being*: hence, whether you like
it or not, you admit a necessary and universal application of the
first principle in its ontological meaning.

All this amounts to saying that our contents of consciousness
always possess some degree of objective reality because they
insert themselves necessarily, in one way or another, in the
absolute finality which animates our action. The object turns out
to be " being " to the extent to which it imposes itself as an
" end."

Hence, the " metaphysical critique of the object " approaches
the object from the angle of necessary finality, and cannot help

positing it in an absolute affirmation. But after this first step it goes backwards and begins to pay attention to the particular *form* of the affirmed object: it analyzes the form (the essence) and according to this form it measures the degree of affirmation, that is, it establishes a hierarchy of beings. However, throughout all this the critique of the form takes place under the guidance of the previous absolute and universal affirmation of being. That is why we speak of a metaphysical critique; it posits the object immediately as an object in itself; it assumes at once its stand before it; only then, in this absolute perspective, does it analyze and modify it from without—dialectically, in accord with the law of identity—without bothering about the genesis of the object in the mind, until this problem of origin will force itself upon our attention in rational psychology. Meanwhile, with the assurance of a realism certain of success, it tries out concepts, endeavoring to make them fit each other as a child would piece together a puzzle, knowing full well that he will be successful. Owing to the initial ontological affirmation, the whole metaphysical problem is whittled down to discovering a state of logical equilibrium for the given elements.

The picture is quite different in the *transcendental* critique of the object, which is, strictly speaking, the modern critique of knowledge.

Here too we start with reflection, but unlike the objectivist critique, this one advances at once against the natural trend of the human mind. It suspends the absolute primitive affirmation of *being,* and instead examines the contents of consciousness in themselves and analyzes the conditions which make them into objects of knowledge. For the transcendental critique interest is at first wholly concentrated upon the *internal genesis of the object as object,* upon the " *fieri* " of the immanent object insofar as this " *fieri,*" far from being only a succession of psychological moments, contains the absolute and universal conditions of the possibility of the objects in general: the necessary structure of the immanent object and the respective origin of its constitutive elements must yield the secret of its logical *value.*

But here, as we said above, an alternative arises: either the structural analysis of the object as such shows only abstract forms, which, on account of their increasing abstraction, extend

logically beyond each other with that immobility which belongs
to purely speculative structures. In this event the transcendental
critique—if it still deserves this name—will not lead us beyond
a more or less subtle phenomenalism. Or, —and this is the
second term of the alternative—the analysis of the object reveals
in it, to immediate reflection helped by an authentic rational
deduction, an active power of unification, a dynamism, a
spontaneity, hence a subject in act: in that case, as we have
stated above and will have to demonstrate explicitly towards the
end of this *Cahier,* the transcendental critique would be legitimately completed only by the rational admission of finality which
reveals to us the existence of an Absolute Being. Kant, the
patient pioneer, would be completed rather than contradicted.

To sum up:

(1) The initial datum of every critique is the objects present
to consciousness, and submitted as such to a reflective examination.

(2) The ontological critique of the ancients starts from the
" objects " considered in the fullness of their objectivity, that is,
posited absolutely, as eventual ends (things); thence it proceeds
to the theoretical classification of their forms (essences, defined
through sense phenomena). It gives itself an objective Absolute
and refers the relative to it.

(3) The transcendental critique of the moderns also starts
with the objects, but as first considered abstractly in their
" forms " (as phenomena). If this critique tried to justify, even
more fully than it does, the objective signification which the
phenomena have in consciousness, it should (as we will show)
rediscover, under the form itself, the affirmation of ends.
Through the relative, which it finds in consciousness, it would
rediscover the ontological Absolute.

(4) The ancient critique coincides with the metaphysical
systematization and is finished only with it: it is the long road
of the critique, but it is also, to our mind, its natural method.

The modern critique claims to discover at once, within the
inner conditions of knowledge, the essential method and the
necessary starting points of every metaphysics. It constitutes an
epistemology which is previous to all metaphysics, a metaphysics in potency. It might be called the short cut of the

critique. It is based upon an artificial method: the phenomeno-
logical point of view—which destroys itself, of course, as soon
as it leads us to admit the metaphysical affirmation under the
phenomena. We believe that it can lead to this point.

These two critical methods, which approach the total object
from two complementary angles, should, if led to their final
conclusion, yield identical conclusions; for the ancient critique
posits at once the ontological object, which *includes* the transcendental subject; and the modern critique considers the transcendental subject, which *postulates* the ontological object.

If it is true—as we try to demonstrate in the present volume
—that the *ontological critique and the transcendental critique,*
although differing in the viewpoint from which they first consider the object of knowledge, converge necessarily towards
the same final result: a dynamic metaphysics, it seems to be a
foregone conclusion that from one to the other there should
exist a strict correspondence which allows us to consider one
as a simple transposition of the other.

But what is the key to this transposition?

The transcendental critique analyzes the *a priori determinations* of the immanent object of knowledge. Since these determinations (functional, modal, or whatever kind they may be) are
not nothing, they fall within the range of the metaphysical critique: hence they must have a place in the system of reality.
It is easy to guess where we will find them. In metaphysics, the
knowing subject himself is posited before the mind as an object.
The metaphysician speaks of the subject and immanent object
as an ontological subject and its real modification; the latter
depends, moreover, for its specific form, on an "object in
itself" which is as real as the two previous terms. Where the
Kantian critique, staying within the immanent object, discovers,
while avoiding all metaphysical affirmation, the "*a priori* determination of a given matter, in an object of knowledge," metaphysics has for many centuries studied a more complex, more
comprehensive, but parallel problem, the problem of "the reciprocal causality of the noumenal subject and of the object in
itself in the production of the immanent act of objective
knowledge."

This problem constitutes the fundamental theme of the *meta-*

physics of the knowing subject and constitutes an important part
of traditional psychology.

And if we wish to proceed beyond Kant, and put together
in one and the same critical justification speculative reason and
practical reason, it is once more in metaphysical psychology, in
the chapter traditionally devoted to the relation between will
and action on one hand and knowledge on the other, that we
will find (as did the ancients) this question examined more or
less completely in ontological language.

The two solutions—the ancient and the modern one—may
be compared with each other, provided we transpose the
metaphysical language into critical language, and vice versa.
The law of this transposition might be condensed in the following short formula.

The transcendental method of analysis of the object is a
precisive, not an exclusive, method. In the object of spontaneous knowledge, it considers *only* the immediate influence of
the faculties which make it a known object. That is, in Kantian
language, it considers the *a priori* which is constitutive of the
object—or again, the transcendental conditions of the possibility of the object (as opposed to its empirical condition,
the sense datum). This amounts to saying, in scholastic language,
that the transcendental method considers the " cognoscible in
act " according to the conditions which constitute it in its
" cognoscible actuality "; or else, insofar as the " cognoscible in
act " is identically the " knower in act "; or again, according
to the functional priority (a limited aspect of metaphysical
priority) of the knowing faculties over their objective operations.

It is not necessary to go on. In the following chapters we will
have the opportunity to analyze in detail this correspondence
between the critical *a priori* discovered through reflection and
transcendental deduction in the immanent object, and the metaphysical *a priori* which is logically deduced from their operations.

Part One (" THE TWO WAYS ") *compared the ancient metaphysical critique of knowledge with the modern transcendental*

*critique. After having explained that he will use both approaches
for the vindication of the absolute value of human knowledge,
Maréchal sets out in this, Part Two, to offer a thorough presentation of the ancient critique by a study of the theory of
knowledge within the framework of Thomistic philosophy.
Since this presentation is admittedly long and complicated, it
will be useful to give a general outline of the author's manner
of proceeding.*

*Is a metaphysical theory of knowledge critically justifiable?
Are we entitled to claim that our knowledge reaches out at
once to the absolute order, that it possesses an ontological
value? Should we not rather suppose that it stops at the
appearances, at the way things look to us? The ancients had
no doubt concerning the metaphysical value of their spontaneous affirmations. Nor was this spontaneous belief wholly
naïve. When challenged, they were able to justify it. Maréchal
will first briefly explain how St. Thomas justified his basic confidence in the power of human reason to reach absolute reality.
Hence the first section—"The Critical Prelude" of the metaphysics of St. Thomas (Extracts XVI–XVIII).*

*The second section, "Analysis of Objective Knowledge,"
examines in great detail the act of knowledge, whose absolute
value has been vindicated. The author explains how the act of
knowledge itself is to be interpreted metaphysically (Extracts
XIX–XX). He establishes that the basic act of knowledge is
the judgment. This is why he devotes considerable attention
to a thorough analysis of all the constitutive elements of human
judgment—its material elements (sensations and concepts)
(Extracts XXI–XXVIII) and its formal elements (synthesis
and affirmation) (Extract XXIX). This lengthy investigation
reveals that one of the elements implied in every human judgment is an affirmation of the whole of metaphysics, including
the affirmation of the Infinite Being.*

*We have thus been shown that man necessarily and unceas-
ingly affirms the Absolute Being. But what kind of necessity
forces him to do so? Is it only a psychological necessity like
the one which makes him see the sun " rising" and " setting"
or admit that there are only three dimensions in space? In that
case his necessary affirmation of God does not prove that God
really exists. If, on the other hand, it could be shown that
" the psychological necessity of the transcendental affirmation
was also a logical necessity, if it could be shown that it is not
only a concomitant or subsequent condition of every affirma-*

tion of an object, but the very condition which renders every
affirmation objective," then we would have demonstrated the
absolute value of metaphysics and the affirmation of God, since
to deny or even to doubt this value would involve a logical
contradiction.

In the third section of Part Two " Deduction of the Onto-
logical Affirmation" Maréchal tries to demonstrate that the
affirmation of the Absolute is implied in every human judg-
ment as a condition of the possibility of such a judgment.
Thus, within the framework of Thomistic metaphysics, *he tries*
to satisfy Kant's strictest criterion of the value of some know-
ledge; he tries to show that the affirmation of the Infinite Being
is a condition of the possibility of any object in consciousness.
In this section he offers us his ideas about the dynamism of
the human intellect; he shows that knowledge involves appetite,
that there is a continual interaction between intellect and will,
between speculation and action (Extracts XXX–XL).

We shall now offer a few representative extracts from each
of the three sections of Part Two.

XVI. COMPARISON OF THE DOUBT OF AQUINAS WITH THAT OF DESCARTES

There is a real but not a total analogy between the two theories
of doubt.

Descartes tries to doubt as much as he can, that is, as
radically and as extensively as it is possible to doubt. He does
not pay much attention to the intrinsic value of his reasons
for doubting. His purpose is to reach at once the solid rock
of an evident " truth," of a truth evident enough to stand
beyond any doubt and capable of serving as an unshaken
foundation for the systematic reconstruction of a philosophy.

The methodical doubt of Aristotle and St. Thomas causes
reflective reason to question the object which it wishes to know
scientifically. By way of a methodic fiction the mind refuses for
the time being to give its assent to this object; it treats it *ad*
modum quaestionis solvendae (like a problem which is to be
solved); it examines all its connections; it weighs all the reasons
which seem to plead for and against its value. This kind of
doubt is more exclusively negative and receptive than that of

Descartes. It requires no artificial effort in order to doubt positively, but only the impartial restraint which befits the objective investigation of a problem. In fact, rather than doubting, the philosopher in this case momentarily suspends his judgment so as to take his time in considering the hypothesis of doubting—*considerando dubitationem*. Although the fact of appealing to the tribunal of reflection momentarily suspends all the prerogatives of spontaneous reason, they will be wholly acknowledged without quibbling as soon as it turns out that they are valid. St. Thomas doubts less thoroughly than Descartes; on the other hand (and this is more important), his doubt is more universal. The purpose of St. Thomas is not, as with Descartes, to reach as soon as possible among all other possible " truths " a privileged one, which is indubitable, well defined and capable of serving as a constructive starting point. His intention is not so particularized, the scope of his doubt is wider and, paradoxical though it may sound, it is more thoroughly " modern." For he aims at nothing less than setting up a general critique of truth as such. That is why the first results of the methodical doubt will not be the same in Thomism and Cartesian metaphysics. The latter reaches the intuitive evidence of the ontological Ego (will it not be imprisoned in it?). The former concludes to the objective necessity of *Being* in general.

St. Thomas understood that the problem of truth must embrace the whole domain of knowledge. He explains, in Summa Theologica (*I, 44, 2, c*), *the manner in which the philosophers of old only gradually became aware of this understanding. For him, however, Maréchal writes :*

XVII. THE CRITICAL PROBLEM: THE EXISTENCE OF TRUTH

The most universal and thorough methodical doubt—in other words, the first and foremost critical problem—should concern the *existence of truth,* or, and this amounts to the same, the *truth of being.*

In regard to this problem we notice at once "that it is self-evident that there is truth in general " (*S.T.*, I, 2, 1, ad 3). Our mind is absolutely forced to admit this evidence. Now, when St. Thomas uses the expression " self-evident " (*per se notum*), he means a proposition whose absolute certitude is undeniable as soon as we understand its terms (see the main part of the article). How can we show that the proposition " Truth in general exists " possesses such self-evidence? St. Thomas admits the perfect validity of the following kind of reasoning which he mentions as an objection (in another context, however): " It is self-evident that truth exists, for he who denies its existence, grants that truth does not exist; for, if truth does not exist, it is true that truth does not exist; but if something is true, then truth must exist " (*ibid.*, ad 3).

We must emphasize the general meaning of this subtle sorites. It looks like a *reductio ad absurdum,* yet basically it is but the discovery of a "transcendental necessity." The relation of truth is inherent to objective thought, for, if denied, it surges again from the very negation. When you say there is no truth, you affirm implicitly that to your present negative statement there corresponds a certain objective disharmony which you admit between thought in general and outside reality. In other words, you admit the existence of a relation of truth in the very act by means of which you claim to deny any relation of this kind. Unless you abstain from every objective act of thinking (affirmation, doubt or negation)—an utter impossibility—you hold willy nilly that truth is not an empty word.

But this entails important consequences. For to admit a relation of truth is tantamount to admitting, outside of your present and subjective thought, " something " which " controls " it, a norm with respect to which it is inevitably true or false. In other words, not only when you affirm anything whatsoever, but even when you believe that you are professing a universal doubt or stating a total negation, you oppose being to your present thought, *the absolute to the relative.*

Our mind is utterly unable to think absolute nothingness, because it is unable to assume an attitude either of pure denial or of pure non-willing. Even when we try to deny as thoroughly, nay as wildly as possible, non-being is always backed up by being, negation is shored by affirmation, non-willing is carried by willing (*S.T.*, I, 11, 2, ad 1).[1] In the speculative order we cannot avoid an objective truth; in the practical order an absolute end. Hence when we think and when we will, we posit *being* unceasingly and categorically.

St. Thomas overcomes scepticism and relativism by his affirmation of the first principle, the principle of identity—Whatever is, is. *This principle is for him not only the norm of all* correct *thinking, it is also the law of all* thinking. *It is not only the first law of* logic, *but also the basic principle of* ontology. *It is not only the first analytic, but also the first synthetic principle. As an analytic principle it forbids us to admit contradictions. As a synthetic principle, it equates that which is in the mind with that which is in reality. It explains why we can never affirm anything without projecting it into an absolute order which is true not only for us, but for every human mind.*

The ancient sophists admitted the first principle in the latter, synthetic sense, but tried to doubt it as an analytic principle. This attitude is so artificial that it has not survived them. Without the first principle as an analytic norm of our thinking, we can no longer think, no longer talk with each other, since every word we use or utter may mean the opposite of what it is supposed to mean.

Kant and the modern agnostics, relativists and analysts admit the first principle as an analytic principle, as the first law of logic. But they reject it as a synthetic principle and thus they shut themselves out of the realm of metaphysics. Maréchal comments on a text of St. Thomas wherein the latter defends the objectivity of our knowledge, hence also the first principle as a synthetic norm of the mind (S.T., I, 85, 2). In this question Aquinas inquires whether we know only our subjective impressions (the species in us) or the things outside us. He answers that if the first is true, there is no more absolute truth since everything which appears to be true is true; since a statement A and its contradictory not-A might then be true for

[1] The French text quotes St. Thomas in Latin. Here and elsewhere we shall simply refer the reader to the corresponding passage in St. Thomas. He will be quoted only when required for the intelligibility of the text.

different persons at the same time and for the same person at different times. But this is not yet decisive. Maréchal continues as follows:

XVIII. THE ABSOLUTE POSED IN EVERY APPLICATION OF THE "FIRST PRINCIPLE"

If the scope of St. Thomas' remarks did not extend further, his line of reasoning would miss the mark. The first principle would only seem to be violated. Two really contradictory judgments would never appear to be simultaneously true, since (against all necessary conventions of language, to be sure, perhaps even despite the psychological structure of the judgment) every statement would then express only my subjective state and the present moment, and would not claim at all to represent any of my other states at any other moment of time. Judgments can be contradictory only to the extent that their respective assertions refer to the same object from the same point of view.

In fact, the thought of St. Thomas is more profound. When he says that to make of the *species* as such (the "subjective state of the faculty") an object of direct knowledge would amount to adopting indifferently statements which are contradictory, he is not only thinking of some temporal instability, but of the basic logical inconsistency which would in that event affect all our judgments.

This logical inconsistency, this conflict with the first principle, may be shown in two ways—one mainly psychological, the other mainly logical.

(1) In the process of knowledge, the passage from the stage *species* to the stage "object of thought" supposes determinations which the *species* as such did not possess, which are precisely those conferred by the first principle. Hence to make the *species* as such into an object means to overlook the first principle.

(2) To claim that the features of the object of thought are merely features of the *species* is tantamount to identifying the necessary and the contingent, to giving up the first principle.

The meaning and the value of the first assertion will be

clarified by the investigation which we shall make below of the function of the judgment in objective knowledge. Hence we do not insist upon it here.

On the other hand, we are directly interested in the second assertion, which is of a logical nature, for it expresses the real meaning of the demonstration outlined in *Summa Theologica* (I, 85, 2, c).

We were told that equating the *species* with the very *object* of the act of intellection, of which it is the *form*, would amount to asserting the coexistence of contradictories; it would mean to withdraw the " object " from its necessary dependence on the first principle.

By its very definition the *species* as such is but an accidental modality of our cognitive activity. It belongs to the subject as an ephemeral glimmer, a brute fact, a mere fluent and inconsistent moment. Of itself it entails no necessity, neither objective nor subjective; it does not exclude variability; it can stop existing, as it could never have existed. It is a relation devoid of any essence or substratum, a mere *esse ad,* a simple *pros ti.* If, as such, without anything added, it should constitute an object of knowledge, it would follow that the object of our intelligence is *contingency itself,* drowned in the mere flux of time.

In fact, such an " object " would not be an object; at the utmost it would be a " phenomenon." Would it, at least, remain under the logical jurisdiction of the first principle? Of course not, for the first principle, as the necessary norm of thought, withdraws precisely the representation from its utter instability as a subjective phenomenon, puts it to some extent beyond the reach of time. The contingent datum reaches the luminous focus of consciousness as a universal and necessary object only because the first principle has grasped and frozen it in its identity with itself, only because it causes us to assert of it something which, by itself, the raw datum does not yet express : that it is, and, since it is, that it cannot not be; that it is such, and, being such, must be such of all necessity. This means, in other words, that every particular datum, by objectivating itself before our mind, puts itself in an immutably determined relation to the absolute norm of being. In itself the datum remains in time, changeable, contingent. But the relation estab-

lished between it and being possesses a supratemporal, unchangeable, absolute aspect. *Id quod est, sub quo respectu est,
non potest non esse* (That which is, insofar as it is, cannot not
be).

Adding the first principle to the subjective datum or to the
species is therefore identical with the very objectivation of this
datum, that is, with the primordial synthesis of this datum with
being. Hence the objective affirmation transcends the brute,
phenomenal content of the *species*.

Thus we glimpse the logical relationship which brings together
in the Thomistic doctrine these four terms: subjective and contingent datum (*species*)—object of thought—being—first principle.

We might put it as follows: the subjective datum (or *species*)
can turn into an object of thought only by submitting itself to
the first principle, that is, by assuming a necessary relation to
the absolute form of being.

In short, pure relativism or absolute phenomenism is one
of these artificial positions which we may really accept and
which we might formulate only at the cost of a hidden contradiction. For the knowledge of the object as object belongs
to the intelligence. And there is no intellectual knowledge
without an application of the first principle, nor such an application without acknowledgment of a necessity which is incompatible with the " pure relative," the " pure contingent."

> *St. Thomas proposes the same doctrine in a different way when
> he affirms both that our intelligence knows only that which is
> necessary and unchangeable and that it knows the objects of
> daily experience which are contingent and changeable. These
> two affirmations can be reconciled only by asserting, as he does,
> that in every object or event, however contingent and change-
> able, there is something necessary and unchangeable (S.T., I,
> 84, 1, ad 3—86, 3, c).*

Hence, according to St. Thomas, every object of thought
assumes a necessary relation to the absolute order of being, that
is, to the ontological order in general. And this relation implies
at least the necessary identity of the object with itself. This also
entails far reaching consequences which will be developed in

the following chapters. But it will not be useless to emphasize the typical trend which shows up in the critical preliminaries of ancient realism. We believe that it may be summarized in the two following statements:

(1) *The necessity of affirming being is identical with the very necessity of thought.* This may be shown as follows: a) the necessity of objective thought (we mean, of an objective content of thought) cannot be denied, even in doubt or negation; b) pure non-being is unthinkable (that is, cannot constitute an objective content of thought). The idea of nothingness is a mere pseudo-concept, a contrived and inconsistent notion, which destroys itself. It amounts to asserting that non-being is being. Since only being, and not mere non-being, can become a content of consciousness, it follows that the necessity of thought is identical with the necessity of affirming being.

(2) *Being which is necessarily affirmed in every thought cannot be reduced to a mere phenomenon,* to a mere subjective appearance, for the phenomenon *as such* possesses no internal element of necessity. By definition it is accidental, variable, relative, contingent. But the primary law of being as affirmed is its " necessary identity with itself " (application of the first principle). But there can be no necessity which is not based upon an " absolute necessity ": an alleged " relative necessity " which should not be based—directly or indirectly—on an " absolute necessity " would no longer be a necessity, but something contingent. Hence every being is affirmed, either as absolutely necessary in itself, or as necessarily related to a being which is absolutely necessary in itself—whatever the further determinations of this absolute being may be.

Therefore, unless we deny the very possibility of thought, something which is subjectively unfeasible and objectively absurd, we must of logical necessity: (1) affirm, in general, the absolute order of being, the ontological order; (2) affirm the relation of every content of thought to the absolute order of being, in other words, the ontological, transphenomenal value of every objective determination of consciousness.

This whole preliminary demonstration—which Aristotle inserted in his *First Philosophy*—appeals to no metaphysical presuppositions. It postulates merely a content of consciousness, objectivated (represented objectively) under the normative law of identity (first principle). These are exactly the postulates of the most rigorous critique. That is why we could rightly claim that the prelude of ancient realism presented, albeit indistinctly, an authentic transcendental deduction of the ontological affirmation. For concerning the latter it demonstrates that it is the *a priori condition of possibility of every object in consciousness.*

Does the ancient Aristotelian starting point in this respect not look infinitely more " critical " or, if one prefers, less " dogmatic " than the Cartesian starting point, a well defined and inborn content of intelligence? Or even more " critical " than Hume's starting point—the pure phenomenon, considered, despite its radical contingency, as an *object,* submitted to the analytical principle?

With regard to Kant the difference is not so clear, since according to the *Critique of Pure Reason* the phenomenon *as such* cannot hold out before reason, but demands the (indeterminate and unknowable) absolute of a Reality in itself.

But let us not insist upon these very inadequate comparisons. The preceding pages constitute only the *preambulum,* a very general justification of an *ontological* theory of knowledge understood in the manner of the ancients. They wasted no time on critical preliminaries and we will, at least for the time being, imitate their example.

Knowledge, once we have discovered an objectively absolute component in its every instance, becomes basically ontological, and its further determinations may be sought in the metaphysical analysis of the contents of consciousness, both direct and reflex. In the following chapters we intend to discover, within the Thomistic metaphysics of the rational subject, the answer to two questions which summarize rather well the critical problem of consciousness:

(1) What exactly is the *object* (objective content) in our knowledge and what elements does it contain? (Section 2.)

(2) What is its necessary relation to the *absolute* norm of the first principle? (Section 3.)

XIX. ANALYSIS OF OBJECTIVE KNOWLEDGE

It follows from the preceding chapter that our contents of consciousness become objective in our thought only when backed by the first principle, that is, in virtue of the very necessity which refers them to an absolute. From this necessity, which derives from the nature of the intelligible object, St. Thomas argued against any relativism which would consider as the immediate term of our objective knowledge the *propria passio facultatis* (the subjective impression in the faculty), the *species* as such, that is, the contingent determination of our subjectivity.

Hence the fundamental principle to which he appealed was this: the object as object (*sub ratione entis,* considered as being) implies necessity. This principle is absolutely universal, for that which is merely contingent does not possess an intelligibility of its own—it amounts to pure non-being.

From this, St. Thomas concluded to an irreducible opposition between subjectivity and objectivity in our knowledge, between the subjectivity of the *medium quo* (*species*) and the objectivity of the *id quod* (object). But he should be well understood. If he had admitted a radical and universal distinction between the subjective and the objective, he would have locked himself up into this unfortunate consequence: since knowledge always goes to the object first, without stopping at the subject as subject, no subject becomes aware of itself except by reflecting upon an object which it opposes to itself. This is precisely the principle of idealistic pantheism. It is one of these deceptive illusions, one of these half-baked axioms which derive from the too easily occurring confusion between our imperfect understanding and absolute reason.

But St. Thomas' idea is different. Far from radically opposing subject and object in knowledge in general, he insists upon the total identity of the subject and the object in perfect self-intuition, the supreme model of all knowledge. The more fully an intelligence is an intelligence, if we may thus speak, the more it is in act through the subjective determination of its very nature, the less it needs an intelligible object distinct from itself. That which in man keeps the *species* or the *propria passio facultatis* (the phenomenon as subjective determination) from being the primary object of knowledge is not so much the subjectivity of this *species*, but its fundamental relativity, the fact that it belongs to the subject in a merely accidental and contingent way. Since in God there is no contingency, since in him the Subject himself constitutes absolute necessity (the ideal of any object), Subject and Object, the Knower and that which is Known, are identified in the luminous undividedness of the Pure Act. Subsistent Intellection is for itself its primary object.

Therefore, if we wish to be faithful to St. Thomas, wherever we meet some knowledge in which subject and object are really opposed, we will acknowledge some imperfection either in the intelligence or in its object; we will admit that we have to do with an intellect in potency, or at least with an " intelligible " in potency. And then we shall face the difficulty which, in various degrees, lies at the root of every theory of knowledge or epistemology: how to reconcile in this knowledge (which is imperfect on account of one of its terms or of both of them at once) immanence and objectivity, or even, in the case of man, the intussusception of the data and their extraposition, the subjectivity of the acquired *species* and the immediate objectivity of that which is known through it. In our opinion the Thomistic metaphysics of knowledge contains the elements required for the solution of this problem.

On page 17 of the present work Maréchal states that the central and guiding idea of his work, as expressed in metaphysical terms, may be found in Chapter I, " General Ontology of Knowledge." The greatest part of the chapter is presented here in literal translation.

XX. THE NOTION OF LOGICAL TRUTH

Let us borrow from the Angelic Doctor a general definition of logical truth to help us understand the exact meaning of his ontology of knowledge.

The critical prelude outlined above has already shown that all objective knowledge, since it refers essentially to the absolute norm contained in the first principle, necessarily claims to express a certain conformity between the subjective determination of thought and an "absolute order of reference," which is extrinsic to this determination. Let us say more concisely that the notion of objective knowledge contains at least the notion of a certain proportion between Thought and Absolute Reality, between Subject and ontological Object.

In fact, this conformity or this proportion between intelligence considered subjectively and an absolute objective norm constitutes the essential part of the commonly admitted definition of "truth"—"*Veritas est adaequatio rei et intellectus*" (*S.T.*, I, 16, 1, c; *Ver.*, I, 1, c).

Let us explain precisely, according to St. Thomas, the meaning of this definition.

It is always in function of some intelligence that something is said to be "true." Between truth and intelligence exists the same relation as between goodness and appetite: "As that towards which the appetite tends, is called good, so that towards which the intellect tends is called true" (*S.T.*, I, 16, 1, c).

Since truth is the proper good, the suitable perfection of the intelligence, a perfect Intelligence—a subsistent Intellection—would possess the fullness of truth. More exactly, it would, in its pure actuality, be the absolute identity of the Known and the Knower, Truth itself. Such an intelligence would be unable to receive any intelligible perfection, any truth from outside. Moreover, it must be both the original source and the supereminent model of any truth which might exist outside of it. Creative "divine truth" is the "first truth" (*Veritas prima, S.T.*, I, 16, 6, c and ad 1; *Ver.*, I, 4, c and ad 5).

Under the first Truth, in the created beings, we attribute truth either to the things or to thought.

If truth is the proper perfection of intelligence, we will call the things true only secondarily and by denomination, expressing in this way their relation to an intelligence. "Truth is mainly in the intellect: secondarily, it is in the things, as compared with the intellect" (*S.T.*, I, 16, 1, c). But this relation of things to an intelligence is of a double kind, one essential, the other accidental. "An object of knowledge may be ordained towards the intellect either *per se,* or *per accidens. Per se* (essentially) it is ordained towards the intellect on which it depends for its being. *Per accidens* (accidentally) it is ordained towards the intellect by which it may be known " (*S.T.,* I, 16, 1, c).

The essential relation—*per se*—is the one by which a being is real according to the degree of being predetermined in a creative Intelligence. In this way the objects of nature " are measured " (*Ver.,* I, 2, c) in their essence by creative intelligence. The objects of art " are measured " in their artificial structure by the artist's idea (*ibid.,* and *S.T.,* I, 16, 1, c). Under this first aspect the truth of the object " terminates " the diffusive and sovereign movement of a thought which extraposes itself partially to itself, thus acquiring a new reality in another " in itself." The absolute intelligibility *per se* of the object is this necessary participation of the object in the perfection of an intelligence : " Every thing is said to be true *absolutely,* in relation to the intellect on which it depends " (*S.T.,* 1, c).

But everything may also, as we have seen, acquire an " accidental truth insofar as it refers to an intelligence on which it does not depend " (*ibid.*), that is, to an intelligence by which it is not foreknown or foreordained, but only *knowable* (*cognoscibilis*). This is the case with objects of nature in relation to our intelligence : " to them *it happens* to be known by us."

We shall, after the scholastic manner, call *ontological truth* the relation of truth considered from the viewpoint of the object, in other words, the sharing of intelligible truth by the things, at whatever degree it may be. It is opposed to the truth of the intellect or *logical truth.*

We must now examine more thoroughly the latter notion in order to find out precisely what St. Thomas means by our human " logical truth," the truth of our imperfect intelligence.

For a perfect Intelligence, logical and ontological truth coincide necessarily and adequately, since this Intelligence is identically its own intelligible perfection and determines in a sovereign manner all the intelligible perfections distinct from its own. That is why in God the principle of objective knowledge does not consist in the always incomplete return of an object to a subject, but in the internal perfection and creative initiative of the divine Thought itself. God knows everything in the pure actuality of his essence.

But wherein does truth consist in an imperfect intelligence? All truth, all intellectual possession of some intelligible content derives from the first Truth. This derivation of the finite intelligences proceeds through two parallel channels: the *intelligences* themselves, and also the *things*.

First, the finite intelligence carries *in its nature,* on account of its having been created, a deficient but inalienable participation in the first Truth, the perfect degree of intelligence as such. This participation may be either the *natural possession of intelligible contents* (essential intuition, inborn *species,* in the pure, angelic intelligences) or only a privative possession, an *exigency of intelligible contents* (activo-passive intellectual power in man). This is the case which interests us mainly.

We must not overlook this: although our intelligence does not, like the angelic intelligences, possess *a priori objects* (inborn *species*), it will no longer be an intelligence unless it presents, in its natural activity, the permanent imprint of the first Truth, at least as a previous rule, as an *a priori condition* of its successive acquisitions of objects. Every intelligence actively defines (*mensurat*) truth to some extent, in this way prolonging the sovereign spontaneity of the perfect Intelligence. Our intelligence too is actively " defining " despite its strict dependence on objects. As its own modest rank it keeps the prerogative of imposing upon the outside data, intelligible only " in potency," the form of the *first principles,* that is, the logical influx of the first Truth. The Thomistic theory of truth would be mutilated and become inconsistent if we ignored this dynamic " exemplarism," which is nothing but a doctrine of the intellectual *a priori* formulated in metaphysical terms.

Let us listen to St. Thomas himself. Nothing could be clearer than this short answer to an objection:

The truth according to which the soul judges of all things is the first truth. As from the truth of the divine intellect proceed in the angelic intellect the inborn forms of things, according to which the angel knows everything; so from the truth of the divine intellect proceeds in an exemplary way into our intellect the truth of the first principles according to which we judge of everything (*Ver.*, I, 4, ad 5; See *S.T.*, 1, 16, 6, ad 1).

On the other hand, the first Truth no longer reaches the finite intelligence directly, as a functional *a priori,* but *through the mediation of objects* distinct from the faculty. Let us here consider only the human intelligence. Although it possesses by its very nature, in a dynamic manner which we will later analyze, the universal type of the intelligible, it must find out from the outside objects how this universal and undetermined intelligibility is distributed among partial and well defined intelligible objects. From this point of view it is no longer a spontaneity which has in itself the measure of its objects; on the contrary, it is strictly " measured " by the things. " The things of nature, from which our intellect receives knowledge, measure our intellect " (*Ver.*, I, 2, c). Since, on the other hand, these same things are " measured by the creative intelligence " (*ibid.*), it is ultimately once more the first Truth which, through them, makes itself known to our intelligence (*Ver.*, I, 5, c).

Hence the truth of our intelligence in apprehending the objects, this truth which we endeavor to justify critically, is the truth which results from the meeting in us of a double participation—interior and exterior—in the divine truth. It is here that metaphysicians as well as critical philosophers will have to start, at this meeting place, at the intersection of the *a priori* and the empirical conditions of our objective knowledge, if they wish to solve, each one in his own way, the epistemological problem.

Let us continue to explore St. Thomas' thought concerning the nature of logical truth. The encounter which we mentioned, however necessary it may appear in Thomistic metaphysics, brings up a series of really disturbing enigmas. The first one is: How does the coinciding of subjective ontological conditions (finite intelligences) and objective ontological conditions (extrinsic data) assume the character of a *prise de conscience* (a becoming aware), of knowledge (whether real or illusory does not matter for the present)? The answer to this question depends on a general ontology of knowledge.

Ontology of Knowledge

" Every being is true." If truth is a transcendental property of being, a universal relation of being with itself (*Ver.*, I, 1, c), we should be able to express it on its different levels, in ontological terms. We explained in *Cahier I* (Bk. II, ch. 3) why and how the realistic point of view imposes a metaphysics of knowledge. Needless to say, St. Thomas teaches a metaphysics of knowledge. For him the perfection of *being* is the perfection of *truth* and also the perfection of *knowledge.*

" Does God know himself? " is the title of one of his Questions (*S.T.*, I, 14, 2). We should notice the principle of the answer developed in the course of this article. God knows himself because, in God, the being without any admixture of potency, subsists the perfect identity of the known and of the knower. The real distinction of both terms can have no other foundation than their relative imperfection, their " potentiality." " Sense and intellect are different from the sensible and the intelligible only insofar as *both are in potency* " (*S.T.*, I, 14, 2, c).

The knower coinciding with that which is known, the subject with the object *in the identity of an act,* such is the whole metaphysical secret of knowledge as such. Knowledge is the prerogative of *act,* of act which is self-luminous, because it is not separated from itself. All opaqueness comes from potency which divides act from itself. Therefore God, the pure Act, must know himself perfectly.

An objection is raised in *De Causis*: It is true that God, as pure Act, is identical with his essence. Does it follow that he knows it? " Every knower, who knows his essence, returns to his essence in a complete return." In other words, self-consciousness, like all knowledge, is a synthesis of object and subject; it therefore supposes a double movement of extra-position out of oneself and of return to oneself. But " God does not step outside of his essence . . . and so it does not belong to him to return to it. Hence he does not know his essence." (*S.T.*, I, 14, 2, 1).

What does St. Thomas answer? Basically this: the proximate ontological condition of knowledge as an act of awareness does not consist in the *union* of two elements, subject and object,

in a common act, but in the internal *unity* of this act itself.
To the extent that a being is really in act, either through its
essence, or in a strictly immanent operation, exactly to that
extent it reaches itself, possesses itself, is aware of itself. We
might add at once: if it carries within itself the type of the
" other " it is also aware of " the other." " To return to its own
essence means only that a thing subsists in itself. . . . Now it
supremely belongs to God to be self-subsisting. Hence, according to this mode of speaking, he supremely returns to his own
essence and knows himself " (*S.T.*, I, 14, 2, ad 1).

The very manner in which St. Thomas handles the privileged
case of divine consciousness already shows us how he will
distinguish and put together the two aspects which belong to
every act of knowledge of the object: the *ontological* aspect
of an immanence of object to subject, and the *psychological*
aspect of consciousness. We foresee how he will interpret the
famous Aristotelian saying to which he so frequently appeals:
" In knowledge the act of that which is known (object of the
senses or of the intellect) and the act of that which knows
(sensing or intelligent subject) is one and the same act." Consciousness is the self-presence of act to itself. It is present
wherever act emerges out of potency, that is, wherever an
activity takes place which is, wholly or partially, its own term.
On the other hand, the immanence of the object will consist in
its total or partial sharing of the subject's internal act. To the
extent of this ontological sharing, the object shares the limpidity
of the immanent act and becomes luminous for the subject. We
see therefore that objective consciousness is an immediate effect
of the immanence of the object.

We will see how this metaphysical meaning of the Aristotelian
formula is worked out in other Thomistic texts, how it contrasts
ever more clearly with a merely superficial meaning adopted by
the nominalistic schools. We beg the reader to allow us to insist
on this point since we stand here at the very source of an
unbridgeable divergence between two major trends of philosophical thought.

" That which is known in act coincides with that which knows
in act." One might object that this is but a harmless tautology,
which may, at the most, mean that the known object *as known*

does not differ from the knowing subject, *as knowing,* that is, considered in the very knowledge which he possesses. Hence the definition of truth would ultimately only affirm *the identity of knowledge* (" in second act ") *with itself.*

If, with St. Thomas, we wish to give due weight to the necessity of a metaphysics of knowledge, we cannot be satisfied with this minimizing interpretation, but we will discern under Aristotle's apparent tautology a much deeper meaning.

It would be superfluous to recall the numerous passages in which the ontological immanence of the known object is affirmed. They are all connected with this fundamental thesis that knowledge is not some kind of passive reflection, a lifeless copy of the object in the subject, but first and foremost the term of an immanent activity of the subject . . . The object will be the immanent term of the subject's activity only to the extent that it will have inserted itself among the dynamic conditions of the subjective activity. This is a strict and metaphysically necessary proportion.

Therefore, when the object is not immanent in the subject through its own reality, it will be known only by substituting in itself, in the subject, a vicarious dynamic principle, a *species impressa,* which bears its resemblance. And once more the object will be known only insofar as the *species* is immanent. The doctrine of the *species* is so intimately connected with the ontological conception of knowledge that the fate of the latter has always depended on that of the former. No wonder then that nominalistic scholasticism did not care for the *species.* On the other hand, they constitute an indispensable element in every metaphysics of the Aristotelian type . . . " All knowledge occurs according to some form which is in the knower the principle of knowledge " (*Ver.,* X, 4, c).

It is not possible to interpret these texts and many more of the same kind as if the " vicarious form " of the object, or, as St. Thomas sometimes says, the *similitudo objecti* (the resemblance of the object) designated full-fledged knowledge in the psychological sense of a conscious representation. Rather, Aquinas means an *ontological* principle, deriving from the object and inserting itself into the dynamic stage of the subjective activity.

Let us have a look at a few texts which are even more explicit. It is remarkable from what angle, in the article of the *Summa* which we commented on in the beginning of this chapter (I, 16, 1, c.), St. Thomas tackles the problem of truth. He declares that the intellect strives towards truth as the will towards good. Truth is not called a simple *reflection* falling into the intellect from outside, but an end which is already alive in the obscure anticipation of a " natural desire ": " Truth is the name of that towards which the intellect strives." But there must be an entitative proportion between a desire thus aroused which sets the activity in motion, and the end which terminates this activity. Truth is *known,* because it is *possessed.*

In the same article, St. Thomas succinctly but decisively rejects the false intuitionism which imagines (between subject and object above the physical relations in being) some kind of direct exchange of ideal luminosities, as if our knowing faculties were simply windows opening upon some " pure cognoscible," or as if the intellectual possession of objects were transmitted to us by some immediate contamination of their ontological truth, by a direct grasping of the influx which creative Wisdom exerts upon them. St. Thomas answers an objection: " It is true that in our intelligence truth is caused by the things, but it does not follow that the attribute of truth belongs primarily to the things," as would be the case if the truth of our intellect formally derived from the truth of the things. For the same text continues. " The being of the thing, not its truth, is the cause of truth in the intellect. Hence the Philosopher says that an opinion or a statement is true from the fact that a thing is, not from the fact that a thing is true " (*S.T.*, I, 16, ad 3). Truth is inseparable from being; it is transmitted only by the relations of being.

Here is how St. Thomas defines in technical language the exact place of the relation of truth in the hierarchy of the ontological relations. Let us go back to the First Question of *De Veritate,* where we can see how the various moments of the cognitive process follow each other. Thus we shall be able to attach a very precise meaning to the definition of truth.

All knowing is produced by an assimilation of the knower to the thing known, so that *assimilation is said to be the cause of knowledge*. Similarly, the sense of sight knows a color by being informed with a *species* of the color. The first reference of being to the intellect, therefore, consists in its agreement with the intellect. This agreement is called " the conformity of thing and intellect." In this conformity is fulfilled the formal *constituent of the true*, and this is what the true adds to being, namely the conformity or equation of thing and intellect. As we said, *the knowledge of a thing is a consequence of this conformity;* therefore, it is *an effect of truth,* even though *the fact that the thing is a being is prior to its truth (Ver.,* I, 1, c).

In this passage St. Thomas assumes the viewpoint of the exterior object presented to an intelligence. We should notice how carefully he mentions the three steps which lead to the knowledge of this object: first the very *being* of this thing, a being which depends on the divine Intelligence measuring it in a sovereign manner. Next, the assimilation or adequation established between the particular intelligence and the being of the thing, an assimilation and adequation which must be understood ontologically since they are called not " knowledge," but " cause " of knowledge. Finally, *knowledge* itself.

It is the ontological adequation, the assimilation, not knowledge as awareness, that St. Thomas properly calls truth: " Knowledge is an effect of truth " (*loc. cit.*). This shows clearly that for him *cognitio,* the psychological property of being known, of becoming luminous in consciousness, is no longer a relative property (a relation) like logical truth, but that it emerges and remains within the very intimacy of the immanent act. It may happen that the knowing subject is too imperfect to bring about his immanent act without assimilation of objects from outside. But even then it is the immanent act, as active unity of the subject, which lights the spark of consciousness.

Thus it becomes easy to see in what sense the commonly accepted meanings of the word " truth " apply to the different stages of the process of knowledge. St. Thomas writes:

Consequently, truth or the true has been defined in three ways.

(1) First of all, it is defined according to *that which precedes*

truth and is the basis of truth. This is why Augustine writes:
" The true is that which is " (*loc. cit.*).

This refers to the ontological truth, the truth of the *res,* a
truth of extrinsic denomination, deriving essentially either from
the divine Intelligence which measures the being of the thing,
or accidentally from the finite intelligence which may " be
measured " by it. The being of the things connects, as it were,
the creative Intellect with the created intellect. In this sense we
may say that the thing, as it participates in the stability of the
creative idea, causes and validates the logical truth of our
intellections.

(2) Truth is also defined in another way—according to *that in
which its intelligible determination is formally completed.* Thus
Isaac writes: " *Truth is the conformity of thing and intellect* ";
and Anselm, " *Truth is a rectitude perceptible only by the mind.*"
This rectitude, of course, is said to be based on some conformity.
The philosopher says that in defining truth we say that truth is had
when one affirms that " to be which is, and that not to be which is
not " (*loc. cit.*).

This *formalis ratio veri* is the relation between thought and
reality which is formally established when the intellect carries
the similitude of the object. In its proper being the object
possessed only an aptitude for such a relation. The classical
definition of truth supposes that it is in fact established according
to the respective ontological conditions of a subject and an
object.
    The last lines of the article distinguish once more the " formal
truth " previous to *knowledge* from some kind of metonymic
truth designated by the features of its proper effect, that is,
by cognition itself.

(3) The third way of defining truth is *according to the effect
following upon it.* Thus Hilary says that the true is *that which
manifests and proclaims* existence. And Augustine says: " *Truth
is that by which that which is, is shown* " (*loc. cit.*).

Hence this third kind of truth is but the awareness which the
subject has of his similitude to the object, or, if one wishes, it is

logical truth—the truth of the intellect—in the strict sense, in the fullness of its properties: " as known in a knower."

Hence there can be no doubt about the thought of St. Thomas: there is knowledge exactly to the extent of the ontological immanence of an object in a subject. The object may be immanent " either through its essence, or through some similitude," that is, either by itself, or through an ontological substitute, a *species* (*Ver.*, VIII, 6, c). And knowledge is but the natural and immediate result of this union of object and subject within the subject.

We still have to explain: (1) of what nature the *assimilation of* the immanence of the object must be, so that knowledge (in second act, consciousness) may derive from it; (2) how the awareness emerging from the immanent act in which subject and object take part can be the awareness of the object as opposed to the subject.

Cajetan discusses the first problem in detail in his *Commentaries of the Summa Theologica* and in his *De Anima*. We have already stated above the principle of the solution: there will be knowledge only when subject and object unite not just in any way, but in the identity of an act. " The known in act and the knower in act are one and the same act." This entails several important consequences which St. Thomas did not overlook.

Let us open Cajetan's *Commentary* on this article of the *Summa* (1, 14, 1), where he points out the metaphysical difference between beings that know and beings that do not know. St. Thomas said that the being who knows possesses not only its own form, but also the form of other beings. To know is to become " the other " while remaining oneself. " Beings deprived of knowledge possess *only their own form*: but it is of the nature of a knowing being to possess *also the form of another* being: for the *species* of that which is known is in the knower (*S.T., loc. cit.*). It follows that the natural form of a being devoid of the power of knowledge is, ontologically speaking, more " restricted " in actual perfection and virtualities than the natural form of knowing beings. But the principle which restricts form is matter. " The restriction of form is through matter . . ." and "As it frees itself from matter, form tends towards a certain infinity " (1, c). And St. Thomas concludes, rather abruptly, it seems to his modern readers: " Hence it is evident that the immateriality of a being is the reason why it can know, and the degree of knowing corresponds to the degree of immateriality " (*ibid*).

What matters for us in this rather difficult but very important text is only this: that the formal immanence of the object, required for knowledge, is made impossible by the " materiality " of the subject, while the latter's " immateriality," that is, the fact that it enjoys the prerogatives of the form as such, makes this immanence possible, so that the degree of immateriality is exactly the degree of the cognitive power.

Cajetan rightly insists upon the necessity of defining exactly the immanence which results in knowledge. For there is a whole gamut of immanences. Let us make it clear at once, he remarks, that a subject united to an object as matter is to form does not fulfill the primary condition of knowledge, namely, the identity of subject and object in one and the same act, according to Aristotle's formula. This is quite evident. " The knower *is* identically the known, in act or in potency. Matter, on the other hand, *never is* its form." And again: " Knower and known are *more one* than matter and form, as Averroes says very well . . . because the union of the knower and the known does not result in a third reality, as does the union of matter and form " (*Comment. in S.T.*, 1, c). Material and formal principle, as complementary elements, remain related and opposed to each other, without coinciding in identity. Hence, if the subject receives the object only in the way in which matter receives form, or *only* in the way in which the substance supports accidents, we shall never discover in their encounter that common, undivided, and wholly actual zone where consciousness emerges. Thus the inorganic bodies and the plants which receive the impression of " the other " only according to their matter, the principle of pure passivity, are certainly invaded by the object, but they do in no way possess it with the degree of immanence required for knowledge. The same material principle which prevents them wholly from knowing themselves makes it impossible for them to know " the other " in them.

Therefore the unity of knower and known can consist neither in the unity of a matter and a form nor in the sole unity of substance and accident. After Aristotle and St. Thomas, Cajetan repeats what this unity must be: " that one be *the same* as the other, while each remains itself " (*ibid.*). The subject remains subject and the object object in immanence itself.

In order to shed some light on this mystery, Cajetan uses two auxiliary principles which (speaking as metaphysicians) we shall take for granted: (1) Everything operates insofar as it is in act " (*ibid.*). Since knowledge is an activity the knowing subject will possess the properties of an " agent." But no agent acts except insofar as it is in act, both from the viewpoint of " exercise " and from the viewpoint of " specification." (2) " The object known is the specifying principle of knowledge " (*ibid.*). The known object makes knowledge into *this* or *that* knowledge. Knowledge is " specified " by its object.

The synthesis of these two principles will yield a definition of the cognitive immanence of an object distinct from a subject. It is true that an object, as distinct from a subject, cannot strictly coincide with the latter considered as the " eliciting principle " of knowledge. Even should this be possible, it would bring about a total identity of nature between subject and object and not the partial identity of objective knowledge. The only way out is that the object, insofar as it is known, inserts itself into the immanent activity of the subject as the specifying form of this activity.

Cajetan writes: " The knower who receives the known object does not first receive it (in the way of some matter) for the sake of the proper operation of some composed, third reality, deriving from their union. Nor for the sake of an ulterior operation of the known object (whose temporary support it would thus be, as the water which receives heat, receives it for the sake of some heating operation; which is not, strictly speaking, an operation of the water as such, for water as water is indifferent to carrying heat. The same thing should be said, adds our text, of every passive reception of accidental forms by some subject), but as the specifying principle of the very operation of the knowing subject " (*ibid.*).

In fine, an object is known only to the extent that, through a series of causalities which we do not have to study here, it is subsumed by the natural form of an active power, in the unity of an immanent operation. Such is, in technical terms, the ontological formula of every knowledge which is neither a self-intuition nor a creative thought. It must strictly apply to the whole of our objective knowledge from direct to rational knowledge, from our direct knowledge of bodies to our analogical knowledge of God.

There is no difficulty in admitting that the objective form, as soon as it has been introduced into the intimacy of the immanent act, enjoys this " autopossession," this elementary reflection, in which *consciousness* consists, if we admit, with St. Thomas, that matter is the only screen which keeps being from being self-luminous.

But we have not yet fully explored the general ontological theory of knowledge implied in our Thomistic definition of truth. The explanation which we have developed covers only the first stage of the process of knowledge, the one which mainly interested the schoolmen. For we have brought the object exactly to the point where, having become the specifying form of the subject in act, it enters the luminous sphere of subjective consciousness. But why is the assimilated form not simply known as a form of the subject, or at least as a " phenomenon " not expressly distinct from the other " phenomenal " peculiarities of the subject? How shall we explain that it stands before consciousness " objectively " according to its opposition to the subject? For it is an immediate datum of consciousness that the manner of our knowledge is *objective*.

Hence, if immanence is the condition and the measure of consciousness, should it not follow that not only the form of the object, but also its very opposition to the subject must first ontologically be imprinted in the intrinsic and actual conditions of the subject's immanent operation? But how shall we conceive such a disjunction within the immanence itself?

Cajetan was aware of this difficulty. Did he not tell us that objective knowledge demands " *ut unum sit idem alteri, salvis rationibus eorum* "—that knower and known be identified, while yet keeping their own entity? (*ibid.*). The actual identity may not end up by creating a confusion of object and subject in our consciousness. That is why he explained this persisting duality within the very identity by invoking, not only the two subsidiary principles mentioned above, but also a third axiom which must explain the evident fact that we do not only perceive in us forms *which* are alien (*alias formas*), but these very forms *as alien* (*quatenus alias*).

Here is the third axiom and the consequence which the commentator draws from it: " If you further consider . . . that *everything exists for its operation,* it follows that a knowing nature is such by itself that actually or potentially it is the very object of knowledge, which means that it is not only itself but also *something else*" (*ibid.*). The context shows that "*alia*" (something else) should not only be understood to refer to the outside origin of the immanent determination, nor to its material resemblance with an object, but to the inseparable outward relation which it affirms within the very immanence of the subject.

We see that Cajetan's answer comes down to an appeal to the *very nature of the knowing subject.* Since objective knowledge is based entirely upon the object's immanence as upon its determining ontological condition, and since, nevertheless, it is the knowledge of an object which is external to the subject, we should, in final analysis, attribute to the (ontological) nature of the knowing subject its strange property of identifying itself with objects without, nevertheless, erasing their " otherness." An ineluctable conclusion, provided we admit the very principle of an ontology of knowledge.

The Thomistic commentator does not push the problem further. Does this mean that we are up against an impassable barrier? Or even perhaps against an antinomy which we cannot not accept? Not necessarily. We should, at the utmost, note for the time being an obscurity which we hope to dispel later in the light of a few fundamental Thomistic principles.

At any rate we notice that Cajetan's authority confirms a remark which we have already made several times and under different forms: knowledge presupposes an ontological bond between object and subject. Between the object of knowledge and the knowing subject, when they are not wholly identical there is always *a priori* to some extent a " complementarity," a " pre-established harmony." One is to the other as the key is to its lock. Every lock may receive an infinite number of keys, yet not every key fits every lock. Hence previous to knowledge, some proportion must exist between subject and object. " There is required some proportion between the object and the knowing power, like between an active and a passive element, and like between that which is perfecting and that which is perfected " (*S.T.*, I, 88, 1). Let us at once draw from this principle an epistemological conclusion which no Thomist will reject.

Through its very design the lock represents the previous rule of the shape of all the keys which are to fit it, whether made of gold or of iron. Hence we shall not say that it would be unwise to look in the subject for some *a priori* knowledge of the objects. Every objective knowledge, lower than an intellectual intuition, arises at the meeting of *a priori* exigencies (which outline *a priori* some of its features) and of empirical *a posteriori* data (which provide it with a content). A knowledge which should be wholly *a posteriori*, wholly " alien " (implicitly as well as explicitly) to the subject, is an impossibility. For in that case the soul would be reduced to the status of an indifferent " matter," hence lacking all power of knowing. This is the absurdity latent in all empiricist systems.

In fact, the " proportion " required between object and subject, which is written in advance in the very exigencies of the subject's nature, constitutes the common basis from which start both the metaphysician when he defines the respective formal object of the knowing faculties, considered as *operative powers* of an ontological subject and the critical philosopher when he defines the respective formal object of these same faculties considered only as *logical functions,* as *a priori* conditions intrinsically affecting knowledge.

There is no incompatibility between these two points of view—the metaphysical (transcendent) and the critical (transcendental)—since the latter is but a precisive aspect of the former. There remains only the question (which we do not have to consider here) whether or not the transcendental viewpoint may lead us to the transcendent viewpoint.

We have seen how Maréchal defines logical truth and interprets it metaphysically. He adds :

This doctrine, borrowed from St. Thomas, assumes in our epistemological demonstration only the hypothetical value of a coherent system of nominal definitions. If we wish to apply it to our objective knowledge, we must analyze the latter in detail, or, more exactly, we must proceed to a reflective analysis of our contents of consciousness *insofar as* they refer, at least indeterminately, to an ontological absolute.

But such contents of consciousness occur only in the judgment. Maréchal's next task, to which he will devote many pages, consists therefore in a detailed analysis of human judgment.

XXI. THE ELEMENTS OF THE JUDGMENT

The judgment is the real center of observation of our human psychology and also the central datum of our human critique of knowledge. This statement, which follows immediately from the Thomistic theses on truth, implies many consequences. If we forget it, we run the risk of bringing up illusory, hence insoluble problems. . . .

Since the judgment is the unity of a diversity, it contains material and formal elements. Insofar as they are involved in constituting the " object," we shall reduce them to the following three :

(1) The *matter* of the judgment, that is, its " terms," considered in themselves as simple concepts.

(2) The *form* which transforms this double material element into a " judgment." It is subdivided in its turn in :

(a) the *synthetic* form of the judgment, that is, the complementary unity of subject and predicate, as such;

(b) the *objective* form of the judgment or the affirmation.

If we abstract from the form of the judgment, the two terms, subject and predicate, are left as simple concepts. But under further analysis the concept itself is seen to be composed of a material and a formal element. For the concept too is, at its level, the unity of a diversity. And if we examine this diversity more closely, we discover finally, amidst a network of associative unities inferior to that of the concept (images at various degrees of complexity), psychological elements which can no longer be dissociated or reduced, the *sense elements,* which constitute the primary matter of human knowledge.

Let us remember that, if this conception of the material

function of the sense elements belongs to Kant, who established
it against Cartesian ontologism, it had formerly been the
common possession of all the scholastic philosophers, since the
most stubborn " dissidents " among them have held the peripatetic tenet that " There is nothing in the intellect that was not
first in the senses." Too many among them went too far along
this line and erred through exaggerated empiricism.

While he affirms with them the sense origin of our knowledge,
St. Thomas carefully avoids suggesting that the intelligence
would only be a transposition and a duplicate of the senses.
Sensation provides intellection with a starting point and some
matter, nothing more. In his seemingly most " sensualistic "
formulas he always safeguards the higher formal point of view
of the intellect.

The primary matter of human knowledge is the sensations.
What do we know through our sensations ? Following is part of
Maréchal's answer to this question.

XXII. THE OBJECT OF SENSE KNOWLEDGE

Hence the formal object of the senses is, according to St.
Thomas, the *exterius immutativum* (that which modifies from
without, not the substantial or accidental ontological reality
which produces this modification, the *exterius immutativum*
taken *materially,* for he has excluded this hypothesis (only the
intellect, not the senses, knows the *nature* of the sense qualities. . . .), but the *exterius immutativum* as such, that is, neither
more nor less than the very form according to which the outside
world (whatever may be the reality of the substances and
qualities which compose it) actively molds our sense organs.
As soon as it is imprinted in the senses, this form, considered in
itself, separated from all the rest, belongs to the subject as well
as to the object. It is one of these " external accidents " (so
called in contrast to the " proper accidents ") which depend at
the same time on two causes, a material and an efficient cause.
But while reacting upon this datum from outside, the sense does
not perceive these relations of causal inherence and dependence.
Its own luminosity only illuminates the very form of the

" immutation," in accordance with the latter's spatial exteriority, without any ontological knowledge of the object.

Hence in the *exterius immutativum* considered as the primary formal object of the senses St. Thomas discovers very clearly the relative element which Kant later will call the " phenomenal datum," that is, the immediate manifestation of the Real, not yet referred by the intellect to the absolute of a Reality in itself. . . .

Hence sensation by itself alone is, strictly speaking, neither subjective nor objective. Insofar as it modifies our organs, sensation supplies an *immediate and relative* representation of the material world, a representation in which the object is *really grasped* (and spatially exteriorized in the case of an external sensation), but not yet *entitatively* distinguished from the subject.

Maréchal devotes several paragraphs to a study of the a priori in knowledge in general and in sense knowledge. St. Thomas did not use the term " a priori " but the idea occurs frequently in his writings. Maréchal tries to show this by comparing the " formal object " of St. Thomas with the " a priori conditions " of Kant.

XXIII. FORMAL OBJECT AND *A PRIORI*

The summary remarks made above on the intermediary, subjective and objective function of the formal object allow us at once to discover an important meeting point between critical philosophy and metaphysical realism.

For it follows from our explanations that the formal object is, as it were, the intersection of two opposed currents of priority. Considered from the viewpoint of the subject, it defines *some general conditions of eventual objects.* The psychological *a priori* can be applied only to a proportionate matter which precontains it in potency (see in Kant the notion of " transcendental affinity "). Considered from the viewpoint of the external objects, the formal object defines *some general conditions of eventual knowing subjects.* The potential universality of the individual objects can be actuated and thus be known only through a psychological *a priori* proportionate to this actuation. Hence the formal object specifies both a degree of *cognoscibility* of the object and a *mode of knowing* of the subject.

It is true that, for the metaphysician, this double series of properties is based upon a series of well defined ontological properties—immediately upon the nature and reciprocal potentiality both of the object (cognoscible in potency) and of the subject (knowing in potency), and ultimately on their deficient and complementary respective participation in the Creative Intelligence. It is a fact, however, that the metaphysician himself, if confronted with the formal object, considered in its proper function, and abstracted from its ontological causes, would already discover in it, if not the ultimate rational explanation, at least the immediate *" ratio cognoscendi"* (way of knowing) of some conditions which are logically required either in the external object or in the subject, supposing that the latter is to know the former. The mere precisive consideration of the formal object would tell us *a priori* something about several necessary attributes of the object and the subject.

Moreover, the " precisive " attitude which we have just mentioned is often adopted by the metaphysician. The method he uses then comes very near that of the critical philosopher.

The latter assumes, before the objects which he explores, the attitude we have described in *Cahiers III* and *IV*. Taking the brute contents of consciousness (rightly or wrongly) as initial data of his investigation, he simply endeavors to define, starting from them, the universal conditions of objective knowledge. In the represented objects " transcendental reflection " shows him the necessary meeting of a contingent datum which cannot be reduced to any general law of consciousness, and some universal and necessary principles of unity. These universalizing principles, which are *a priori* with respect to the datum, define for him the knowing subject and his faculties. For the subject is really knowing as such only to the extent that he formally takes part in the edification of the object.

What is the difference between the *" a priori* conditions " which, from a purely functional and precisive viewpoint, represent in the *Critique* the " faculties " of the knowing subject and the formal object of the scholastics abstractly recognized in the diversity of the "material objects" as a common character " to which the power *refers per se* "? For all essentials and considered precisively, the two considerations seem to cover each other. Hence, whether from the transcendental viewpoint of the subject or from the (abstractive) viewpoint of the formal object of the powers, we notice a wide and common boundary between critical theory and the scholastic metaphysics of knowledge.

It is rather embarrassing to make these obvious statements. Would it not have been enough, in order to establish the reality of some *a priori* in every knowledge, to say in two words: If knowledge is the act of that which may be known, and if act is logically prior to potency, there is some *a priori* in all knowledge? This should indeed have been sufficient. But when we remember in how many strange contexts the notion of *a priori* has occurred for a very long time, we might perhaps be excused for slightly exorcizing it. Besides, the difficulty consists not so much in discerning the inevitable role of the *a priori* in every exercise of the powers, but in recognizing exactly the nature and scope of this *a priori* at the different levels of our knowledge of objects.

XXIV. SPATIALITY AND TEMPORALITY AS THE LAWS OR UNIVERSAL RULES OF SENSATION

The sensible and extended qualities of the outside world are imprinted in the senses according to the laws of physical interaction. As noted by St. Thomas, the sensible quality exchanges the materiality of the object for that of the sensing subject. But this " natural immutation," which establishes in the sense organ an alien form, does not make the latter " cognoscible in act."

Every act of knowledge occurs through the unification of its raw data. What kind of unification does the form passively received in the senses need from the subject in order to reach intentional unity, a unity which must be simple and which we may already call " immaterial "?

Of course, first a synthesis of its spatial dispersion. For

at this first moment, the extension of the form, materially received in the organ, is still but the point for point coincidence, we might say, the disjunctive coinciding of the subject's extension with that of the environment. But the only possible type of immediate synthesis of extension (or space) in a knowing subject —or, speaking like the scholastics, the only mode of unity which extension (or space) may receive so as to become the " specifying form of a strictly immanent act "—seems to be the formal unity of the inner scanning which would successively take up the juxtaposed parts of this extension (or this space), fusing and totalizing them in a well defined temporal continuity. The synthesis of *space* occurs through *time*.

But this elementary synthesis of the spatial form by time can *totalize* the mentally scanned space in sense consciousness only under the following condition : that the scanning activity, as it develops, keeps and accumulates that which has been collected before according to the very order of the successive acquisitions. Since the sense qualities, however elementary, are always given to us in connection with some definite extension, the unity of their immediate perception would already require the intervention of some kind of rudimentary, preconscious memory.

Should we admit, even though only as a hypothesis, this successive intervention of space and time in the operation of the senses? We do not see how any other hypothesis would safeguard the necessity, commonly admitted by the scholastics, of some participation of the " internal senses " (especially of the " common sense ") in external sensation itself. We will not have much trouble expressing a share of the *a priori* in sensibility. It would simply consist in the *combination of a double exigency* imposed *a priori* upon every " sensible in act ": the exigency of the *spatial* mode and the exigency of the *temporal* mode. Let us explain this in more detail.

A " succession " in the wide sense, that is, some unilinear series of acts, is not incompatible with the proper perfection of the finite forms, even though they be subsistent. But let us suppose the form of an agent which, although exceeding matter to some extent, is intrinsically tied to it, so as to be unable to subsist except as the form of a material composite being. Since " as a being is, so it acts," the operative powers of such a composite being will present in their acts the " mode of succession " (a universal property of finite form) only as inseparably connected with the " concrete mode of extension " (the formal effect of prime matter). The functional association of the pure " mode of succession " with the " spatial mode " constitutes precisely the *temporal mode*.

Hence, adopting Kant's terminology, we might say that the " *a priori* formal condition " virtually latent in the sense power is the *pure synthesis of space by time*. Of course, this synthesis, as the word " pure " indicates, belongs to the " first act "[1] of the power and designates only a natural combination of the dispositions (rules, laws) which rule the " second acts."

These considerations may help us understand: (1) how that which is " sensible in potency " (the exterior object of the senses) may, on account of its materiality, become " sensible in act " only if, in the sensing subject, it receives both the forms of space and time; (2) why a sense endowed subject (" sensing in potency ") may, on account of its materiality, corresponding to that of objects, become " sensing in act " only if it receives the outside data according to the double mode of space and time.

Hence the requirements of the sense object and the nature of the sensing subject impose upon the sense faculty an *a priori* rule of operation, namely, the temporality and the spatiality of the eventual acts of this faculty. But this brings up another problem.

Apriority and Objectivity of Space and Time in Sense Knowledge

If we admit the apriority of space and time, do we not endanger their true objectivity? On the contrary, at least within the metaphysical framework in which we have defined the *a priori* of the senses.

As soon as we put the problem of sense *a priori* in metaphysical terms, we must admit that the subject's spatiality and temporality require similar conditions in the object. An

---

[1] The scholastics call the " first act " of an operative power the formal disposition of this faculty previous to its operations or " second acts."

unextended and timeless object would be totally incapable of being received and arranged under " *a priori* forms " of space and time. We should even say that we call these forms " *a priori* " because—logically and psychologically—they demand in advance, in every possible object of sensation, a strictly corresponding aptitude, which can only be the concrete extension and the temporal mutability of the object. Thus we understand why the *a priori* of the senses . . . does not affect the objectivity of knowledge. . . .

Let us once again compare the partial apriority of the senses with the total apriority which St. Thomas attributes to the pure spirits. We are told that the reason why the pure spirits can know each other *a priori*, by means of innate principles, is that from angel to angel there exists some essential *order*, some *relation* of affinity and hierarchy, which explains why the very knowledge of the subject necessarily leads to that of the object.

According to Cajetan and St. Thomas himself, we must extend to every created subject capable of objective knowledge the central principle of explanation which applies to pure spirits. And this supposes that there should correspond to the different degrees of objective knowledge in the knowing subjects as many natural degrees of " relation " or " ordination " to the objects— as many degrees of apriority.

Let us restrict ourselves to the lower level of the cognitive functions, to the sense faculties. What will be the characteristic " order " which, on this level, keeps the subject " oriented outwards " towards possible objects? Only one *a priori* disposition of this kind is compatible with the shared *materiality* of the sensible subject and object, namely, their reciprocal " otherness " according to concrete quantity.

How does the quantitative relativity of the senses introduce into sensation some objective *signification*, some kind of *extroversion*?

We said that in order to possess an objective signification, the sense act must render manifest the natural " order " which unites and opposes the sensing subject as sensing and external reality. This order should be both an " affinity " and a " difference." But quantitative relativity, the *a priori* rule of the sense act, verifies this double condition.

Let us first consider *affinity*. Since the sense is material, it can assimilate only material forms. Since the object is material, it can " move " and directly " inform " only a material faculty. This affinity through matter, this two-sided material condition manifests itself on both sides in the mode of being and operating, which is the formal effect of materiality, that is, in concrete quantity, according to its double expression, spatial and temporal.

The second element, the *differential* element, which gives the immanent operation of the senses a first degree of objective " signification," is also based upon the material community between sensing subject and outside reality. For, as soon as they enter into contact, in an actual sensation, this material community imposes on them the " order " or the " relation " which is characteristic of concrete quantity : reciprocal *otherness* according to spatial and temporal characters.

For *space* and time *separate* as much as they *unite*.

Is it not a property of a point in space to lead into the next point without coinciding with it? And of a moment of time to flow towards the following moment without coinciding with it? Wherever there is spatial and temporal representation, every discernible element calls for others and leads into them. One subsists only tied to the other, one is posited only in function of the other. That is why we might conceive, but certainly not imagine, an ultimate limit of space or a last moment of time. The boundary line of a limited space always looks like the transition to another extension, and the moment in which a definite duration stops opens for us a new duration.

In virtue of its quantitative structural law every sense representation virtually " extraposes " on either side of itself a space and a time in which all other possible representations must fit. We shall not insist upon the differential value of the form of time. Since its study would have to be based on an analysis of the internal sense, it would lead us beyond our immediate purpose. We shall only consider the relations of space. If the sensing subject acquires a spatial representation of itself, this representation will necessarily possess the property of exteriority with respect to all other spatial representations. No spatial confusion will be possible between the image of subject and

objects. This mutual exteriority of the subject to the objects and
of the objects to each other—a fact of daily experience—was
demanded in advance by the quantitative law of the sense
faculty; a Kantian philosopher would say, by the "*a priori*
form*" of sensibility.

But we must push even further the analysis of the proper
objectivity of the senses. The sensing subject, when concretely
representing extension (and duration) to itself, is not itself
placed outside of space (or time). It remains inserted in it, not
only objectively as an image, but also subjectively as an agent.
With respect to the environment which invades it and upon
which it reacts, it stands as a material agent in the same relation
which an element of extension has to the surrounding points.
Hence it will be dominated by the laws of concrete extension
even in its very attitude, in the mode of its operation, in the
form of its reaction to the object whose imprint it receives.

From the very start and by *a priori* necessity the attitude of
the sensing subject must be exteriorizing, " extroverted "; it is
a projection into the surrounding space. Although the external
sense does not perceive its own *ad extra* (outwards) relativity,
it directly perceives its object in the perspective of this relation
to exteriority, somewhat as an observer, standing at the center
of a convex surface and looking towards it, would at first see
in it only the concavity of the environment.

Hence sensation is objective. But it is slightly objective, since
its objectivity consists merely in spatial exteriority. Yet sensation is also subjective, that is, it reveals the sensing subject to
itself. But it is slightly subjective, exactly as it is slightly objective, or, better still and in one word, as it is slightly immanent.

Among the cognitive faculties, the senses are those in which
the strict immanence of a knowing activity—which is always, to
some extent, a reflection of the subject upon itself—is reduced
to a minimum. The subject knows itself only according to that
surface of itself which is also that of the objects: " *sensus
haeret in superficie rerum* "—the sense clings to the surface of
the things. In order to be clearly self-conscious the subject
should be capable of a perfect reflection, reach itself at a
point which it occupies all on its own, and not only at a point
which it occupies undividedly with the object. This higher

degree of immanence remains beyond the reach of a material faculty. That is why the senses, whose movement goes straight to the object (*terminatur ad objectum*) do not, nevertheless, know the distinction between subject and object.

Thus we may understand—that is what we have in mind here—why the objectivity of the senses, far from being impaired by the quantitative *a priori* of the sense faculty (spatial and temporal *a priori*) is rather logically demanded and psychologically caused by it. We have shown, according to St. Thomas and Cajetan, that, provided only it contains somehow a relation to the object, the *a priori* is no longer an obstacle to objective knowledge and becomes even a means of it (*medium quo* or *in quo*). It does not matter much in this respect whether the *a priori* is immediately *knowable* in itself (as with the essence and the " inborn species " of the angels) or simply " lived " as a functional disposition, and *recognizable* only when it has combined with an objective content (as with the " forms " of sensibility). In neither case does it hide the object. On the contrary, we shall later demonstrate that objectivity increases and decreases in direct proportion to apriority understood in this way.

After studying sensation Maréchal investigates the higher material element of the judgment, the concept. *Here he meets the famous problem of how we can pass from sense knowledge to intellectual knowledge, from sensations to concepts. The traditional Thomistic answer is through abstraction, as performed by the agent intellect upon the phantasm.*

The following extract considers the relation of the agent intellect to the phantasm, first in terms of formal and efficient causality, and then within a general theory of the mental powers, the abstraction of the species *and the nature of the* species.

XXV. RELATION OF AGENT INTELLECT TO PHANTASM IN TERMS OF FORMAL AND EFFICIENT CAUSALITY

St. Thomas not only describes the natural relation between agent intellect and phantasm by metaphor, he also tries to formulate it in terms of *metaphysical causality*. He uses two kinds of causal relation: material and formal causality, and efficient causality, both principal and instrumental. . . .

In a first series of texts we see the relation of agent intellect and phantasm reduced to *a synthesis of form and matter, of act and potency*. " But since the phantasms cannot of themselves immute the possible intellect, but require to be made actually intelligible by the agent intellect, it cannot be said that sensible knowledge is the total and perfect cause of intellectual knowledge, but rather is in a way *the matter of the cause* " (*S.T.*, I, 84, 6, c).

This means that the *total* cause which will introduce the intelligible determinations into the possible intellect contains the phantasm as some kind of material element of which the agent intellect would be the form. Of course, this is true only in an analogical way. For, if we understood it literally, the operation of the agent intellect would be intrinsically dependent on matter, and would lead not to something which is intelligible in act, but to something concrete, belonging to the sense level.

Elsewhere St. Thomas explicitly states that the " light " (the actuality) of the agent intellect is the *very act* of that which is intelligible in potency when it has become intelligible in act. " [Our intellect] is made actual by the species abstracted from sensible things, through the light of the agent intellect, which [light] *is the act of the intelligibles themselves* " (*S.T.*, I, 87, 1, c). What is meant here is an actuation in the intelligible, not in the natural order. Nevertheless, since the intelligible order itself is but an aspect of ontological reality, the text of St. Thomas, taken literally, would mean that the agent intellect becomes ontologically the act of that which is intelligible in potency, that is, of the phantasm. Once more this statement is true only when transposed, for an agent intellect that should identically become the act of a phantasm would become a higher *material* form. The product of this association of act and potency would be a material composite being, not an " intelligible in act."

Shall we then give up altogether this way of speaking? Not necessarily. The subordination of two faculties within the unity of one and the same *suppositum* necessarily possesses some of the characteristics of a relation of matter to form, of act to

potency. " Some of the characteristics " only, for while taking
into account the radical unity of the faculties, we should not
overlook their formal distinction.

When he considered this distinction, the Angelic Doctor, using
the terminology of *efficient causality,* proposed the famous formula which many of his disciples have raised to the status of a
theory : the cooperation of the agent intellect and the phantasm
in the production of the intelligible species is that which exists
between a *principal* and an *instrumental cause,* where the former
moves the latter :

When the possible intellect receives the *species* of the things from
the phantasms, the latter act in the way of an *instrumental and
secondary agent,* while the agent intellect acts like the *principal and
first agent.* That is why the effect of this action in the possible
intellect has some of the features of either agent (*Ver.,* X, 6, ad 7).

In the instrumental causes which we know through direct
experience, the instrument's own efficiency always carries the
action of the main agent. Of course, in the process of intellection, the material phantasm exerts no direct efficiency whatsoever upon the possible intellect. Its function consists only in
providing the agent intellect with a diversified form, a " specification." Only in this sense may we say that the phantasm is the
instrument of the agent intellect.

Moreover, St. Thomas does not insist much upon this analogy,
which he mentions briefly in the *Quaestiones Disputatae,* and to
which he does not come back, to our knowledge, except in a
rather indirect way, in the *Summa Theologica.*

Everyone knows the objections of Suárez against the theory
of the instrumental causality of the phantasm, which he considers impossible. These objections would hit the mark if agent
intellect and phantasm were considered by Thomists as two
supposita, two principles of operation, radically distinct although
subordinated to each other. They lose all their strength if
intelligence and the senses are distinct only as two *faculties*
deriving from the same root and sharing the same being.

But, if in its deeper being the phantasm is not distinct from
the agent intellect, is it still a true instrumental cause, sub-

ordinated to a true principal cause? It is, in a refined and analogical sense. But we must admit that the mutual relation of agent intellect and phantasm is difficult to pigeonhole in the rigid framework of " predicamental " causes, defined after sense objects. If we wish to translate this relation in categorial concepts, we must associate at least two kinds of concepts and correct one through the other. For an agent intellect which, within one and the same ontological subject, moves a phantasm as a principal cause moves an instrument, is also to some extent with respect to this phantasm like a form which " informs " some matter, because an immanent action has something both of an efficient and formal cause, and may thus, albeit inadequately, be expressed in two different languages.

We have seen that St. Thomas alternately employs these two languages without being deceived by the apparent precision of either.

In short, if we do not wish to misinterpret the meaning of the Thomistic formulae, we must keep in mind the impossibility of considering the " operative powers " of the same subject, either *only* as forms which fit statically one in the other, or *only* as autonomous dynamic entities whose solidarity would not go beyond the extrinsic relation of an agent to a patient.

The Function of the Agent Intellect Interpreted through the General Theory of the Mental Powers

The case of the natural solidarity between the agent intellect and the phantasm comes under St. Thomas' general doctrine of the vital intercommunication of the powers in a being which is substantially composed.

It is a common presupposition of almost all scholastics that man's bodily and spiritual composition constitutes in the strictest sense *one* substance, *one* nature, *one* radical principle of action and passion. We might for the time being consider that substantial unity as a hypothesis which would turn into an established thesis if it became evident that no other hypothesis would supply a possible metaphysical reason for the necessary cooperation between the agent intellect and the phantasm. Let us then consider how the powers must be related to each other within the unity of the substance.

According to St. Thomas the powers emanate from the essence and constitute the natural dynamic explicitation of the essence. Let us suppose a substance which is composed (but strictly one, subsisting under only one " first being "), in which the form's perfection would transcend the purely material level. The presence of this double level within the essence will manifest itself through a hierarchy of perfection in the powers. Such is the case with human nature, in which the soul, although spiritual, is nevertheless the form of the body (see *S.T.*, I, the whole of Q. 77). Keeping this in mind, it will be useful to read the actual text of the *Summa:*

" Since the soul is one, and the powers are many, and since a number of things that proceed from one must proceed in a certain order, there must be *some order* among the powers of the soul " (*S.T.*, I, 77, 4, c). This order may show itself from different viewpoints. We are interested only in the order considered "according to the dependence of one power on another " (*ibid.*):

Now the dependence of one power on another can be taken in two ways: according to the order of nature, *inasmuch as perfect things are by their nature prior to imperfect things*; and according to the order of generation and time, inasmuch as from being imperfect, a thing comes to be perfect. Thus, according to the first kind of order among the powers, *the intellectual powers are prior to the sensitive powers; wherefore they direct them* and *command them.* . . . In the second kind of order, it is the other way about (*ibid.*). . . . Those powers . . . among which these two kinds of order exist, are such that *the action* of one depends on the other (*loc. cit.*, ad 3).

A little further on, St. Thomas gives more details about the hierarchical dependence of the powers and expresses it in terms of causality:

In things which proceed from one according to a natural order, just as the first is the cause of all, so that which is nearer to the first is, in a way, cause of those which are more remote. . . . There-

fore one power of the soul proceeds from the essence of the soul
by medium of another. But since the essence of the soul is compared to the powers both as *an active and final principle*, and as a
receptive principle, either separately by itself, or together with the
body; and since the agent and the end are more perfect, while the
receptive principle, as such, is less perfect: —it follows that those
powers of the soul which precede the others in the order of perfection and nature *are the principles of the others after the manner
of an end and an active principle*. For we see that *sense is for the
sake of the intellect*, and not the other way about. Sense, moreover,
is *a certain imperfect participation of the intellect*, and therefore,
according to its natural origin, it proceeds from the intellect as the
imperfect from the perfect. But considered *as receptive principles*,
the more imperfect powers are principles with regard to the others;
and thus the soul, according as it has the sensitive power, is considered *as the subject, and as something material* in relation to the
intellect. . . . (*S.T.*, 1, 77, 7, c).

These passages will determine our interpretation of the
Thomistic doctrine of the agent intellect. Let us emphasize the
scope of some of them.

First, a principle which is absolutely general: just as the
multiplicity of the powers shows the *imperfection* of the essential
form, so the *order* of the powers expresses its unity.

If the form, neither wholly subsistent nor wholly immersed in
matter, possesses both a material level and one which is more
or less completely independent of matter, the powers which
correspond to these levels of perfection will be arranged in an
order of *subordination*. Their subordination reproduces in a
hierarchy of virtualities the intensive degrees of the essence
itself.

According to whether we wish to consider the respective order
of the powers *statically,* insofar as they are arranged on a common stem, or *actively* insofar as they engender and command
each other, we shall define this order through relations of
material and formal causality or through relations of efficient
causality. On the one hand, the lower powers—or, more exactly,
the subject insofar as it possesses these powers—will operate as
a *principium susceptivum* and *materiale quoddam* (some kind of
receptive and material principle). And the higher powers, in

their turn, will operate as a *formal element*, as a principle of *actuation*. On the other hand, from the other point of view the higher powers will appear as a *proximate cause* and an *immediate end* of the lower powers, *sicut principium activum et finale*. St. Thomas explicitly attributes this double series of relations—formal and dynamic—to man's intellect and will.

We find here again, between the subordinated *powers*, the two couples of relations formerly discovered between their respective *activities*, that is, between the agent intellect " always in act " and the senses in exercise (phantasm); a formal couple: " the *act* of that which is intelligible in potency " as opposed to " the *matter* of the cause "; and a dynamic couple: " principal cause " (which moves, which actuates) as opposed to an " instrumental cause " (which is moved, actuated). Besides, it is evident that the reciprocal properties may be transposed from the powers to their acts and the other way around, since " as a being is, so it acts." St. Thomas explicitly admits this transposition. He says that in subordinated powers " the *act* of one power depends on the other." One group of powers directs the activity of the others.

Let us for awhile overlook the static subordination of the powers " as they stand to each other like matter and form," and consider only their dynamic subordination.

St. Thomas affirmed that the intellect is an active principle with respect to the senses, that is, it insinuates itself continually into sensibility as a cause insinuates itself in the effect which it shapes into its resemblance. Under this permanent influence, the senses will be radically finalized towards the intellect. The end of sensibility as moved by the intellect will coincide in this respect with the very end of the intellect, will be an " intelligible " end. " The end of the agent is the end of the action." And the higher powers are " the principles of the others in the way of an end and of an active principle " (*loc. cit.*). Hence in man the " inner finality," the " natural appetite " of the sensibility, is not confined to that which is spatially or temporally concrete. Beyond this concrete reality it strives towards the intelligible. That is why in man, unlike what happens in animals, the higher product of the imagination calls, by its very nature, as a normal complement, for *intelligibility*. This is expressed in the traditional formula—" the phantasm is intelligible in potency." For in a real subject potentiality does not merely designate the negative side or the pure possibility of an act, but the *positive aptitude* and, as it were, the vague desire of this act. " Potency has an appetite for act; matter is an appetite of form."

The fact that the senses are continually moved by the intellect is so clearly within the horizon of the scholastics that they have expressed it in the very name they apply to the internal sense. In man the estimative power becomes " the cogitative power " and memory becomes " reminiscence."

Hence throughout the ordered system of the essence and its faculties the striving towards the subject's total end spreads from level to level, evoking at each level a tendency towards the perfection of the next higher level. The operation of the vegetative powers prepares and fosters the activity of the sensitive powers, and the latter collaborate with the exercise of the intellectual faculties (*S.T.*, I, 77, 4, c).

Let us try to discover the exact point where this rising finality *immediately* affects the intellect. We said above that in a certain sense there is some intellectuality diffused all the way down to the lower levels of our human nature, to our bodiliness and the peculiar mode of our vegetative life. But the influence of the intellect reaches that far only indirectly. Even external sensibility does not border on intelligence and does not carry its *direct* stamp. We meet an immediate intellectual influence and not merely its repercussion; we see the intellect at work, as St. Thomas says, " directing and commanding," only on the highest level of innermost sensibility where the *synthesis of the imagination* is effected.

We do not have to present here a psychological analysis of the syntheses of the imagination. It will be enough to make a distinction between a lower imaginative synthesis which we might call passive, a mere effect of automatic associations deriving from spatial or temporal contiguity or from the work of memory. This *passive* synthesis cannot enter as a unit into consciousness unless it is accompanied by an *active* constructive or reconstructive synthesis. The product of this second synthesis —or more precisely of this active and spontaneous stage of the syntheses of the imagination—is precisely the " phantasm " of the scholastics; it is the image with its global pattern and the connection of its parts.

The question has been raised whether any *constructive* synthesis of the imagination would be impossible without some directing intelligence. We do not wish to claim that it is, since even according to the scholastics the instinctive and appetitive tendencies of the animals already introduce in the associative automatism a " constructive " principle whose importance should not be underestimated. But, leaving the animals aside, in man the " constructive synthesis," the highest act of the imagination, occurs *under the natural and steady motion of the intellect,* the immediate principle and the proximate end of the imagination (" *principium activum et finale* ").

Thus the specific finality of the active imagination and the internal unity of the phantasm are *raised* above the level of sensibility, not as if the image itself stopped being material and concrete, but because its constitutive unity within matter itself depends directly on the intelligible unity. Exactly to the extent in which the phantasm undergoes this influence, it acquires new properties. " Just as the sensitive part acquires a greater power by its conjunction with the intellectual part, so through the power of the agent intellect phantasms *are made more fit for the abstraction of intelligible intentions from them* " (*S.T.,* I, 85, 1, ad 4).

The Abstraction of the "Intelligible Species"

However subtle it may seem to be, a further precision becomes necessary.

When St. Thomas notes that the intellect *dominates* and *moves* the phantasm, he does not claim that the intellect constitutes, in and with the sense faculty, the proximate eliciting principle of imaginative knowledge. Every knowledge " *in actu secundo,*" that is, every " intentional " reaction, every " reflection," however elementary it may be, of a faculty upon its actual content, belongs to the inviolable domain of the *strictly* immanent operation of this faculty. Neither the agent intellect nor any other active principle may insert itself here.

Hence, as soon as the objective determinations have entered the sense faculty as its ontological modifications, their *last* actuation as acts of knowledge depends only on the formal perfection of sensibility itself. Hence, whether or not the phantasm is " intelligible in potency," constructed under the motion of the intellect, the imagination knows it only according to its sense concretion, as a particular image. And in this " autonomous " activity the sense faculty shares nothing with the intellect. The unifying action of the intellect upon the senses ends on the level of the *natural esse* of the phantasm. At this preconscious stage nothing prevents the phantasm, although it is inherent in the imaginative power, from depending also on other actual causes. St. Thomas states that the ontological dependence of the phantasm with respect to the intellectual faculty is a *necessity of nature.*

Hence it is not in the phantasm as already known by sense consciousness, it is not in the " image " that we will look for the corresponding " intelligible," but on the boundary line where imagination and intellect cooperate as natural agents in the synthesis, the genesis of the image. We might say, since the scholastics use the terminology, in the " phantasm *in first act.*"

But how can the " phantasm in first act " become " intelligible in act," or, to use another expression of St. Thomas, " such that an intelligible intention may be abstracted from it "?

Of course, as we said above, the answer is: to the extent and only to the extent in which it actually happens to be the term of the intellect's natural activity. The phantasm becomes intelligible only when bathing in the very light of the agent intellect which is always in act.

Let us then briefly consider again the active participation of the intellect in the synthesis of the phantasm. The following questions occur at once.

First, how is it possible that between the spiritual intellect and the intrinsically material phantasm there should occur the contact required so that the former's activity really should affect the latter? Would we not, after all, face the difficulty which baffled Descartes, namely the necessity of admitting that a material reality may act upon a spiritual one?

St. Thomas has already given us the principle of the answer. " The agent intellect is always in act, it is in act according to its substance." Only in the material agents *(as material,* not as agents) " passion " precedes and elicits action. " The agent, *as agent,* is not modified." When the agent intellect starts acting, when it operates, it merely extends its own permanent actuality to a patient (or, in general, to some subordinated determinations). This is the way in which spirits operate, by pure spontaneity, without having to undergo any previous "alteration."

Yet the actuality of a spirit can extend to a new content and thus become " action," " operation," only if between this spirit and the object of its activity there pre-exists *some physical relation,* some " affinity." Let us say in one word with the scholastics : the object (the patient) must be *proximately in potency* of the act which is offered to it. Hence, when explaining the action of the pure spirits upon matter, St. Thomas supposes that the original perfection of their essences puts each one of them in advance in relation—a physical relation, a relation of active power, of efficacious domination—with a more or less extended domain of bodily realities. We cannot insist here on these strange theses of angelology. Let us only note their principle : the action of a finite agent always presupposes a physical bond between agent and patient.

In the case of the intellect moving the senses, the pre-existing physical bond is simply *the substantial union of soul and body.* The natural and immediate domain wherein our spiritual soul can influence matter is the body united to the soul in one same being. Because the soul is the formal cause of the body, the higher powers which emanate from the soul as spiritual have an essential relation and a solidarity in action with the lower intentional powers which emanate from the composite being as such. That is why as soon as the sense elements enter the precinct of the imagination they enter also in the immediate zone of the influence of the intellect. With respect to the latter they are then in a real sense " the matter on which it operates."

Yet we might wonder whether the analogy between the action of the intellect upon the senses and the external operation of a pure spirit is not very slight. The pure spirit is led in its actions by its previous knowledge of the object of its activity. There can be, for the agent intellect, no anticipated knowledge of sensible matter, since—as our intellect does not have, like the angelic intellect, any inborn species—such a knowledge itself should demand another agent intellect, and so on *ad infinitum.*

The objection is well taken. That is why the causality of the agent intellect on the senses must operate, as the scholastics say, *per modum naturae,* unconsciously, with an absolute necessity, according to an unchangeable rule, without knowledge or choice.

This entails important consequences. If it should happen that the intervention of the agent intellect brought to our concepts not only the possibility of originating and a subjective mode (*modus quo*) but even some *content* (*id quod*), the latter element, since it would not result from any selection operated *a priori* upon the sense data, would totally respect their natural relations. With respect to their diversity, it would be of itself totally indifferent, wholly universal. Hence the problem of the intellectual *a priori*—should it arise here—would in no event refer to the delimitation or the distribution of the material essences, but only to something which would belong to the intelligible representation of all these essences, whatever they may be.

A third question arises. In the above context what is the relation between the natural, unconsciously exercised influence of the intellect upon the imaginative synthesis and the *illuminating* function attributed to the agent intellect?

This relation is extremely intimate. Let us again consider the theoretical elements implied in the transitive action of a spiritual agent. Of course, the latter knows the object of its action before influencing it, but once the action is finished it possesses in another way, in the specifying form of its own operation (*specificative et terminative*), the very outline of the latter's objective term. To a finite agent, even an immaterial one, every external action brings something new, and this acquisition does not imply in the active subject a real passivity, a " predicamental passion," in the line of matter, that is, an invasion from without, with alteration of the subject. It is not a *real* passivity, but the immaterial passivity which corresponds to the power of expansion of the form as form. For if, on one hand, the term of every action is precontained in the agent insofar as it is produced by the latter, on the other hand, insofar as it is not produced by the agent, it marks an actual limit of the latter's expansive power—and can be found in it, as it were, in reverse relief. While exercising its active powers, the finite agent explores itself in its own limitation, and, by so doing, explores the reality which surrounds it. It follows that, in order to *know* the external object in another way, that is, through the form of the operation exercised on it, it is enough for the immaterial agent to become aware of itself according to the particular mode of its present activity, which supposes, of course, a power of " complete reflection " upon itself.

The case of the intellect in its causal influence (efficient, final and formal, all at once) upon the syntheses of the imagination is absolutely analogous—but for the fact that the activity of the agent intellect is directly ruled by the substantial unity of soul and body without previous knowledge of the term of the action. Once the *actual* contact has been established between the two faculties with respect to some sense matter, the intellect, whose natural activity has adapted itself spontaneously to this matter (*materia circa quam*), possesses in its very adaptation the formal type of the effected term, a dynamic type, intrinsically immaterial, yet having a relation to the qualitative diversity of a sense matter and itself diversified according to this relation. In its intimate and active union with the phantasm which it moves intrinsically and fills, as it were, with spiritual finality, the intellect gives up its first indetermination. As a result, since it is immaterial and in act, it becomes self-luminous according to the immanent determination which it gives itself. And this determination fulfills all the conditions of an "intelligible species."

In short, owing to the substantial unity of the sensitivo-rational subject, the intellect acquires, through its transient (or quasi-transient) and unconscious action on the imaginative synthesis, the internal determination which makes possible its own immanent and conscious operation (intellection).

It is on purpose that we mention here but very concisely

the last stage, the conscious stage of the intellectual act. For it raises several problems which we can consider with profit only later. We wish to show only how the theory of the powers allows us to explain in more detail, from the metaphysical point of view, the kind of solidarity which binds the phantasm to the agent intellect in the actuation of the possible intellect, according to some " intentional *species.*"

Before continuing our investigation, it will be useful to define, in line with the above interpretation, a few of the traditional expressions of Thomistic ideogenesis.

In the first stage of its intervention the *agent intellect* is the intellect itself inasmuch as (owing to the substantial union of soul and body and to the active subordination of the powers which follows from it) it exerts upon the imagination a causal influence which is both formal and efficient.

The *phantasm* is the concrete result of the constructive or reconstructive synthesis of the imagination, as effected in the imagination itself according to the laws of sensibility, but under the influence of the agent intellect.

From the necessary and unconscious encounter of the agent intellect and the phantasm, as the former actively subsumes the latter, a dynamic determination results in the intellectual faculty which corresponds to the qualitative structure of the phantasm, the term of this activity. This is the *second stage* in the operation of the agent intellect.

The new, enriching determination (*impressed intelligible species*) affects the intellect in its " immaterial potency " that is, as *possible intellect*. The proximate conditions of *intellection,* which is an act of the possible intellect informed by the *species,* are then realized. Later we shall have to show how this intellection is " objective," and not merely " consciousness of the subject."

Coming back to the general technical formula to which we must always return in this matter, it seems to us that the Thomistic theory of the powers explains, as no other theory can, why, actually informed by the agent intellect, the intelligible in potency offered in the concrete phantasm has become intelligible in act—not in its singular concreteness, but through an " abstraction " of those features which were potentially intelligible.[1]

When we speak here of an " explanation," we do not, of course, use this word in the sense which it has in experimental psychology, but in the sense in which, in metaphysics, a system of *necessary relations* may be called an " explanation." And even within this order of metaphysical relations we will keep in mind that, although the specific causality of the agent intellect may be defined by us *analogically and negatively,* through a concatenation of rational necessities, in its intimate nature it remains for us much more inaccessible than the material essences. Who will show us not only that there *must* be a subordination of powers in the human composite, but *how* this subordination is possible? The ultimate secret of our sensitivo-intellectual knowledge remains sealed for us, in the very depths of the substantial unity of body and spirit. No finite being can fathom the depths of its own nature.

The "Intelligible Species"

The immediate effect of the activity of the agent intellect is the presence in the possible intellect of " *species,*" that is, of " determining forms " which make possible the passage of the intellect from potency to act.

At the stage in which we consider them these *species* are not some kind of intellectual image, a copy of the phantasm. They possess in the possible intellect a *dynamic and formal* function (*id quo*), not an objective one (*id quod*). St. Thomas compares them with the " specifying form " of the external action; they determine and specify the immanent intellectual action (*S.T.,* I, 85, 2, c). In fact an immanent action creates nothing physically except for its own form. In this sense the

---

[1] Let us not forget that, according to St. Thomas, abstraction supposes no physical transferring of " forms," but only a purely precisive " conformation " of the intellect to some of the phantasm's features. The abstraction in question is nothing but the very setting up, within the possible intellect, of dynamic relations (*species*) according to the qualitative diversity of the phantasm.

species is also the term of the immanent action. We might call
it the characteristic line of an attitude (but of an " objectivating "
attitude).

An error which is frequently committed because of the inexact-
ness of language consists in introducing stealthily, within the
very concept, the sense representation which gave rise to it. It
is a fact that our thought is always accompanied by some
image, more or less vague, more or less schematic, more or
less symbolic, upon which our attention always falls back as
soon as we try to represent clearly to ourselves the object of our
thought. . . .

Hence the concept, insofar as I am aware of it, is not sufficient by itself as representation. It remains always in a *necessary relation* to the concrete image. What kind of relation?

If the intellect gave us, in the concept, an intelligible representation which should be self-sufficient as such, like a more
or less sublimated copy of the image, the collaboration of the
phantasm would be required only as a necessary starting point
for the act of understanding to set the agent intellect in motion.
Once the " *species* " is in the possible intellect, such a collaboration would become superfluous since the species would intelligibly represent by itself all that the image represents on
the sense level. But, according to St. Thomas, not only no single
primary act of intellection, but also no use whatsoever of the
species is possible except *in the presence of the phantasm, in*
the phantasm. . . .

[Hence] the *species* is by itself only a *dynamic* disposition
of the intellect, qualitatively diversified in function of the
phantasm. . . . Thus the intelligible species never enters our
consciousness alone, like a complete intellectual representation
which screens off the sense representation, but always according
to a dynamic relation to an actual phantasm.

A dynamic relation to the phantasm. But a relation supposes
two terms. Relation of *what* precisely? Hitherto we have defined
the *species* only through the qualitative diversity of this relation
itself. But what is ultimately referred to the phantasm, and
projected upon it as on a phosphorescent screen which becomes
luminous at the points of impact?

To this question we shall answer in a word that the higher term of the relation imposed upon the phantasm by the intellect is the *speculative unity of being*. . . .

In the particular intellections, the conceptual unity may be generic or specific. . . . But these are only partial, subordinated unities, whose diversity still proceeds from the very diversity of the phantasm. If we wish to know on what *last universal unity,* the real share of our intellect in the intelligible *species,* depends the whole hierarchy of the abstract unifications, we must decidedly remove every particular representation and suppose *any* imaginative datum *whatsoever,* noting what happens to the concept in this case.

As a result of this operation we are left, according to Kant, with *the categorial unity of the real,* specified only by the " transcendental," purely *a priori* relation of the intellect to the senses, without intervention of any determined content except the *a priori* intuition of space and time. We would thus have uncovered the formal object of *human* understanding (if not that of every possible understanding).

St. Thomas likewise stated that after these successive abstractions we are left with the *unity of quantitative being* as such, which corresponds to the proper and immediate object of our intellect, to the " quiddity or nature which exists in corporeal matter " (*S.T.,* I, 84, 7, c). Since all material *quiddities* are essentially quantitative, identically multipliable, their common unity will have the features of undetermined numerical unity, of the *ens principium numeri* (being as origin of number).

Hence on the ascending line going from the multiple phantasm to the concept, if we abstract from the diversity of the sense qualities, the pure universal unity which we meet in the intellect expresses the immediate relation of the latter, in its most general content, *being,* to the most basic property of every phantasm, *concrete quantity.*

Suppose we call " element of representation " in the concept all that which, in the latter, derives from its relation to the phantasm or from an abstraction practiced on the phantasm. We may then say that the supreme unity of the concept as " representation " (that is, conceptual unity embracing not this or that sense content, but any sense content whatsoever) does not go beyond the abstract unity of number. Should the concept's *objective* function wholly coincide with its *representative* function, as supposed by the *Critique of Pure Reason,* we would have to conclude that the spontaneity of the agent intellect in the formation of the intelligible *species* comes down to a formal power of numerical synthesis. Intelligible unity would not differ from abstract numerical unity.

But this conclusion manifestly contradicts St. Thomas' statement on the extension and comprehension of intelligible unity . . . This unity will certainly not stand below the original virtuality which belongs properly to the agent intellect. But what does properly belong to the agent intellect, what does it contribute to the *species,* and hence to the objective operations of the possible intellect?

" To know the *first intelligible principles* is an action belonging to the human species . . . the power which is the principle of this action . . . is *the agent intellect* " (*S.T.,* I, 79, 5, ad 3).

" For in every man there is a certain principle of knowledge, namely the *light of the agent intellect,* through which certain *universal principles of all* the sciences are naturally understood as soon as proposed to the intellect " (*S.T.,* I, 117, I, c). " In the light of the agent intellect, *the universal science (omnis scientia) is somehow congenitally inborn in us . . .*" (*Ver.,* 10, 6, c).

But it is evident that in the terminology of St. Thomas the universal science, *omnis scientia,* comprises also the analogical knowledge of the transcendent being; that the *first intelligible* principles comprise within their extension the wholly unquantitative objects, all the way up to the pure act of being; that the " universal principles of all the sciences " are mainly the fundamental principles of metaphysics.

On the other hand, if there is a science whose revelation must be "inborn " in some way to our intelligence, it is without doubt the philosophy of the *metempirical* world. Did we not mention previously that in the order of objective knowledge, the agent intellect is by nature endowed with an unlimited constructive universality—*est quo omnia facere?* The same Aristotle who used the latter expression, also uses (and

St. Thomas after him) another typical expression when speaking of the inborn nature of the " first principle," which is not only the principle of quantitative being, but of being *as such*: among " the conditions of this very certain principle . . . the third one is that . . . *it comes from without to someone who, as it were, possesses it by nature,* as if it were known naturally, and not from any learning. For the first principles are known through the very *light of the agent intellect*" (*In IV Metaph.,* lect. 6). *Advenit quasi habenti ipsum:* " it comes from without to someone who, as it were, possesses it by nature "; this is the very formula of the virtual, dynamic *a priori,* as it becomes explicit, under the impact of the outside data in some objective knowledge. The agent intellect possesses *a priori* the supreme rule, not of number, but of being in its whole extension.

This clearly shows, therefore, that St. Thomas does not restrict the influence of the agent intellect to mere quantitative syntheses; starting from the very origin of the concept, he attributes to it the virtual scope which Kant reserved not only to the " understanding," but to metempirical " reason ": the agent intellect really abstracts, and gives rise in this way to the universal and repeatable element of the concept; but it does so on account of a *principle of unification* which is as wide, not as quantitative being as such, but in some way as the whole amplitude of the " knowable."

After having examined the sensation and the concept, Maréchal devotes a chapter to the intelligible unity of the concept. Our concepts are universal, the unity of a diversity. This diversity comes from the phantasms and the senses, and our pragmatic interest in everyday activities turns mostly in this direction. The unity derives from a higher unity which, according to St. Thomas as interpreted by Maréchal, is ultimately the unity of the Infinite Being itself. We do not know the Infinite Being by means of an adequate concept of it. We know it analogically, because we implicitly refer to it all the objects we know. The following selections set forth some of Maréchal's views on the analogy of the intelligible being.

XXVI. THE ANALOGY
OF INTELLIGIBLE BEING

But how can we "reach" God if not *through an objective concept?* It is true that our knowledge can extend all the way up to God only through the intermediary of an objective concept. Must this objective concept necessarily be the proper, direct, "quidditative" concept of God? If we reply affirmatively, we are led either into ontologism, which attributes to our intellect a rather vague, but direct and intuitive knowledge of the divine being, or into one of these powerless theodicies which make God and the creature coincide in a univocal concept and are thus unable to demonstrate the real transcendence of God. A middle road is difficult to follow. According to St. Thomas, although we do in fact know God through an objective concept, the whole objective content of our concepts (*omnis "ratio objectiva"*) directly represents a created object and must therefore, when we attribute it to God, be *corrected* by us.

But, once more, how could we perform this correction, since, not knowing God directly, we have no way of comparing him with his creatures?

Here we hit the most difficult element in analogical knowledge. We can, in a very real sense, compare God with the creature without knowing him immediately in himself. Let us suppose that a well determined relation connects the creature with God and that this relation, as such, should be known to us in its lower term. Then, knowing the lower term *as relative,* we would, in this very knowledge and to the same extent, have some notion of the higher term, somewhat as when we see an arrow leave the bow, we have in the direction of its flight an indication about the position of the target. That is what happens to us: we know the creatures *as relative* to an absolute Principle, as *contingent* and in this way and only in this way do we know God.

But the objection returns as soon as we have answered it. In the Thomistic doctrine all our concepts are originally concepts of material quiddities: the contingence of the created

being—inasmuch as it reveals to us the divine transcendence—
is given to us neither in the representation contained by these
concepts, nor in their abstractive and universal form. The
former is but a diversified relation to the phantasm, the latter a
process of objective generalization which does not rise above
the level of representation. Hence there seems to be in the
objective concept no hint of a " transcendental relation " such
as the contingence of finite being would be.

We must grant the objection if the concept is *only* a representation and a mere generalizing abstraction. For how
should the absolute and transcendent term of the relation
of contingence—God—reveal himself, even analogically, in
finite representations or in their simple generalization? Does
St. Thomas not say that the peak of our knowledge of God
is " to know, that he exceeds all that which we should be able
to conceive of him " (*Q. Disp. de Pot.,* VII, 5, ad 14)? Hence,
the transcendent God cannot be represented by our concepts;
neither can he even be hinted at as the limit towards which
the generalization of these concepts would tend. It would seem
that we could have an awareness of the radical contingence of
the created objects only if we could transcend their finiteness
through the awareness of an absolute supereminence of their
principle with respect to every *possible* object of our thoughts.
But on what might such a consciousness be based if it is
neither the analysis of a sense intuition, nor the abtract consideration of a material form?

Thus we are induced to postulate in our objective knowledge
something more than the static reception and the abstractive
analysis of " data," a movement of thought which would bring
us constantly " beyond " that which may still be represented
by concepts, some kind of metempirical anticipation which
should show us the objective capacity of our intellect expanding infinitely until it exceeds any limitation of being. Otherwise
there can be no analogical knowledge of the transcendent.
Hence in order to explain and safeguard the latter we are
induced to take our stand on the domain of the *dynamic
finality* of our spirit. For only an " internal finality " of the
intellect may make it constantly exceed the present object and
strive infinitely towards a wider object.

XXVII. ABSTRACTION

The problem of analogical knowledge at times arises in a very clear way as an insoluble objection in the mind of philosophers who look at Thomism through stereotyped formulas whose exact scope they do not yet grasp.

They may speak as follows: You scholastics claim that every intellectual knowledge comes to us through an *abstraction* performed upon material objects. But we can abstract from an object only that which it contains. Suppose we grant (although even this might be too much) that a material object—presented by the senses!—somehow contains a corresponding " quiddity " whose comprehension may through successive abstraction be extenuated until it finally yields the most general attribute of every material quiddity, " univocal being," *ens principium numeri* (being as the principle of number). But what sounds utterly unintelligible is that you also claim to abstract from the material quiddity the transcendental concepts which, by definition, extend beyond it and which no longer have any common measure with it. And these philosophers conclude that, if the transcendent is to be within the reach of the human mind, this will not be the result of an analytical process of abstraction, but of some process of progressive and conquering dialectic.

To this objection we reply that it involves a misunderstanding of the meaning of abstraction in scholastic philosophy. This one term refers to a series of successive processes which, although showing some similarity with each other, are far from being homogeneous. Let us try to explain St. Thomas' doctrine on this topic.

In the line of intellectual knowledge, St. Thomas distinguishes *three degrees of abstraction*—of the abstraction which the scholastics call " total abstraction," to distinguish it from the particular abstraction of the senses.

Next Maréchal explains the meaning of the two first degrees of abstraction, the direct abstraction of the universal and mathematical abstraction. He then gives us his interpretation of the third degree of abstraction.

XXVIII. ABSTRACTION
OF THE TRANSCENDENTAL CONCEPTS

The highest degree of abstraction described by St. Thomas is heterogeneous with respect to mathematical abstraction, as the latter was with respect to simple universalizing abstraction. " Some things may *even* be abstracted *from common intelligible matter*; such as being, potency and act, and other similar things. They can even subsist *without any matter*" (*S.T.*, I, 85, 1, ad 2).

The object which remains after this third abstraction is clearly indicated. It is the transcendental concepts.[1] Let us, in some content of thought, drop the individual determinations and the differentiation coming from the senses, let us drop every abstract relation to quantity. What do we keep then? The empty capacity of consciousness, the " pure transcendental object " as purely undetermined? Kant will answer that, speculatively speaking, there is indeed nothing else. St. Thomas, on the other hand, answered that there remains a plurality of objective determinations whose differential features stay on even when all the diversity deriving from pure quantity and the sense qualities has disappeared.

Where will we look for the psychological principle which sets this higher differentiation " in act " in the subject? The physical contact of the outside object gives us only that which is concrete and perceivable by the senses. The lowly *a priori* of our senses performs only a differentiation of sense qualities. The constructive *a priori* of the imagination does not explain any abstraction superior to quantity. In its universalizing function the understanding simply dematerializes that which is quantitative and sense perceivable. It seems then that, in order to explain the origin and the differentiation of the transcendental concepts which we obtain through the third degree of abstraction, we can turn to no other subjective principle than *an* a priori *diversity of the intellectual faculty itself*. In other words, the intellect must be not only the immaterial and the universaliz-

---

[1] We must bear in mind that these concepts are transcendental only in virtue of their *analogical signification*. At first and directly, they *represent* attributes of material essences.

ing support, but to some extent the constructive principle of the immanent intelligible object, somewhat in the way in which the imagination was shown to be the constructive principle of the mathematical object. Might we not push this comparison further and admit that the intellect's transcendental object is, on its level, some kind of " pure intuition " (an *a priori* content of representation) as the formal object of the internal sense would be, at a lower level, a " pure intuition "? This excessive conclusion is unacceptable for Thomistic scholasticism. It would put us directly in touch with the transcendent object and thus agree, if not with the extreme tenets of ontologistic innatism or intuitionism, at least with the fundamental conception of Wolffian rationalism, which ascribes to our intelligence the power of obtaining *a priori,* through a process of synthesis, the formal representation of *objectively* possible essences.

What are we then to make of an " *a priori* intellectual diversity " which is neither an ontological intuition nor a " pure intuition "?

Here we run into the difficulty which was brought up previously by our effort to reconcile these two Thomistic affirmations: (1) we can objectively know the transcendent Being; (2) however, we do not possess in our knowledge the proper form of the transcendent Being. Here, likewise, we meet a dilemma. Either our intelligence really contains transcendental determinations which may be objectively applied beyond the categories of experiences (but in this event our intelligence is intuitive, or at least it contains within itself a formal " quidditative " idea which is directly applicable to the transcendent, and an *a priori* synthetic metaphysics becomes possible), or metaphysics is purely analytic, and our intelligence contains no objective *a priori* determinations, since its whole formal content is borrowed from experience. But in this hypothesis whence comes the possibility of abstracting transcendental concepts which extend beyond the most extreme generalization of experience? Can we escape the alternative of ontologism or agnosticism?

To get out of this pressing dilemma we should show that the intellectual *a priori* which is at work in third degree abstraction can give us *an objectively valid knowledge* of the transcendent without being its *formal representation.*

It is obvious that such an enterprise is perfectly impossible for any philosopher who, on account of his method or of his system, would reduce all knowledge to static or formal conditions. Such a thinker would have to choose between ontologism and agnosticism. Hence only the adoption of a dynamic viewpoint completing the formal point of view can provide a possibility of explaining the analogical value of the transcendental concepts. Let us once more gather this hint. It is still negative and confused, but it at least shows us the direction which we must take if we do not wish our epistemology to endeavor in vain to accomplish an impossible task.

After his study of the material elements of the judgment, sensations and concepts, Maréchal proceeds to the investigation of its formal elements : the synthesis of subject and predicate, or the synthetic form of the judgment, and the affirmation, or the objective form of the judgment. Affirmation occupies a central position in Maréchal's system. The following selection exposes some of his ideas on this topic.

XXIX. THE NATURE OF AFFIRMATION

We have noticed to what extent St. Thomas multiplies the expressions which introduce assent in general, and even purely scientific assent, into the domain of *finality.* The following text will confirm this. To the assents which it is in our power to give or to refuse, St. Thomas opposes the necessary, absolutely evident assents: " When we apprehend things to which the intellect naturally gives its assent, like the first principles, to assent to or dissent with such principles is not within our own power, but *in the order of nature*; hence, strictly speaking, it underlies the power of nature " (*S.T.*, Ia-IIae, 17, 6, c).

It is well known that, for the scholastics, *nature* is but the " radical principle of operation and passion," the " internal finality " of the agent. Hence our evident assents occur ultimately, according to St. Thomas, under the decisive influence of this "natural appetite" which moves our reason even before it carries our volitions.

From these passages, compared with many others—especially those which explain the "reciprocal causality" of the intellect and the will—we may derive the following conclusions:

(1) That the assent in question here designates one and the same final psychological attitude of the knowing subject, whether we have to do with a firm belief or with a rational certitude. Only the causes which determine this attitude differ from case to case. Hence we may formally identify *assent* and *affirmation*.

(2) That the *assent* or *affirmation* is an act of the intellectual faculty, not of the will.

(3) That the *assent* or *affirmation* is determined by an antecedent finality.

This is evident in the case of faith or belief because assent is explicitly commanded by the will.

But the decisive influence of the antecedent finality exists also in the case of the rational assent determined by the presentation to the intellect of its "proper object," with or without intermediary reasoning.

For, according to the most authentic Thomistic teaching, the proper object of an assimilating power, like our intelligence, measures exactly the *natural finality,* the basic exigency of this power. The *natural finality* refers to the dynamic value of the proper object, the formal term of this finality. For the objective end "moves because it is desired."

Hence everything St. Thomas says here of the causality exercised by the proper object of the intellect upon the assent should be understood in a strictly dynamic sense of the very dependence of every rational assent with respect to the "natural" antecedent finality of the intellect. St. Thomas is thinking of this antecedent finality when he writes: "the assent puts to rest [the intellect of the knowing subject]"; or again: "the movement of the thinker stops [in the assent] and rests in it" (*Ver.,* 14, 1, c); or finally "the assent [of him who thinks or knows] underlies the power of nature" (*S.T.,* I^a-II^{ae}, 15, 1, ad 3).

The internal "natural finality" or the "natural appetite" of a rational being may be called "natural volition" as contrasted with "elicited volition" or simply "the will." Using this terminology in the very precise meaning which St. Thomas himself occasionally used, we might take up again and widen his formula and say "that the intellect assents (or affirms) insofar as it is moved by volition (either natural or elicited)" (*S.T.*, Ia-IIae, 15, 1, ad 3).

(4) Should we push our interpretation even further, we would discover that the assent determined by antecedent finality determines in its turn a further finality, a *consequent finality*.

The intellect does not find a complete rest in any particular affirmation, since none of them constitutes its last end. Hence the assent means the reaching of a subordinated end, a simple stage or means in the pursuit of a more comprehensive end.

Thus we see that the affirmation stands at the common boundary of the two orders of intellectual finality whose meeting point in us is called understanding. It is both the result of a previous exigency and the starting point of another one, a "formal" acquisition and a value for possible "action"; in a word, a partial quieting and an immediate reawakening of the very desire which constitutes the core of our intellectual nature, the deep and never resting desire for Being.

We might add that this double finality, antecedent and consequent, explains—we will later show that it alone can explain—the exclusive property possessed by judgment, of producing the relation of logical truth in our understanding, the knowledge (at least implicit) of the object *as object*. For, a representative form which has already been assimilated and unified in a subject must also oppose itself somehow to this subject if it is to function as object. But we have just mentioned that a form grasped by a "becoming" inserts itself in it, both inseparably as some good which is already possessed and as a still desirable good, as a *form* and as an *end*. Hence it will possess at once the logical properties of a form and those of an end; that is, while immanent to the active subject, it will be opposed to him as an end is opposed to a tendency. For nobody acquires or pursues that which he is or has. If the faculty (in which the represented form exists in this way in a state of indivision between the two successive stages of the same becoming) is spiritual, capable of complete reflection, the dynamic properties of the representation—hence its opposition to the subject—will emerge directly or indirectly into consciousness.

Is this not precisely the mechanism of the affirmation? Is it not on account of it that affirmation necessarily " objectivates "? Considered as a moment in the intellect's ascent towards the final possession of the absolute " truth," which is the spirit's " good," it implicitly (*exercite*) projects the particular data in the perspective of this ultimate End, and by so doing *objectivates* them before the subject.

But let us proceed further: if affirmation objectivates the partial data only by projecting them into the perspective of the ultimate End, would we not possess in this dynamic relation the middle term we were looking for in order to pass from the knowledge of the finite objects to that of the *infinite Being?* For in this case the affirmation is no longer a simple " categorial " function, opposed to negation, a simple formal aspect of the synthesis of subject and predicate; it becomes a *transcendent anticipation.* Because of this the transcendental relation of the objects to Being which is posited implicitly in direct knowledge will undoubtedly manifest itself to reflection.

St. Thomas alludes several times to this still hidden stage of our knowledge of God—the " main analogate "—in our very knowledge of the " lower analogates," the finite objects. " All knowing beings *implicitly* know God *in everything they know.* For as nothing is desirable but through some resemblance with the first goodness, so nothing is knowable but through some resemblance with the first truth " (*Ver.*, 22, 2, ad 1).

Not only is God hinted at by us in every object as an Ideal of intelligibility, his very *existence* is given to us in a confused and implicit way in the primitive exigency of our intellectual nature. " To know *that God exists* in a general and confused way *is implanted in us by nature,* inasmuch as God is man's *beatitude.* For man naturally desires happiness, and what is naturally desired by man *is naturally known by him* " (*S.T.*, I, 2, 1, ad 1). Therefore the transcendent term of the analogical relations,

which constitutes before our mind every object as object (as
" being "), is implanted in some way in our actual consciousness.
It is given *implicitly,* and the whole problem consists in making
this implicit datum explicit. Many human intelligences do not
succeed in this analytical enterprise.

But is this supreme term, intended by the obscure anticipation which carries our affirmations, only a *subjectively* postulated
reality? Is it, on the contrary—as St. Thomas claims—an absolute *objectively* necessary Reality? The answer to these questions will become clearer from the following chapters, which
will also introduce us more deeply, and from another angle,
into the logical structure of the object of knowledge.

*In the conclusion of the last section, it was stated that in
every one of his affirmations man implicitly affirms the existence
of the Infinite Being. Maréchal will now try to show that the
necessity which induces man to affirm the Transcendent is not
merely a psychological necessity, but a logical one as well.*

*Kant would have admitted a psychological necessity of this
kind. He calls the " transcendental illusion" unavoidable. But,
according to him, we affirm God's existence only subsequently
to our affirmation of the objects of our experience. Maréchal
will try to show, in the section that follows, that the affirmation of God is not subsequent to, but constitutive of our every
affirmation.*

XXX. DEDUCTION
OF THE ONTOLOGICAL AFFIRMATION

Between the preceding chapters and those which are to follow
there is the same difference as between the *analytic* (dissociating)
and the *deductive* (synthetic) stage of the transcendental proof
in the critical philosophies.

Hitherto we have mainly been looking, in the objective contents of consciousness as observed in ourselves, for the " *a
priori* conditions " which rendered them logically and psychologically intelligible. We have borrowed the elements of this
rational induction from the metaphysical context in which St.
Thomas offered them to us. This is where we had to study them

if we wished to carry out our exegetical task. We were entitled to do so, since we have established with the ancient realists the necessity of attributing an ontological meaning to every content of our affirmation. Yet, as we frequently hinted, one might easily discover, under our ontological inferences, the precisive outline of a " transcendental reflection " in the modern sense.

Henceforth and without overlooking the fact that our first task is to interpret faithfully a metaphysical doctrine, we will adopt the strictly *deductive* method demanded in order to complete a critical demonstration. We endeavor to establish *a priori,* " through concepts," that for *every* non-intuitive intelligence the means and the only means of representing the contents of consciousness as *objects* is their strictly metaphysical affirmation, that is, their well determined, at least implicit, relation to a transcendent Reality, so that a rejection of such an affirmation would amount to a denial of the very possibility of objective thought. If we succeed in presenting this demonstration, we will have connected the affirmation of the metaphysical value of the objects as *noumena* to the necessity of the " minimum " postulate of every critique—*objective thought* as such. We will, within the framework of Thomistic metaphysics, have made a " transcendental deduction of the ontological affirmation."

XXXI. THE ACTUALITY OF THE OBJECT AS THE MEASURE OF AFFIRMATION

Should we be able to embrace in one glance the logical and ontological conditions of the real, we would clearly and continually see that every " abstract " content is secondary, that is, that it is originally but the immaterial form of our perception of concrete individuals. We would also see that that which is merely " thought," even *ideal* existence, is only " possible " and that the knowledge of the " possible " is by no means a necessary stage for the knowledge of the " existent." That, on the contrary, the " possible " is given to us at first only in the " existent." Finally, we would see that the " existent " itself is " intelligibly " knowable only through its experienced relation to the absolute act of being. We must use reflective analysis and dialectical effort in order to see this implicit series of conditions latent in every attribution of being.

Does it not look as if we had come back to Descartes' notion of the clear and distinct idea or to Spinoza's adequate idea? The *clear and distinct* idea guaranteed its own objectivity; the *adequate* idea implied reality. For an idea is fully " distinct " and " adequate " only when it saturates all the natural affinities of reason. And in this case it reaches the Absolute. Would Cartesian rationalism, especially after the manner of Spinoza, be in this sense a nextdoor neighbor of Aristotelian-Thomistic rationalism?

Despite the fact that both accept the principle of intelligibility (or rationality) of the affirmable objects, a radical divergence subsists between Aristotelianism and modern rationalism. And once more this divergence sheds light upon the peculiar epistemological difficulty which we meet in the knowledge of a transcendent object.

The rationalist will argue as follows: If we are to build the rational edifice all the way up to its necessary peak, which is the Infinite or the perfect Being or the pure Act, should we not possess, for lack of a real intuition, at least a faithful image and reproduction of this supreme element—a concept that is homogeneous to the subordinated concepts which it must render coherent? It is inadmissible that the keystone of knowledge should be something Unknowable.

To which we reply that—even if we overlook the fact that rationalistic metaphysics, in strict logic, leads to immanent pantheism and is powerless against Kant's critique—we know that the pure Act can be thought only as the " beyond " of our thought (*Pot.*, VII, 5, c and ad 14). None of our concepts represents it as it is. And once more we face the profound mystery of a Reality *posited* in all our objective affirmations without being *represented* by any form which properly belongs to it.

. . . Although objective affirmation is indifferently applicable to all finite essences, demanding none and excluding none, it nevertheless obeys a law of strict progression insofar as it expresses the *degree of actuality* of the objects. For when we affirm matter (which we can do only because we share it physically), we affirm at the same time the form, the act of matter. When we affirm the essence, we likewise affirm *esse*, the act of the essence. When we affirm finite *esse*, limited act, we implicitly affirm pure *esse*, the necessary perfection of act. When we affirm pure Act as the supreme rational condition, as the Ideal par excellence, we logically affirm the pure Act as absolute Reality, for an *ideal* pure Act, which would not be posited as a *real* pure Act, would mean a potency of actuation declared to be the summit of act. Hence every affirmation which would stop at one of the lower rungs of actuality would enter into conflict with the affirmed content and ruin itself. On the rising line of act, a transcendental dialectical law, a law of nature, carrying as a sanction the ever imminent threat of logical incoherence, marks in advance the great stages of objective affirmation up to the very last one which can no longer be represented in concepts.

Affirmation as a Dynamic Substitute for Intellectual Intuition

Since all knowledge is an immanent operation, the conditions which proximately determine the objective or subjective value of knowledge for the subject's consciousness must be found *in* the subject himself. Conditions which should remain totally extrinsic to the subject would be nonexistent as far as consciousness is concerned. . . . The general axiom of " immanence " or of " interiority " which is recalled here receives different applications in the different categories of knowing subject.

A subject which should be at once the prototype and the author of things in the fullness of their being would possess in itself eminently the totality of all existent and possible objective determinations. He would know *everything* by knowing *himself*. Such a fullness of knowledge could belong only to a pure actuality, for only the pure Act envelops and dominates the infinite extension of the " possible." Hence it is only in God that the known objects have their full interiority, the interiority of the effect in its adequate cause. For the divine intellect is the adequate measure of the things, of their essence as well as of their existence. "The divine intellect is measuring, not measured " (*Ver.*, I, 2, c; compare *S.c.G.*, I, 44, 53, 57; *Ver.*, II, 7, c).

Thus divine knowledge realizes the perfect type of *intuition* which creates its object. If we wish to distinguish partial aspects in this infinitely simple act, we might say that the form of things is prefigured in the divine intellect while their existence is predetermined in the divine will. But these are analogical ways of speaking: " The divine intellect knows through no other *species* than its essence " (*S.c.G.*, I, 53). And this divine essence is nothing but the pure Act of being, pure subsisting Idea: " God's knowing is the divine essence; and the divine Being is God himself: for God is his essence and his being " (*S.c.G.*, I, 45, 1).

But as soon as we descend to the finite intelligence, the outside object is no longer known in and through the very essence of the knowing subject. Hence a certain degree of " passive potency " has entered the intelligence, which must *receive* its intentional principles of objective knowledge from the *species*.

    . . . Human intelligence occupies the lowest place; it is not only not pure actuality, but it is not even—as knowing—a potency which is always in act (like the angelic intellect). Our acts of knowledge happen intermittently according to the rhythm of our sense knowledge.

Later we will try to define that which persists, in our intelligence, of the connatural participation which all the spirits possess of the creative idea. In any event, this participation is not sufficient to produce " objects " in us, and an external action must supply for the insufficiency of the internal determination. Hence the interiority of the object in the subject has decreased to the same extent in which the excellence of the knowing subject decreased, that is, to the same extent as the penetrating value of its knowledge decreased. . . .

Human intelligence is affected by " passivity "; it is a " passive power " at least with respect to *some* objects. This is evident from the very flux of our intellections, which succeed each other, appear on the threshold of consciousness, emerge into full light, then disappear into darkness. But does the " pas-

sivity " of our intellect extend to *all* objects absolutely? Do
we have no " intellectual intuition "?

Thomism answers: none whatsoever, thus closing all possible doors to any manner of essential intuition.

We do not possess any inborn ideas. St. Thomas notes the
fact and demonstrates the necessity of this lack in a spirit
which is the form of a body (see *S.T.*, I, 84, 3).

We do not directly perceive in themselves any subsisting
forms or ideas, any exemplary types of lower realities (*ibid.*,
a. 4). The immaterial world reveals itself only through the
analogy of matter.

Nay, although our intellect " has a share in the uncreated
light " (*S.T.*, I, 84, 5, c), it enjoys in no way and to no extent
that " objective vision in God," that intuition of the intelligible form *in rationibus aeternis,* which Malebranche and
after him the ontologists of the nineteenth century tried to
revive. Already in the thirteenth century St. Thomas rejected
this too Platonic interpretation of a few Augustinian texts
(*ibid.*, a. 5). . . .

Intellectual Intuition and Objective Affirmation

We may now institute a more detailed comparison between
intellectual intuition and our objective intellection.

Since our intelligence exercises the power of passing to its
last act, objective knowledge, it possesses this power. But in
exercising this power it depends on conditions which are partly
interior, partly *exterior.*

Interior conditions: When St. Thomas after Aristotle calls
our understanding *tabula rasa,* he means that by its very
nature it possesses none of these differential determinations
(essences) which formally constitute and distinguish from each
other the " objects " of our thought. But he is far from denying that the transcendental principles applicable to every object
indistinctly, and present in the data of the senses only " in
potency," pass into act within the concept through the active
intervention of an *a priori* of the intellect. We have already recalled and we shall again recall in a more significant context

these meaningful formulas, so dear to the undisputed master of medieval Aristotelianism: " For in every man there is a certain principle of knowledge, namely the light of the agent intellect, through which certain universal principles of all the sciences are *naturally* understood as soon as proposed to the intellect " (*S.T.*, I, 117, 1, c; compare *Ver.*, X, 6, c).

By its very nature, our intellect possesses the transcendental principles which allow us to reconstruct a unity that is " intelligible in act " on the model of a representation that is only intelligible in potency. In modern terminology this amounts to saying that it contains a " synthetic *a priori* condition," which is not quantitative and sensible, but which starts operating only with the effective cooperation of the senses. The sense cooperation *materially* completes the transcendental determinations, inborn to the intellect, thus, allowing them to express themselves in objective representations.

Hence, of the intuitive, perfect interiority properly belonging to the pure Act, human intelligence keeps at the utmost the inborn presence not of Ideas, nor even of merely virtual ideas, but rather of a *transcendental mode* of unity calling for some matter to which it may apply. In other words, human intelligence, possessing naturally, " privatively "—if we may speak that way—not " objectively," the type of being, is extrinsically limited by " things in themselves " (*res*), whose successive data it must assimilate through the senses in order to pass to its objective act.

It is evident that none of the material data deriving from the " thing in itself " *equals* the " potency " of the intellect. It is true that their accumulation *tends* to fill the abyss which separates the intellectual power from the fully saturating cognitive act. But as this " potency " possesses the whole objective capacity of being, its full actuation, by means of material data, looks like an inaccessible *limit* . . . which means that the transcendental unity, inborn to our intelligence as a functional disposition, will never be totally objectivated in our concepts.

We are unable to reach this ideal and chimerical limit; we meet, instead, only limping, unfinished concepts, whose demand for unity is too wide for their " matter "—and whose production does not bring the intellect all the way to the end of its power.

What allows us, nevertheless, to " objectivate " them categorically and to refer them in our judgments to the absolute order
of being, as if they occurred, each one in its respective place,
within a totalizing intellectual intuition? What is the element or
the activity which substitutes here for the lack of intuition?

The answer is twofold :

(1) *Psychologically* speaking, the substitute is the affirmation.
We have demonstrated this above *a posteriori* and through exclusion.

(2) *A priori* and *deductively,* we can establish that the objective function of the affirmation substituting for intellectual
intuition is *necessary in every non-intuitive knowledge.*

*Maréchal spends four chapters of this section in building this
deduction " with elements borrowed from St. Thomas." This is
the famous study of the finality of human intelligence, of the
dynamism of the intellect, within the framework of Thomistic
philosophy.*

*After having carefully delimited the problem (XXXII), he
studies first movement and finality in general, next the finality
of man's intellect (XXXIII). Finality implies striving and
belongs properly to the domain of appetite. That is why the
author devotes quite a number of pages to a thorough study of
the reciprocal causality of the intellect and the will in human
intellection. This reciprocal causality is considered not only
in the second acts of both faculties, but, more signifi-
cantly, in their first acts (XXXIV). There follows the important
study of the final end of the dynamism of our intellect and of
the relation existing between this end and our supernatural
destiny (XXXV). After these preliminary investigations and a
study of Thomistic exemplarism (XXXVI), Maréchal tackles the
main object of this whole section, the deduction of the ontological affirmation (XXXVII). The last chapter of this section
examines the nature of objective evidence. We have translated
here the passages about the evidence of Form and the evidence of
Act (XXXVIII), the passages about the reconciliation of constructivity and objectivity in intellectual knowledge (XXXIX), and,
finally, the pages which discuss whether the necessity which we
experience of affirming the basic metaphysical principles is*

subjective or objective (XL). These pages present a transcendental demonstration within a metaphysical framework.

XXXII. DELIMITING THE PROBLEM

What remains to be demonstrated? That every statement, in order to be objective (in its very form of a statement), must contain the implicit affirmation of a *determined absolute reality*; in other words, that the *noumenal absolute* belongs to the logical presupposita of the object as such. Now, if we should be able to establish that the datum of knowledge is objectivated in our mind only by assuming implicitly (*exercite*) the value of an *end,* our thesis would no longer be so difficult to prove. For the domain of *ends*—the " practical " domain—is *absolute,* not phenomenal. To be objectivated as an end means also necessarily to be objectivated in the absolute, according to a *definite* form. In order to finish our general demonstration, it would then be enough to clarify the traditional, too much neglected idea of the necessary interpenetration between the practical and the theoretical order, and to show under what conditions this compenetration would by no means impair the speculative value of the rational evidences. . . .

Before studying, in St. Thomas, the final middle term of our demonstration, the intellect's finality, let us remind the reader of a few conclusions which have previously been gathered. We have shown:

(1) That the " datum " represented in us was constituted as an " object " in our mind through the judgment of *affirmation.*

(2) That the affirmation is an intellectual act expressing, in the assimilation of a particular datum, the repose of the *natural or elicited tendency of the intelligent subject* towards his end.

Hence it follows that either the datum, by itself, satiates this finality, or, failing this, the tendency can be put at rest with respect to this datum only insofar as it is subordinated to a more comprehensive and truly saturating object. We feel thus how important it will be for our study to analyze the finality of the human intellect and to measure the amplitude of its final and adequate object.

(3) That the adequate object of our affirmation extends beyond any conceptual representation, beyond any content which may *statically* affect our intellect. Since, nevertheless, the universal object of the affirmation must be imprinted in some way in our intellect, it should be imprinted dynamically, as an end which is anticipated in a tendency—one more reason for us to examine intellectual finality.

(4) Finally, we have seen above that the judgment or affirmation is, in its own way, a substitute for the objective function of the *intellectual intuition*. In the intellectual intuition the subject precontains all the determinations of the known object and opposes this object to himself as an efficient or exemplary principle opposes its effect to itself.

But a non-intuitive intellect, which does not *a priori* possess this fullness of determinations, is obliged to pass *progressively* from potency to act. Affirmation is wedged in, like an intermediate stage, between the initial passivity and the full intuition, which would be the perfect objective act. The affirmation constitutes a " moment " in a movement.

How can it, under these conditions, be a substitute for the objective intuition? We shall show in the following pages that it can do so from two points of view. Intuition means *interiority* of the object's determinations. Since there is no previous interiority of the object in the subject, the affirmation provides, at every step, the penetration of a datum into the intellectual faculty. Next, intuition means immediate *objectivation*. The affirmation objectively refers the interiorized datum, or, better, immediately projects it into objective reality not as a produced *effect*, but as an intended *end*. There is indeed no other logical possibility. We are caught in a dilemma. A form which is immanent to a subject can in the subject itself detach itself from this subject, in order to be objectivated, only in two ways: through a creative or productive act, which would realize it ouside of the subject—that is, the *intuitive* way—or through the act of striving which would establish it as an outside end, as " object " of a possible assimilation—that is, the *affirmative* way.

We see that from all sides we are led back to intellectual finality, both in order to render the datum immanent, and in order to project it outside of us as an object. The interiorization of the datum must occur according to the " antecedent finality " of the intellect. On the other hand, the " objective projection " of the datum, the apperception of the " other " as " other in itself " is likewise conceivable only in the order of ends. Hence the total reaction of the intellect, receiving the intelligible *species,* must introduce it into the current of an ulterior finality: the datum is objectivated by becoming an element of the " consequent finality " of the affirming subject.

XXXIII. THE DYNAMISM OF THE INTELLECT

Let us take up again, while insisting this time on the *dynamic point of view,* the great lines of a demonstration which is latent throughout St. Thomas.

The awareness which we have of the objects present to our thought is not, or is not only, the ecstatic intermittent contemplation of a number of pictures presented to our mind's eye. Perceiving " intelligible objects " does not go without some reflective perception of the intellectual activity exercised on them, or, to put it better, exercising itself in them.

How shall we, in this intellectual activity which we surprise in exercise, grasp the radical *a priori* which delimits the formal object of the intellective power as such?

Even the spontaneous and, as it were, the pre-philosophical reflection of common sense can discover rather extensively under our eyes the field of our intellections and thus reveal to us, step by step, the huge extension of this " formal object." Yet, if we wish to measure this field with technical precision, we dispose of a faster and surer way, which is a true *inner experimentation.* This is a perfectly legitimate experimentation. For it is reason's privilege—celebrated by Kant—that it can observe itself in its operations and undertake to control them. Every critique of knowledge rests on this faculty of reflection.

Let us then try to assign to our intellectual capacity limits which are gradually expanding. As long as any condition whatsoever will look to us as " limiting," we shall be certain that the absolutely last end of our intelligence lies beyond it, or, which amounts to the same, that the formal object of our intelligence extends beyond this limitation. For the awareness of a limit as limit contains logically, within the very order where the limit occurs, the knowledge of a further possibility.

But the most elementary inner experience shows our intellectual activity embracing more and more objects without ever reaching its saturation point. The intellect's capacity seems to expand as new data enter into it. When we notice this steady movement, should we not be justified when we conclude, by some kind of extrapolation: " Our possible intellect has the same relation to intelligible objects as primary matter has to physical things; for it is in potentiality as regards intelligible objects, just as primary matter is to physical things " (*S.T.*, I, 14, 2, ad 3).

Everybody has the vague feeling that the active and passive capacity of our intellect is without any limit in the intelligible order, as the capacity of prime matter is unlimited in the order of things quantitative. But an extrapolation based upon a vague feeling is not a demonstration.

Can we determine, at least negatively, the end of the anticipation which carries our intellect towards its adequate object? It is evident that this term will not be this or that spatial extension, this or that length of time, since not even our senses are *a priori* affected with such a limitation of their formal object. Would the ultimate boundary of our intellectual power not be exactly designated by the famous scholastic formula: " The proper object of the human intelligence is *the quiddities of material things*? " In this event the objective and dynamic infinity of our intelligence would remain wholly relative, it would be restricted to the field of " predicamental abstract being," that is, of " being as principle of number."

Once more, inner experience protests against this premature limitation. It is true that we can *represent* only quantitative objects, but our faculty of *signifying and of affirming* carries much further, even as, borne by it, our faculty of desiring and of willing strives much higher. Rightly or wrongly, it does not matter. We are not discussing the " objective value " of the intellectual appetite. But the inner fact is undeniable.

Moreover, this fact does not shock reason. For the quantitative character (the " intelligible quantity ") of the proper and immediate object of our intellections is imposed upon our intelligence by a condition which remains *extrinsic* to it: its natural coordination to a sense faculty. Although every non-intuitive intellect needs with physical necessity to borrow from the senses the matter of its knowledge in order to pass from potency to act, it does not follow that every *possible* activity of this intelligence, hence that its proper form, should be strictly enclosed within the extension of the matter thus received. Does Kant himself not admit at least the negative possibility of the metaphysical object, of the noumenon?

But again there is more than this mere possibility. We are positively aware that the movement of our intellections does not stop at the intelligible unity of the material objects, that the latter do not constitute *the intelligible which is totally in act*, the saturating act of our intellectual power, that, after having surveyed them, there remains in our intelligence a balance of unused power. Hence the adequate form of our intellectual activity would not be correctly expressed as " abstract being, numerical unity " or as " predicamental abstract being." It is wider and extends to a domain of being which exceeds our experience. Let us continue to make hypotheses in this metempirical domain and we shall discover that the only insurmountable limitation which stops our thought is not this or that objective limit of being, this or that degree of finite essences, but the " absolute limit," non-being as such. But if we understand this well, to conceive non-being as the sole possible limit amounts to conceiving *the absence of a limit*. Hence, since the total objective capacity of our intelligence rejects every limit but non-being, it extends as far as being pure and simple. To such a formal capacity there can only correspond one absolutely last and saturating end: the *infinite* Being.

Thus internal analysis confirms the formula which St. Thomas borrows from Aristotle in order to designate the absolute universality of the intellectual power " *id quo est omnia facere— id quo est omnia fieri.*" While presenting the great lines of this, as it were, experimental proof, we were thinking of the (quite similar) major premise of the demonstration of God's infinity through the objective infinity of our intelligence: " Our intellect extends into infinity in knowing. This is shown by the fact that whatever finite quantity may be presented, our intellect can think of a greater one " (*S.c.G.*, I, 43, 7).

This text brings to mind St. Anselm's famous " ontological argument." But this similarity does not tend to weaken the value of the above line of reasoning, since from St. Thomas' text as from St. Anselm's argument there follows at least this conclusion: that the *ideal* activity of our intelligence extends beyond any assignable limit. This suffices for the time being.

It follows that the " form " of our intellectual dynamism, considered as an immanent activity, is adequately expressed only by the transcendental concept of being. But, unlike the predicamental concept of being, this concept is *analogical, by no means univocal*. This brings up difficult problems, which we have mentioned several times already, without having as yet found a decisive solution.

XXXIV. RECIPROCAL RELATION OF THE FIRST ACTS OF THE INTELLECT AND THE WILL

The first act, a permanent disposition of the faculty, should be discovered in a pure state, without admixture of adventitious features, immediately before the first performed operation. It represents in the agent the totality of the *a priori* conditions of possibility of this first operation.

Since the operation of the *will*, as elicited appetite, is directed by the good as objectively known, the first voluntary operation presupposes an intellection which specifies it. But on what does this first volition depend for its exercise? On some previous dynamic condition, of course, but on which one?

A previous volition? But we wish precisely to explain the very first volition. Hence the dynamic tension required by the latter must be rooted in nature, and precede every operation. It realizes the definition of an *actus primus* (first act).

But St. Thomas goes further. Since this first act is the imperfect act of a finite essence, it can consist (in virtue of the analytical relations of act and potency) only in a motion coming from an extrinsic agent.

" We must admit that, insofar as the first motion of the will is concerned, the will of every being which does not always actually will, must be moved by an outside agent " (*Quaest. Disput. de Malo*, VI, art. unic., c).

And it is easy to demonstrate then—we shall come back to this later—that this outside agent, which provides the will with its first act, is the universal Cause: " Hence . . . that which originally moves the will (and the intellect) is something which stands above will (and intellect), that is, God " (*ibid.*).

But previously we had read in St. Thomas that the natural motion *ad exercitium* imprinted by an outside agent is directed towards an end. And insofar as this end must be reached by a movement of the being which receives the motion, the latter's natural form specifies it. Hence the natural motion *ad exercitium* imprinted by the first Cause upon the will of the intellectual subject tends to realize an end whose specifications are written by anticipation in the natural form of this subject. But the natural form of a subject—that is, the essential law of its operations—is immediately expressed in the formal object of the powers of this subject. Hence (to take the simplest case) in a purely spiritual subject, whose natural powers consist merely of intellect and will, the natural form which should direct the first act of the will can only be the first act of the intellect.

If we likewise go back to the series of the elicited acts of the intellect, St. Thomas warns us that we meet an initial objective apperception which is not influenced by any motion of the will.

There is no need to go on indefinitely, but *we must stop at the intellect as preceding all the rest*. For every movement of the will must be preceded by apprehension, whereas every apprehension is not preceded by an act of the will; but the principle of counseling (*al.* of consideration) and understanding is an intellectual principle *higher than our intellect—namely God* (*S.T.*, I, 82, 4, ad 3).

Through and beyond the first intellection we vaguely perceive the *a priori* conditions which define the intelligence in first act. Once more it is a natural motion, imprinted by an agent distinct from the subject, a motion which should be ordained towards an end and which presents therefore undividedly two aspects: a dynamic aspect and a formal aspect. As a dynamic impulsion *ad exercitium,* considered independently of any specification, the motion which constitutes the intellect in its first act does not differ from the natural motion *ad exercitium* imprinted upon the will by the universal Cause. But what will, in this case, be the *formal and specifying* principle of the transcendent motion?

The essence of the intellectual subject, of course. But according to the profound Thomistic doctrine of the operative powers, every finite essence causes, by its very nature, its " powers " to emanate from it, subsisting in them and being in first act for its operations only according to the coordination and the subordination of their formal objects. Now, as we have just said, the essence of an intellectual subject, as intellectual, demands and contains only two powers: the will, a dynamic power directed by the intellect, and the intellect itself, the power of specification of the voluntary dynamism. Hence the specifying or formal principle of both faculties must be looked for *in the line of the intelligence.*

Although intelligence itself is *specified by the object* which it apprehends, and since the intellectual apprehension of the object is activity and not mere passivity (since, in other words, intellectual passivity is the passivity of a form, and not of matter), we must admit that before the first act of objective apprehension the intellect possesses its own formal determination, some kind of " formal first act " which it possesses by nature, that is through a specifying motion of the universal Cause.

St. Thomas clearly indicates this *formal motion,* logically previous to the external impression coming directly or indirectly from the object. Thus in the following text (which treats primarily of supernatural illumination):

To know truth is a use or act of intellectual light. . . . Now, every use implies movement, taking movement broadly, so as to call thinking and willing movements. . . . Now in corporeal things we see that for movement there is required not merely the *form* which is the principle of the movement or action, but there is also required *the motion of the first mover.* . . . But it is clear that . . . all movements, both corporeal and spiritual, are reduced to the simple First Mover, Who is God. And hence no matter how perfect a corporeal or spiritual nature is supposed to be, it cannot proceed to its act unless it be moved by God. . . . Now, not only is every motion from God as from the First Mover, but *all formal perfection is from Him* as from the First Act. And thus *the act of the intellect* or of any created being whatsoever depends upon God *in two ways*: first, inasmuch as it is from Him that it has *the form* whereby it acts; secondly, inasmuch as it is *moved by Him to act*. Now every form bestowed on created things by God has power for a determined act, which it can bring about in proportion to its own proper endowment. . . . And *thus the human understanding has a form*, viz., *intelligible light*, which of itself is sufficient for knowing certain intelligible things, *viz*., those we can come to know through the senses. . . . (*S.T*., Iᵃ–IIᵃᵉ, 109, 1, c).

It is almost superfluous to observe that the " intelligible light," the inborn form of our intellect, designates identically these " first intelligible principles " about which St. Thomas claims several times that they are dynamically inborn in the agent intellect.

Hence under the transcendent motion, our intelligence possesses a first natural specification, according to which it will pass to its second act as soon as the extrinsic conditions of an operation are presented to it. The first act of our intelligence consists in this primitive specification.

These considerations define the relation of the will " in first act " to the intellect " in first act." *The first act of the intellect is to the first act of the will as specification is to exercise, as form is to dynamism.* And since the first act is not a particular operation, but the *a priori* condition imposed upon every operation whatsoever, the whole series of the intellectual and voluntary second acts will, under adventitious determinations, possess the same fundamental relation as the respective first acts of the two faculties.

Let us slightly develop this idea.

The natural motion " in the order of exercise " is by itself but the undetermined impulsion, the pure striving towards the

End and the Good, defined only as that which is correlative
to the tendency. The good is that towards which everything
strives in some way. Every activity whatsoever, and under whatsoever modality it presents itself, stands under the dynamic influence of a good or an end. But it is obvious that a wholly
undetermined impulsion, an amorphous tendency, an undefined
exigency, a mere *Sollen* (Ought), cannot be realized any more
than a " prime matter." Dynamism demands a form, a tendency
necessarily assumes a specification. To the tendency in first act
there should correspond a specification in first act, that which
St. Thomas calls a " first principle in the line of the formal
cause " (*De Malo*, VI, c). But the characteristic feature of the
rational tendency, which differentiates it from the lower ap-
petites, is not to have any limit this side of the End which
comprises all that which is desirable and of the good which
exhausts all goodness. The specifying form which allows for
all the possibilities of this comprehensive tendency can only
be the most general form possible, the one which excludes no
other one : *being as such.*

Hence our intellectual nature *must,* before any elicited act,
possess in itself, that is, in the correlative unity of our two great
faculties, considered according to their respective first acts, an
a priori condition which is both formal and dynamic, namely
the capacity and the desire, both of them unlimited, of *being.*

What happens at the next moments? As soon as the intellect,
meeting an external datum, passes to the second act under the
formal motion of this datum and the permanent impulsion of
the natural appetite, we have a particular, positive determination subsumed under the universal form of *being,* which previously was only the framework of and the call for all possible
determinations. An " object " profiles itself before consciousness. And this objective representation, grafted upon the natural
form of the intellect becomes for the dynamic (appetitive) faculty
a new specification, a new formal starting point, but this time
the appetite's impulsion will be strictly voluntary. It will take
place " according to some good known by the intellect." Let
then, on reflection, the good object, thus represented, formally

reveal its appetibility, and the will no longer unconsciously follows the brute representation of the object, but the explicit representation of its appetibility or goodness. At this moment is born the proximate possibility of a deliberation and of a free volition. And since intellectual reflection may emphasize in consciousness the appetibility of the representation or, even more generally, of every knowledge, as a good of the subject, the natural appetite will not only continue to push the intellect blindly and necessarily to more objective assimilations (man *naturally* desires . . . the knowledge of the true, which fits the intellect [*S.T.,* I^a-II^{ae}, 10, 1, c]), it will also become capable of formally (*signate, sub ratione boni*) commanding the intellectual operation itself (" we use our intelligence when we will it "). As psychological life grows, the process whose course we have outlined becomes more and more complicated, without losing its basic characters.

As, under the ceaseless invasion of the outside data, the partial ends and the particular specifications of the rational tendency increase in number, its initial potency or indetermination diminishes. For in a spiritual faculty nothing gets lost; the acquired science persists in our intelligence in the state of a *habitus,* say the scholastics. The *habitus* is, as it were, a second nature, interposed between the first act and the second acts. It is the blind pressure of the past upon the present activity. The *habitus* is added to the natural form of every power and influences its every activity.

Hence the manner in which we actually react to the new data which enter our consciousness depends on complex influences, affective and voluntary, strengthened or modified as experience goes on. A *logical* theory of intellectual operations *as such* may abstract from these contingent factors. A *psychological* theory of the operations which *effectively* succeed each other in us should, on the contrary, take into account the speculative and practical *habitus.* It is quite true—as among the schoolmen the Franciscan philosophers like to emphasize—that love, or an upright or biased or evil will, even our feelings, will influence to some extent our apprehension of the truth.

XXXV. INTELLECTUAL DYNAMISM AND SUPERNATURAL END

The ultimate *end* of intellectual becoming can be read in the natural *form* (formal object) of this " becoming," and it has been shown " that this natural objective form " was expressed in our concept of " transcendental being " (*ens qua tale*). Since the formal object of a tendency is the measure of the amplitude of the end whither this tendency keeps striving, we know that the ultimate and satiating end of the intellect must be a reality possessing no limiting determination, that is, a transcendent object, a *subsisting Infinite*.

> *Maréchal shows further that, according to St. Thomas, only an intuitive knowledge of this absolute Being would entirely fulfill our deepest appetite, and that such an intuitive knowledge of God is beyond the powers of a finite nature.*

Hence the ultimate perfection of our intellect supposes not only that it be free from all material bonds; it requires also an extrinsic condition, standing above our nature: a divine initiative; an active communication of the absolute Being, whose sovereign independence is incompatible with any obligation towards its creature; we might say in one word, with the theologians, that it supposes a " supernatural grace " (*S.c.G.*, III, 52, 1 and 5; *S.T.*, I, 12, 4; I^a-II^{ae}, 5, 5).

The Supernatural Factor of Our Destiny

Let us briefly pause here. We should not forget that our inquiry about the ultimate end has been conducted from the critical point of view. If we really hoped to discover in this way the unshakable foundation of an epistemology, is it not rather embarrassing to discover that our absolutely ultimate end depends on the free bestowal of a supernatural grace?

If the nature of the intelligent subject—with or without the help of extrinsic conditions, which were physically or morally " demanded " by this nature—would have been sufficient to reach the ultimate End, there could have subsisted no doubt about the reality of this End as the object of our intellectual tendency, nor about the epistemological consequences thereof.

Unfortunately, as we have seen, the realization of our ultimate End stands in total dependence on a factor which we cannot control, neither speculatively, so as to foresee it, nor voluntarily, so as to secure it. We mean the free bestowal by the absolute Being of the intuitive knowledge of himself. Will God bestow this gift? Are we even certain that this gift is really possible? True, we have shown above that it is *negatively* possible; but how should we know that this seeming lack of internal contradiction does not simply derive from the lack of light which casts a haze in our intellect on the outline of the transcendent objects. The fact that we desire an end is not an evident sign of its real possibility.

Might it be then that the problem of our rational certitudes demands the previous solution of the problem of our supernatural destiny?

We do not think so, but obviously a few distinctions should be made here.

First, it is undeniable that the full satisfaction of our higher faculties cannot be discovered in the order of our purely natural possibilities. What may we conclude from this fact?

Not the reality of a supernatural end for man. St. Thomas claims—and it is an evident truth—that this reality can be known by us only through the revelation of the design which God might have of communicating himself supernaturally to us (*S.T.*, I^a-II^ae, 1; *De fide*. arts. 1 ff.). In fact, God has revealed such an intention. Should we, however, base our whole objective certitude upon our belief in the supernatural object of a revelation, this would be " fideism," not a rational critique.

Yet, even independently of a " revelation," St. Thomas does not claim that we know nothing about the supernatural destiny. It is not only " negatively possible," but some *positive* conclusion about it is virtually contained in the dynamism of our faculties, as in purely natural premises. Although only faith can tell us whether or not God wishes to become our supernatural beatitude, we deduce legitimately, from the radical disposition of our faculties, *the absolute* (positive) *possibility* of this beatitude, that is, the *existence of the remote objective causes which render its realization possible.*

This demonstration is based upon the axiom, universally admitted by the scholastics, *Desiderium naturae non potest esse inane.* Which means that the natural finality—the fundamental law of Becoming—reveals at least the *possibility in se* of the end towards which it strives. Otherwise, the " natural volition " should be conceived as the volition of the impossible: being would strive towards nothingness; position would be negation; non-being would become being. Hence it would be logically contradictory to hold that a natural[1] impulsion should move a being towards something which is *impossible in itself.* Once we accept this principle, we are left with two hypotheses:

(1) The adequate causes of the impulsion received by the being may be *blind and necessary* forces; in this event, if no interference from without stops their action, they will necessarily push the being towards the term of its movement: the ultimate end would not only be possible in itself, it would also be *realized.*

(2) On the other hand, if the first causes of the motion are, at least in part, *free agents,* they may create, in the subject who is in motion, an initial orientation whose full development remains subordinated to a new free intervention coming from them. In this event it is not certain that the subject in motion, whatever may be its natural " desire," will be able to reach its ultimate end. Reaching this absolutely ultimate end would belong only to the domain of remote *possibilities.* The only thing which would be certain is *the existence of all the factors required for this possibility.*

Our " natural desire " for the vision of God belongs to this second category. . . .

With St. Thomas we shall conclude that the natural impulsion of our intellectual faculties drives them towards the immediate intuition of the absolute Being. It is true that this intuition exceeds the power and the exigencies of every finite intelligence, left to its sole natural resources. Yet the radical impul-

---

[1] As contrasted with *elicited* volitions, which may strive for impossible ends.

sion which drives it to this intuition is not conceivable without the objective, at least remote, possibility of reaching it.

But this objective, even remote, possibility implies two necessary conditions: *the existence of an absolute Being,* which is capable of communicating itself, and the *capability of our intelligence* for receiving this communication.

But if this is the case, if the " vision of the divine essence " is not a utopian perspective, but something which is " possible in itself," we know now to what " absolutely last end " our intellectual representations refer during the dynamic and implicit stage of objective knowledge.

XXXVI. THOMISTIC EXEMPLARISM

We have already said that the " natural form " which is logically previous to every elicited act of the intellect—hence the form of the intellectual " first act "—is the universal and abstract form of *being.*

At this primary stage it does not yet represent an " object," not even a virtual object, but only the form of an assimilating virtuality, an " *a priori* formal condition," the previous rule of our apprehension of eventual objects. It can objectivate itself in our consciousness only after first meeting, in some matter presented by the senses, an " intelligible in potency."

Whence comes to the intellective subject this " formal principle " which rules all its particular intellections?

As in corporeal movement that is called *the mover which gives the form that is the principle of movement,* so that is said to move the intellect which is the *cause of the form that is the principle of the intellectual operation* called the movement of the intellect. Now there is a twofold principle of intellectual operation in the intelligent being: one is *the intellectual power itself,* which principle exists also in the one who understands in potentiality; while the other is *the principle of actual understanding,* namely, the likeness of the thing understood. So a thing is said to move the intellect, whether it gives to him who understands the power of understanding, or impresses on him the likeness of the thing understood. *Now God moves the created intellect in both ways (S.T.,* I, 105, 3, c).

*Of this double motion Maréchal considers only the first one,
by which God gives the intellect the power of understanding,
and he considers it not as a mere impulsion, but in its formal
aspect. He shows that it corresponds to the* agent intellect,
*about which St. Thomas said that it is in us " some kind of
shared resemblance of the uncreated light "* (S.T., *I, 84, 5, c*).

The " uncreated light " designates the purely intuitive intelligence which creates its external objects. According to St.
Thomas, like the pure spirits we receive something of this intuitive power which creates its object. That is, our intelligence
itself, although extrinsically dependent on the senses, introduces into the immanent object, into the " mental word," a
higher, metempirical element, which it possessed by itself, virtually. Of the " intelligible in potency " it makes an " intelligible
in act." . . .

If anything represents, in our intellect, a participation in the
intuitive power of the absolute intelligence, it must be the virtual possession of the " first principles," of the " principles of
being." . . . Hence sense experience by no means brings to us
from without the " first principles of being," it only embodies
them in objective representations. They themselves surge from
the very bottom of our intellectual nature and this surge is
divine in its primordial origin. They are at once a *subjective
virtuality* and a *virtual objective principle,* and they constitute
in us something remotely analogous to the " first truth." . . .

Thus we understand in what sense it is correct to compare
Thomism with ontologistic or Platonic *exemplarism.*

Both sides profess that man receives some participation of the
divine Truth, of the divine Ideas. But unlike Platonic ontologism,
Thomism admits only a participation restricted to the " first intelligible principles "—to the transcendental attributes of being
—and by no means a participation according to the generic and
specific types.

Moreover, this participation which, in the ontologistic
language, would mean that ready made, although latent, ideas
are inborn, designates here a natural disposition of a dynamic
nature, which demands a material complement. The " first intelligibles " are first imprinted in our Ego as the lived form of

a natural tendency. Next, they are objectivated in the way in
which for us the form of such a tendency can be objectivated,
that is, by revealing themselves, through connaturality, in the
very objects met by the concrete exercise of this tendency.

In short: Thomistic exemplarism is a *dynamic exemplarism
restricted exclusively to the " first intelligible principles."*

XXXVII. OBJECTIVATION IN FINALITY: DEDUCTION OF THE ONTOLOGICAL AFFIRMATION

The act of intellection occurs in a " becoming " whose universal
form, original *principle* and last *end* we have defined in the line
of St. Thomas. We shall now use these analytic results to finish
bringing out the conditions which necessarily rule in our consciousness the " apprehension " of the object as *object.*

*After remarking that such an apprehension implies an opposi-
tion of the object to the subject, Maréchal continues:*

But every awareness of an opposition is based on the awareness of a *relation.* Moreover—this is essential—in the present instance the knowing subject itself is one of the terms of the
relation which is perceived.

What kind of relation is capable of disjoining from a subjective activity some of the conditions inherent in it? How is it
possible for a subject to represent, as separated from itself and
extraposed in an outside absolute (*en soi*) the very form of its
immanent activity? This is the heart of the problem of the constitution of the object *in* consciousness and *for* consciousness.

Internal Finality as the Basis of the Opposition Between Object and Subject in Consciousness

Can the intentional " form " of our intellection—the *species* of
the scholastics—become, in its immanence, the term of some

ontological relation which implies the opposition of subject to
object?

First it would seem that, through its empirical elements (or
through its " representational " content) the form should be, in
the subject, the term of a relation of receptivity, of passivity,
of a *passio,* which refers it to an outside agent, to a non-Ego, a
thing-in-itself, as to its efficient cause. Would this not constitute
a possible foundation for the conscious opposition of subject
and object?

This is doubtful, or at least, it is doubtful that this foundation
is sufficient. For the intellect in its second act, the only one of
which we are aware, is not directly passive with respect to sense
objects. Such an immediate passivity belongs properly to the
senses. It is true that the intellect models itself after the form
of the sensation. Yet, ontologically speaking, there is passivity
in the intellect only with respect to itself, of the possible intellect to the agent intellect (guiding the phantasm). Such a passivity introduces an *immediate* relative opposition only within
the intellect, between its active and its passive function.

Let us even suppose that this intra-intellectual relation should
become conscious in the direct act of intellection—which is not
the case. It would project neither of its two terms into some
absolute (*en soi*) outside the intellect, hence it would not provide
us *directly* with an objective knowledge.

It would do even less to confuse, like the empiricists and the
semi-empiricists, the objectivity of the intellect with the imperfect objectivity of the senses, as if the former were only an intellectual transposition of the latter. The senses give us merely
spatial extraposition, not *intelligible reality.* Even were one to
suppose—as might be done without incoherence—that the intellect, associated with the senses, should somehow perceive intelligibly the passivity of the latter, one would at the utmost
have to admit with Kant that the intellect, in its collaboration
with the senses, refers their phenomenal contribution to a *thing-
in-itself,* which is absolute, but wholly undetermined, a mere
logical counterpart of the sense phenomenon. Such a solution
would not sufficiently justify the " relation to the object," which
is essential in each direct act of the understanding. Moreover, it
would be unable to extend its " objective value " beyond the

material realities manifested in the phenomena. It would never lead us, even indirectly, to a transcendent object. We might as well admit it: if the natural objective function of our intellect is measured by the undetermined " thing-in-itself," by a reality which is nothing but *the limit and the counterpart* of the phenomenon, Kant has correctly set down the boundaries of our knowledge. All the constructions of our reason, in search of a *transcendent* absolute beyond experience, are " *a priori* syntheses " in the pejorative sense, lacking any objective guarantee. They may be useful in many respects but, speculatively speaking, they remain empty. In that case we cannot escape theoretical agnosticism.

Let us add this rather abstract remark, which we consider decisive for a Thomist: the subject's passivity before the outside object can, at any rate, not appear to consciousness as a total passively, but only as the *limitation of an activity* of the subject itself. For, as demonstrated by Cajetan interpreting St. Thomas, although knowledge may—on account of the imperfection of the knowing subject—require the previous reception of a form in matter, of an accident in a substance, it does not take place according to this very relation of matter to form or of accident to substance, but according to the identity *of an act*. Hence, in any event, if the sense passively contributes something to the awareness of the object as object, this can only derive from the perceivable repercussion of this passivity in the very exercise of the subjective activity. But this steers our problem in a quite different direction. We are no longer inquiring whether a *potency* perceives itself *as potency* in the very actuation which it undergoes (an absurd supposition), but whether an *act* may perceive the terminal limitation by which it is affected (which does not seem wholly impossible).

Besides the relation of a patient to an outside agent, we meet in the process of objective knowledge another kind of relation which, unlike the former, intrinsically affects the specifying form (*species*) of the intellectual act itself, and, moreover, extends beyond the restricted limits of the phenomenon. We mean the *relation of finality*. Without wholly overlooking the function of finality in knowledge, Kant limits it to the " reflecting judgments "; he excludes the " tendency " from any intrinsic participation in the structure of the " determining judgment," that is, of the judgment through which we exercise our natural, primary power of objectivation. In this respect the Thomistic thesis, as understood here, is radically opposed to the Kantian thesis.

A form may refer to an end in two ways: first, as the *exemplary type* (*idea, forma factiva*) of a reality which is to be produced. Such is the ideal design which directs the artist's hand, such are the eternal ideas of creative intelligence. Since such a form can belong only to an intellectual subject, who is aware of himself, the latter intuitively knows in it the real or possible effect which it outlines or projects. The knowledge of the object (as real or as possible) coincides here with the awareness of the exemplary form as a productive actuality or virtuality. We are outside the critical hypothesis; an intuition stands in no need of a rational justification of its proper object.

On the other hand, the finality which we meet in our intellectual dynamism is that of an immanent action through which the subject *acquires and assimilates* new determinations.

We have shown several times . . . that the specifying form of our intellection, the *species,* is not a mere static ornament of it, but, at every moment, the actual form of a movement, of a tendency striving towards its end. Caught up in the natural desire which draws our intellect from empty potency to integral act, every acquired *species* assumes clearly a dynamic value. Since it constitutes at least a temporary term of the intellectual activity, it possesses the attractiveness of an *end* with respect to this activity. On the other hand, since it does not exhaust the active potency of the intellect which, having assimilated it, looks out for more knowledge, it cannot be the intellect's ultimate end. Now, when an end is not an ultimate end, it refers to the latter as a *subordinate end,* as a means or as a stage.

Our problem is then to find out how this relation of finality, which intrinsically affects the successive forms of our intellectual activity, might be the very basis of their " objectivation."

The first condition required for the " objectivation " of an immanent form is, of course, that it be somehow separated from the subject as such, and that, as so separated, it should acquire a value in itself (*un " en soi "*) and qualify " a thing."

We wish to insist upon the exact terms of our problem: the subject to whom the immanent form should be opposed, if it is to be perceived objectively, is the " subject as such " or the knowing function in exercise (*cognoscens in actu*), not the subject in its full ontological reality. Before this kind of limited subject the extraposed form must, in order to possess the character of an intelligible *object*, refer, at least in general, to some absolute (*un " en soi "*), to a subsistence. This first degree of objectivity does not at once imply that the " in itself " of the objectivated form be distinct from the ontological reality of the subject itself. The metaphysical opposition of two subsistences, that of the subject and that of the object, presents a more complex problem than that of the *objective* apprehension (*sub ratione entis*) of the content of the representation. In the present case it is enough that the subject as *function* be opposed to the object as *in itself*.

Hence we set up the following thesis: in a discursive intelligence, the assimilated form is opposed to the subject and acquires an " in itself " insofar as it constitutes, for the subject, a *dynamic value, a moment of an active becoming*.

We say: an *active* becoming. In every becoming, whether active or passive, every moment, by its very definition, saturates something in an antecedent tendency, and gives rise to a consequent tendency.

But when an immanent form is experienced as an end, both retrospectively and prospectively, in that fleeting moment when aspiration turns into possession, and a still imperfect possession is overtaken by further desire, is it not then immanent in the subject according to a relation which distinguishes it from the latter? A value is distinct from the need which takes hold of it as well as from the need which still craves it. And since this relation is posited in the order of ends—the absolute order of the *noumenon*—the immanent form refers also *ipso facto* to a subsistence, to an " in itself " and takes on in our mind the essential features of an ontological object.

Thus the enigma of objective knowledge can be solved, if we can show that the *ad extra* (outward) relations of the immanent form are not only *in us* real attributes of this form, but also *for us* attributes which we can know.

Yet, should we stop here, we would have solved only a *psychological* problem. Our real problem, which is a problem of epistemology, a problem of *logical* value, would only be halfway to its solution. In the natural impulsion itself, which projects the immanent form outside of ourself, as an end, we should be able to discover not only a dynamic exigency, but also a *logical implication* of the " in itself " reality of the end. Now, there are two ways in which, from a natural tendency to an end, we may argue to the reality of this end:

(1) Through a *moral* inference, based on our confidence in the general finality of the world, so that we immediately apply the scholastic axiom: *a natural desire cannot be frustrated.*

(2) Through an *analytical* demonstration, which shows that the tendency's rational coherence and the ontological possibility of the end depend on each other, so that, should the logical incoherence of the tendency be unacceptable, the ontological possibility of the end must be accepted. It is, of course, this second kind of demonstration which we must use.

To facilitate the reader's task, we shall once more summarize *our whole argumentation.*

(a) In virtue of the " first principle " every content of thought is ontologically *affirmable* (critical *preambulum*).

(b) The content of a non-intuitive (discursive) mind may be affirmed only *objectively,* that is, in opposition to the subjective function exercised upon it (relation of " logical truth ").

(c) This " objectivity " in immanence, the necessary condition of the exercise of a non-intuitive thought, is itself logically and psychologically possible only if the content of this thought is inserted in an *assimilating movement* which tends towards an absolutely final end.

(d) This finality, without which there can be no non-intuitive thought, dynamically posits the " reality in themselves " of the (objective) ends intended by it. But, from the strictly critical point of view, a dynamic exigency, however ineluctable, establishes only, by itself alone, a *subjective* certitude.

(e) Therefore, we must still show that the " reality in themselves " of these ends, which are necessarily intended in the very exercise of every discursive thought, is for the knowing subject not only a dynamic exigency, but a *logical necessity.*

When this point has been established, our task will be ended. For, through critical reflection, we would have rediscovered the indissoluble vital unity which exists between the intellect as speculative faculty (as formally knowing) and the intellect as an assimilating dynamism (as some reality, whose good or end is the true itself).

Towards Objective Affirmation

Let us therefore consider even more attentively, so as to bring out its logical implications, the intellectual operation in which an immanent intelligible form is referred to the domain of ends.

We know that the basic tendency which carries the intellectual becoming exists before any objective apperception, as a "natural tendency" (natural appetite). It is finalized towards act and starts moving as soon as the senses provide the indispensable "matter." It is precisely in this elicited activity, where the "natural form" of the tendency and the determination coming from outside meet for the first time, that, for the first time too, are realized the immanent conditions of objective knowledge.

Let us restrict ourselves to this first elicited act of our intellectual faculty . . . It combines, as mentioned above, a natural dynamism and empirical determinations. But, in order to be grasped by the original dynamism, these determinations must be subordinated to the proper end of this dynamism. A tendency, even a "natural tendency," intends only its own end or that which leads to it. Hence the native dynamism of the intellect grasps the empirical determinations as a beginning or a participation of this end, and the dim volition by which it assimilates them is but the very volition of this end itself. Thus the "empirical determination" of the first intellectual act enters into the mind's dynamism not only as *assimilated to the natural form,* but also as *referred to the proper end* of this dynamism.

The whole secret of objective knowledge lies in the logical necessities implied in this respective situation of the "form" and the "end."

The adequate subjective end of our intellectual dynamism—perfect happiness, the possession of the perfect Good—consists in a saturating " assimilation " of the form of *being,* in other words, in the possession of God. Although this end is supernatural, it must, *in itself,* be possible. Else the basic tendency of our intellectual nature turns into a logical absurdity, the appetite for nothingness.

But the *possibility* of the *subjective* end *(finis quo)* presupposes the *reality* of the objective end *(finis cujus).* The first condition for the possibility of the assimilation of the absolute Being is the *existence* of this Being.

Moreover, the knowing subject guarantees, of logical necessity, the existence of this being. To posit any intellectual act whatsoever in virtue of the natural tendency towards the subjective ultimate end of the intellect is tantamount to implicitly or explicitly willing this end, hence to adopting it *as at least possible.* Strictly speaking one may intend an end without being certain of reaching it, even with the certitude of never reaching it. But it would be contradictory to strive towards an end which one considers *absolutely and in every respect* unattainable. This would mean to will nothingness. This logical incompatibility, in the subject himself, between willing some end and affirming its total emptiness, applies as well to the implicit as to the explicit domain of reason.

Hence, even if one rejects the immediate metaphysical value of the " natural " tendencies, a value which is admitted by the scholastics, it would still be true that to posit any intellectual act whatsoever means to affirm *implicitly* not only the possibility but the reality of the " objective end," of the *finis qui, vel cujus,* as the logical condition of the possibility of the " subjective end."

When the " objective end " is a *finite object,* its mode of reality is not totally determined by the sole fact that it objectively " terminates " a tendency. A subjective end may be intended, without logical incoherence, even should the object whose possession one desires be actually nonexistent. It is enough that this object *may* exist when and in the conditions in which the subjective end would be reached. Nothing prevents us from desiring to acquire a thing which is not, but which will be (which exists in its causes). I may even, without contradiction, although rather whimsically, desire to possess an object which is merely possible, provided, of course, that I suppose it to be really existing when my subjective end is hypothetically achieved. The degree of reality, logically postulated in the object of a tendency in virtue of this very tendency, does not, by itself, go beyond the pre-existence of the object " in its causes," or its reality as " possible."

But when this object is God, when the objective end is identified with the Being which is *necessary by itself* (the pure Act), which has no other mode of reality than absolute existence, the dialectical exigency implied by the desire assumes a new scope, not merely on account of the natural desire, but on account of the nature of the desire's *object*. To affirm of God that he is possible is the same as to affirm that he exists, since his existence is the condition of every possibility.

Hence we may state, in strictest logic, that the *possibility* of our subjective last end presupposes logically the *existence* of our objective last end, God. Thus, in every intellectual act, we affirm *implicitly* the existence of an absolute Being. " All knowing beings implicitly know God in everything they know " (*Ver.,* 22, 2, ad 1; to be interpreted according to *S.T.,* 84, 5 and 88, 3).

But it is not enough to discover the logical implications of every contingent *fact* of knowledge. In the present instance the *fact* implies a radical *necessity,* which does not depend on the fact which reveals it to us. Our implicit affirmation of the absolute Being was *necessary a priori.* For the " objective end " is affirmed exactly to the extent that the " subjective end " is explicitly or implicitly willed. If we willed the subjective end contingently, we would only *in fact* adopt the possibility of this end, hence *in fact* affirm the (necessary) existence of the objective end. But when the subjective end is the ultimate end, it is necessarily intended, in virtue of an *a priori* disposition, of a natural volition which precedes logically every contingent activity. But if we necessarily and *a priori* will the subjective end, we necessarily and *a priori* admit its possibility, hence we affirm *necessarily and a priori* the (necessary) existence of the objective end. Therefore our implicit affirmation of the absolute Being is *a priori* necessary. This is exactly what we had to demonstrate.

Of course, the presuppositions which we have made explicit are not immediately known by us; they are at first implicit. Yet, as such, they provide the assimilated object with its *logical* characteristics.

What exactly is their influence upon our original awareness of the object? At the first moment of the direct intellection, nothing is " in act " in consciousness, hence nothing is directly known but an *empirical content* which provides the assimilating movement of our spirit with an actual specification. Hence we are not aware of the general form of our intellectual power (potency is not directly knowable as potency), but we know the form of the mental becoming insofar as it is right now " actuated " from the outside, we know the totality of the determinations actively assimilated by the intellect at this particular stage of its progression towards the ultimate end.

Hence we are aware of the " form of an active movement." It is important to realize what this means for a consciousness which is not, like sense consciousness, totally obstructed by the form which it receives, but which remains capable of penetrating, beyond the given form, to the vital activity which animates this form.

We should remember that, at every moment, the form of the intellectual becoming is at once the form of a *fieri*, of a *factum esse* and of a new *fieri*. It is the point of transition of a dim desire which finds in it a temporary rest, only to surge forward again towards the infinite. This dynamic state, with its bilateral orientation, is present here in *proximate potency* of distinct consciousness. All its active and formal elements are " cognoscible " elements which are already immanent, they are virtually known; only a glance of reflexive consciousness is required to make them fully conscious.

Objective knowledge, in its first moment, is the total and complex expression, both implicit and explicit, of this state of affairs:

(1) The qualitative content which is actually assimilated (the " representative " content of the direct concept), insofar as it is the form of an " *operari* " (activity), realizes all the conditions required for distinct consciousness. Hence it can be explicitly known *according to its proper diversity*.

(2) But this content can be assimilated only if the intellectual faculty has assumed and keeps before it the dynamic attitude of an agent before a partial end, projected in the perspective of an ultimate end, that is, an actively and actually *objectivating* attitude. Thus the represented form stands really before the intellectual subject *in the situation of an object.*

It does not follow that the subject is at once aware of the two terms of this opposition. Psychological experience shows us and reason confirms that the orientation of consciousness is always ruled by the impulsion of its appetite (whether natural or elicited), which St. Thomas calls the " *intentio.*" This " *intentio* " varies with the agent's interest. For an assimilating faculty, which has to look outside itself for that which fills its need, the first interest lies in the good which fills this need. Hence the first *known object* can only be the assimilated object, not yet formally the activity itself of the assimilating subject.

Thus the content which is represented in the direct act of knowledge is at once known *objectively* (although not necessarily formally known as an object), because, impelled by his nature, the subject assumes first before this content a dynamic attitude, which, logically and psychologically, implies *objectivation*. . . . The undeniable property of extroversion in immanence—so hard to explain by nominalistic logic—is no longer a worrisome paradox, if one admits that every intellectual knowledge of objects is carried by some dynamism, whether creative or assimilating. Both a *creative* will and the *tendency* towards an end, more generally a finality *diffusive* of the good and one which *strives towards* the good, introduce into the subject the principle of an immanent disjunction of subject from object. Lacking such a finality, there is no *possible* psychological foundation for the objectivating function of the knower in act.

We should remember here that the *judicative affirmation,* which we have analyzed above, constitutes in objective consciousness the bilateral dynamic moment according to which the intellectual assimilation of the data takes place, according to which they are introduced into the absolute domain of ends. Thus the dynamic function of affirmation coincides with the imperfect *objective function* which belongs to discursive intelligences.

In what order does a dynamic explanation of knowledge bring the representations up to clear consciousness?

(1) In line with the natural finality of an immaterial power, which looks for being and intelligibility, it is first the new acquisition, the actual content of the intellect, that is aimed at by the "*intentio*" and focused in consciousness, not as a form of the subject, but as something opposed to him. From this first stage on we know objectively, we possess an objective representation. This is the classical stage of the "direct concept": a universal, objective concept whose universality and objectivity are not yet explicitly grasped. The initial moment of intellectual knowledge presents only the formal diversity of the phantasm, the "intelligible in potency" as illuminated before us by the objectivating light of the abstractive understanding.

Is this direct concept a "simple apprehension" or is it already an "apprehensive judgment"? We answer with a venerable scholastic distinction, which keeps all its value: the direct concept is not an apprehensive judgment (a judgment of reality) *signate* or *representative,* but *exercite*. It is not an explicit judgment, but a "lived" one. In other words, at the very moment when the conceptual content lights up in our consciousness, the activity exercised by us contains all the logical and psychological elements of a judgment of reality. Hence that which penetrates first and at once into our explicit consciousness is an objectivated content, a "something," object or being. *Primo ens:* first being.

(2) But the immanent form is objectivated as being (*ens*) only in virtue of the objectivating attitude of the subject. His natural inclination pushed him towards the object. But afterwards, he may reflect, and know himself as an objectivating activity molded on the object and opposing himself to it. Starting with this first step in reflection, there emerges in consciousness the *relation* of the intellectual subject to the represented object. The intellect recognizes itself, albeit dimly, in "something of its own" (*quoddam proprium*), as St. Thomas put it. In other words, the relation of "logical truth" itself, which was first dimly exercised, suddenly becomes luminous. *Secundo verum;* in the second place, the true.

Then, as reflection goes on, there emerges before conscious-ness not only the mere relation of logical truth, as an opposition of subject and object, but also the *dynamic value* of this rela-tion. The objectivated form is seen as the term of the subject's inclination. It stands out, explicitly, in the wide open perspective of desire, as an end which stands in itself, as the term of a pos-sible action, as a good (in the transcendental sense in which every being necessarily is good). *Tertio bonum:* in the third place the good.

Of course, these first stages of reflection do not yield the con-cepts of being, of the true and of the good distinctly, as uni-versal. We grasp these transcendental properties and relations, these primordial *a priori* conditions of the object, only as actually experienced in a particular content of consciousness. If we look for a formal representation of the *ratio universalis entis, veri aut boni* (universal notion of being, of the true or of the good), we shall have to use the comparative process of analytic and reflective generalization, which reveals to us the exact scope of this whole gamut of " total abstractions " (specific, generic and transcendental) which have already been performed uncon-sciously in the assimilation of each object. For the comparative process of generalization *does not bring about* abstraction, as supposed by the nominalists; it *reveals* it and explores all its degrees. This exploration in depth uncovers successively the respective " formal objects " of the various faculties which work together in direct intellection. . . .

Deduction of the Ontological Affirmation

If we have reasoned correctly thus far, we would really have made the " objective deduction " of the metaphysical affirmation according to the very principles of St. Thomas.

Let us present this deduction in a different and shorter way, so as to put in better light its necessary connections:

(1) For a non-intuitive intelligence, which receives formal determinations (*species*) from outside, these immanent deter-minations will have the immediate value of *objects* only if the

very mode of their immanence to the subject *opposes* them to the latter (principle of the necessary immanence of all the determinations of knowledge).

(2) Opposition in immanence is possible only according to a *relation* which inheres in the subject. And this opposition can affect consciousness only if the relation inherent to the subject is implicitly or explicitly knowable by him. But only that is knowable for a subject which is immanent to him according to his *ultimate actuality*.

(3) The only immanent relations which fulfill the above conditions are the relation of *cause to effect* and the relation of *tendency to end*. Both of them and no other put in the creative or appetitive activity of a subject an immanent principle of disjunction. To know oneself as a cause means to distinguish oneself ontologically from the effect. To know oneself implicitly or explicitly as a tendency means to know oneself implicitly or explicitly as really distinct from an objective end. The former relation is the foundation of creative intuition, which does not concern us here. The secret of *our* objective knowledge lies in the dynamic relation of *finality*.

(4) If it is to extrapose immediately, before the intellect, an object corresponding to the immanent determinations, the dynamic relation of finality must affect the *very act* by which they are assimilated, so that the act which assimilates is identically the act which opposes. Hence the assimilation itself must project and keep the immanent form opposed to the subject, in the domain of ends. This is possible only if the assimilation occurs under the initial and permanent influence of a wider end, with respect to which the assimilated form is grasped and held as a *subordinated end,* as a beginning of possession, as an eventual means or possible approach. And this already introduces the immanent form within the ontological order, since the ends are noumenal.

But once they are posited, subordinated ends possess exactly the same necessity as the higher, superordinated ends on which they depend. Hence we must demonstrate—and we may do so either *a priori* or psychologically—that the primordial motion which causes the intellectual dynamism is the motion of the absolutely ultimate objective end, of the *Good in itself*. The particular forms, immanent to our intellect, derive their objective value from their final subordination to an absolute necessity. They are contingent in their existence and through their differential features, but they receive from this subordination the " hypothetical " necessity which is the share of absolute possessed by all things under God. The absolute end introduces them virtually into the rigorous concatenations of *Metaphysics*.

(5) Let us call " affirmation," in the widest sense of the word, the active referring of a conceptual content to reality (*ad rem*). Then the above remarks lead us to assert that the representations which are immanent to our thought possess in it the value of objects only in virtue of an *implicit affirmation*; not of any affirmation, however, but in virtue of a *metaphysical affirmation* which connects the object with the absolute realm of being. Hence the metaphysical affirmation, as a dynamic attitude, is really the condition of the possibility of the object in our mind, that is, in a discursive mind. This is precisely the point which we promised to demonstrate.

(6) A few more remarks may be useful.

a) At the outset of the act of objective knowledge, affirmation is " exercised," not yet " known " with all its logical properties and consequences.

b) The ontological conditions postulated by the objective affirmation are *really implicit* in it, are objectively " constitutive " of it. Something is *implicitly* (*exercite*) known in an elicited act of knowledge when it is immanently " knowable in it without being actually perceived." In an intellectual representation there are two kinds of implicit contents. One is the *purely analytical implicit,* that is, all that which may be found in this representation by analytic dissociation. The other is the *subjective implicit* (a real transcendental implicit in the Kantian sense), that is, the totality of the *a priori* conditions, of the functional exigencies of the intellect as such, actuated in objective knowledge, whose subjective conditions of possibility they constitute. They may be discovered by the subject through self-reflection and introduced into a rational deduction which renders them *objectively* necessary.

Reflection and Metaphysics

The reflective exploration of the transcendental implicit combined with strictly analytical reasoning would gradually unfold before us the whole of *general metaphysics* (including the metaphysics of the Transcendent) as a system of absolute conditions which objective thought cannot reject without destroying itself through logical contradiction. But the possibility of objective thought is the *minimal* point of departure, which every critique, however radical, must accept.

We cannot, in a couple of pages, make an inventory of the huge speculative wealth hidden in the subjective implications of every human act of knowledge. Besides, this would mean to build a metaphysics, not simply to discover its threshold. Yet, in order to obviate a difficulty which has not yet been sufficiently solved above, we would like to consider briefly a rather restricted sector of the domain of the necessary implicit.

When, as mentioned above, reflection discovers the opposition between subject and object in the very opposition between tendency and end, it shows us the conscious " form " (the " cognoscible in act ") divided, as it were, between two subjects of inherence, the *in itself* of a subjective activity and the *in itself* of an objective end.

Considering next the successive acts of the intellect, reflection discovers in them, through an authentic inner experimentation, the correlation of a basic dynamism which is at work everywhere and of an ultimate subjective end which is always intended. Now, unless one be willing to deny being and to adopt contradiction, the admission of a necessarily intended ultimate subjective end entails the affirmation of a necessarily existing objective ultimate end. Thus we not only know implicitly, but we discover clearly and explicitly, in the *a priori* conditions of our primitive apperception of objects, the at first latent revelation of the absolute Being as universal End.

Moreover, when it returns to the matter of knowledge, reflection shows us the empirical elements grasped successively by the basic tendency which leads us to the universal assimilation of Being. Each one of them is seen, in its own form, as the specification of partial ends depending on the ultimate and

absolute End. Since each one of them had to be implicitly
willed by us according to its specifying form and its necessary
relation to the ultimate End, we are led to measure " theoretically " their objective reality with the yardstick of this form and
of this relation.

Thus there arises before our reflective mind, under the leadership of the infinite Being, the keystone of metaphysics, a huge
system of objects : some subsisting in themselves, others connected with some subsistence; some are physical beings, modalities or relations, others are mental beings, modalities or
relations. All of them, beings, principles or modes of being or
abstractive aspects of beings are more and more distinctly
discovered by reflection; they constitute possible rungs for our
ascension towards God; they are real *essences,* all meshing in
each other while subordinated to the absolute Being, the *final
End* and the *universal Cause.*

Causality and finality are analytically connected. In a moving
object the striving towards the last end is identically the motion
of the first cause. Knowing the former, we know the latter.
Thus to know God as universal End means to know him as
universal Cause. Whatever may be the exact relation of the
principle of finality with the principle of causality in the
" predicamental " order, it is a fact that, in the transcendent
domain, when we wish to ascend from finite beings to God, it
does not matter which of the two principles we use. They
constitute the two sides of one and the same relation. Do we,
in the natural order, have any other revelation of the transcendent God than the *radical love* which he produces in us and in
all things, as first Mover and ultimate End of all things. *Kinei
ôs erômenon* (" he moves by being loved "), said Aristotle. And
after him St. Thomas repeats : " As God is the first unmoved
mover, he is the first object of our desire " (*S.c.G.,* I, 37). This
love is hidden in us and it operates as mysteriously outside of
us. We discover it *in ourselves* only through the intermediary
of the finite objects in which it is infinitely refracted, without
ever being absorbed. We discover it *in the things* only because
they react when we try out on them our own striving towards
God. That is, we discover it by knowing and loving these things.

Human metaphysics consists mainly in discovering and

exploring this universal love in which transcendent causality
expresses itself. Therefore metaphysics is the science of love.
However, Thomistic Aristotelianism adds at once: this love
is not a blind impulsion, but an *intellectual love*. The ultimate
end of the universe is identically the end of the intellect.
Thomistic voluntarism is an intellectualism. Let us briefly
insist on this consideration which, it seems to us, reveals the
very core of the theory of knowledge which is fragmentarily
exposed in the works of St. Thomas.

The Finality of Our Intelligence in the Finality of the Universe

St. Thomas claims that the last end of the universe can only
be the *truth*. For both the end and the principle of all things
necessarily reside in the Act which is not mixed with any
potentiality. Now in the pure Act there is complete identification—without opposition or synthesis—of the intelligible in act
(*object*) and the intellect in act (*subject*) (*S.c.G.*, I, 1) . . . If the
divine truth, as unity of the first intellect and the first intelligible,
is the end of all things and also their origin, it constitutes also
the absolute norm, subjective as well as objective, of all
intelligences, including human intelligence (*ibid.*, I, 62). . . .
Hence, according to St. Thomas, the " first truth " is really the
perfect prototype, the principle and the end of our " human
truth." Hence our last and beatifying end and our supreme
perfection consists in rising all the way up to and *objectively*
reaching through our intellectual acts the principle which, from
within, animates and carries them (*Quaestio disput. de Anima*,
q. 1, art. 5, c). . . . Our intellectual nature would have fully
fulfilled its destiny when, exactly as it receives its *dynamic
impulsion* from the " first truth," it also contemplates this same
truth as its immediate and saturating *object*.

The Theory of Knowledge and the Problem of the Supernatural

Meanwhile, we strive for this possession of the " first truth "
with all the operations of our intellect and of our will. We strive

for it *in an efficacious way,* if grace makes up for the basic
powerlessness of our nature. Without grace we strive for it but
in an inefficacious way. On the natural level the " first truth "
gives us only the initial impulsion towards an end which is
possible in itself, but which we cannot demand, which lies
beyond the reach of every created agent. The effort we make
to reach it, our " natural desire " remains powerless until it
encounters the complement of supernatural grace.

Without this complement our internal finality is limping. On
the one hand, our radical capacity extends to a remotely *possible* ultimate end, which is the intuitive assimilation of God
himself. On the other hand, our natural power stops at a
realizable last end which consists only in the indirect assimilation of God through the intermediary of the creatures. On the
one hand we have then the beatific vision of God as the ultimate
end of our deepest tendency and on the other hand, the analogical
knowledge of God, however perfect, as the extreme term of our
efficacious action. The natural tendency goes beyond the possibilities of action. Without the help of grace, the different stages
of action, although finalized by the tendency, do not reach the
latter's ultimate term. The action is somewhat like the trajectory
of a projectile: the shell is launched horizontally towards a
target which is too far away, and it deviates towards the ground
because there is no steadily acting force to counteract the force
of gravity. The initial aim pointed towards the target, but the
power at work is too weak and the motion deviates downwards.

If this is the case, if our intellectual finality shows a disproportion which no created agent is able to compensate—a
disproportion between the basic capacity and the natural power
—we understand why, for pure reason, man's real destiny is
hazy and uncertain. Whatever definition of human beatitude we
may accept, this beatitude cannot be absolutely perfect as long
as it derives only from an indirect knowledge of God. Yet, as
creatures, we cannot demand more. What right do we have, by
nature, to the intimate sharing of divine life? The transcendence
of the infinite Being peremptorily explains both our physical and
" juridical " powerlessness to possess him directly. Therefore, in
a purely " natural " order (an order which excludes all the
" supernatural ") there would be a basic disproportion, in man,

between what he desires and what he can reach. May we conclude from this that an "order of pure nature" would be
impossible? By no means, because this disproportion is, by
itself, not necessarily irrational. We might add that, even should
it not be compensated by supernatural grace, it would still
derive from the goodness of the Creator. For the deep and
necessarily unfulfilled desire of an illimited surplus of beatitude
would be the condition and, as it were, the ransom, of the
marvelous privilege of intelligence. "All things strive to resemble
God," says St. Thomas (*S.c.G.*, III, 19), each one according to
its own nature. But our intellect, although burdened by matter,
is capable, because it is an intellect, of discovering in us this
natural and objectively infinite tendency and thus to suspect,
negatively, a happiness which we remain radically unable to
secure for ourselves. Only one being would have the power of
conferring it upon us, by giving himself. This being is God. Is
he morally obliged to do so? We do not see why, since the
merely natural beatitude of intelligence is already, in itself, an
incomparable gift, and since this very gift would have been
impossible without opening up before our eyes the dim perspective of an even greater gift.

However, although the problem of human destiny remains
mysterious for natural reason, this does not entail any essential
uncertainty about the critical problem of objective truth. For
the critical conclusion which we have developed is based solely
on the "possibility in itself" of the absolutely ultimate End
whose hidden desire sets our whole mental activity in motion.
Whether or not this possibility can be realized without a free
and gratuitous supernatural gift, it remains implicitly affirmed
as a possibility in itself, with all its logical presuppositions, in
every one of our rational activities. Therefore, not only can we
know objects objectively—as is quite obvious—we can even
justify their objectivity without first having, even implicitly,
established whether the vocation to a supernatural end is for us
a fact or a mere possibility.

The *critique of knowledge* may leave the problem of man's
supernatural destiny undecided. But an *ontology of the knowing
subject* may not do so, for the ontological principles of the
intellectual dynamism must be qualitatively different according

to whether the operations which they direct can or cannot reach their absolutely saturating end. If they cannot, the intellect's " nature " is self-sufficient as the first internal principle of the movement of our mind. If they can, we must admit that to the natural dynamism is added a complementary virtuality, a gratuitous gift from God. The " reality " of the intellective subject is not the same in the two cases.

That is where a theory of supernatural grace would find its place. If it is to be complete, the metaphysics of the knowing subject presents an *option* about which reason cannot decide by itself alone. Moreover, a metaphysics which would try to be self-contained would be a *rationalistic* and virtually a pantheistic metaphysics. The history of philosophy provides us with famous examples of such systems, starting with the Alexandrine doctrines of emanation and going over Spinozism all the way to Hegelianism.

At any rate, and whether or not they be supernaturalized, our intellectual activities constitute, although at a more or less exalted level, a gradual progression towards the " first Truth," which, like a common peak (accessible from one side, merely visible from a distance from the other side), towers above the field of faith as well as over the domain of rational knowledge. In himself the " God of the philosopher " is no other than the " God of the Christians." . . .

In fact, according to Christian dogma, human truth considered in its totality, according to all its principles, is both natural and supernatural. St. Thomas describes it very widely in a formula which admirably summarizes his metaphysics of " truth." It applies to merely natural knowledge, but it reaches its full meaning only in the hypothesis of a nature which is backed and illuminated by grace: " The ultimate perfection of the human intellect is the divine truth; other truths perfect the intellect in order to reach the divine truth " (*S.c.G.,* II^a-II^{ae}, 180, 4, ad 4). Which means, if we take into account the full meaning of these words: the supreme perfection which the human intellect is looking for is nothing but the divine truth, the truth which is immanent to the subsistent Intelligence. The other truths may perfect human intelligence only in order to reach the divine truth, that is, as approximations to and fragmentary participations of this truth.

In the *corpus* of the same article, a few lines higher, Aquinas, consciously mixing the natural and the supernatural perspectives, had put it as follows: "This contemplation [of the divine truth] will be perfect in the life to come, when we shall see God face to face, wherefore it will make us perfectly happy; whereas now the contemplation of the divine truth belongs to us imperfectly, namely *through a glass darkly* (I Cor., XIII, 12). Hence it bestows on us a certain inchoate beatitude which begins now and will be continued in the life to come; that is why the Philosopher (*Ethic.*, X, 7) *places man's ultimate happiness in the contemplation of the supreme intelligible*" (*ibid., corp.*).

This combination of a theological formula from St. Paul with the best Platonic background of Aristotle looks like a fine symbol of the most comprehensive Thomistic intellectualism.

XXXVIII. THE EVIDENCE OF FORM AND THE EVIDENCE OF ACT

Knowledge which is certain, which is evident, puts us in touch with reality. Its object is not exclusively the *Form* of reality, but more exactly *Reality* according to its Form. For reality, whether existing or only possible, always refers, directly or indirectly, to the concrete line of *Act*. Knowledge which would only grasp the form of reality, taken absolutely in itself, as a mere qualitative representation, would not be a real knowledge of *objects*.

Hence, under the objective light of evidence, reality must reveal itself both as form (logical, ideal essence), and as reality of this form (actuality or necessary relation to actuality).

Let us review different conceivable modes of the manifestation of reality (form and actuality) in knowledge.

Intellectual intuition, which is an immediate communion of the knower and the known, does not abstract in perceived reality the form from the act. Our discursive intelligence cannot claim this higher form of evidence; our intelligible representation is "conceptual."

But why should the conceptual form—whether inborn to our

understanding (Descartes) or synthetically constructed by putting several attributes together (Wolff)—why should this form, a logical essence present to our thought, not directly represent in it some ontologically *possible* reality? This is the claim of the realism of the essences or of the possibles, a favorite tenet of the various forms of ontologistic rationalism. According to these philosophers, every one of our clear and distinct concepts should, as an *ideal* essence, be the expression of some corresponding reality, that is, of a possible object, of an objective aptitude for existence. Should this possible, this aptitude for existence be, by definition, a necessity of existing as happens in the concept of God, the conceptual form would imply the actual existence of the object it represents.

For a Thomistic philosopher, every solution which makes the form alone reveal to us directly or indirectly the existential act is absolutely unacceptable, because it adopts and dogmatically asserts the fundamental error of the Anselmian paralogism: the transition by pure analysis from the objective concept (logical essence) to that which is ontologically real.

The "clear and distinct" representation of the essences, far from implying as such their aptitude to existence, or even in the case of the divine essence, their necessary existence, tells us at the utmost that the finite essences are not incompatible with the *representation* of existence, and that the idea of God necessarily comprises the *representation* of existence. But how can we pass analytically from the simple representation of an actual or possible existence to an *absolute* positing of this existence as actual or as possible? The conceptual representation of *esse* does not yet go beyond the order of the *ideal* essences and of the formal predicates; the conceptual representation of the act is but the formal image of actuality. We can confuse the immediate evidence of an act with the formal representation which we call a "predicate" of being or of act, only if we unwittingly accept the ontological paralogism, or, at least, only if we dogmatically assert, like Descartes, the exact parallelism between the imperfect ideas of our understanding and reality (basic principle of rationalism).

Besides, when rationalistic ontologism transforms into an explicit axiom the presuppositions implied in the ancient proof

which is called St. Anselm's proof, it errs not only by putting a
dogmatic affirmation at the basis of realism (after all, a dogmatic affirmation may be true), but it also implicitly asserts the
absolute primacy of form over act, of essence over *esse*. And
this reversal of the order of priority between act and potency—a
priority so well analyzed by Aristotle and St. Thomas—contains
in germ pantheistic monism, realistic as well as idealistic.

Hence if objective evidence gives us reality, it cannot consist
only in a *formal* representation of the object.

While the ontologistic rationalists, overlooking the abstractive
character of our concepts, have a too high opinion of our
understanding, attributing to it real "angelic ideas," *a priori*
principles of knowledge of reality, other philosophers who are
likewise too exclusively attached to the formal aspect of knowledge, but immune—or cured—of the ontologistic illusion, err,
on the contrary, through defect. We mean Kantian criticism.

Kant puts at the basis of his *Critique* a methodological
exigency which we shall formulate in these terms: every *objective* evidence derives from an intuition or from the analysis of
an intuition. Therefore man, who lacks an ontological intuition,
does not possess any objective evidence outside of the formal
intuition of the primitive datum (sense datum) and the application of the analytic norm to the concepts of experience (logical
identity). But a sense intuition reveals to analysis no other
reality than its own. It remains a pure phenomenon. Likewise,
our later elaboration of the phenomena or *a priori* syntheses of
essences—formal constructions—offer the critical philosopher no
undeniable claim of representing any kind of ontological reality.
They simply refer the phenomena to the unity of consciousness,
nothing more.

Yet there subsists in Kant some remnant of the Wolffian
dogmatic inheritance—and this slightly complicates our problem. He believes that accepting the representation or the form
as phenomenon means accepting the *undetermined absolute*
logically demanded by the phenomenon in order to become
affirmable. For every affirmation posits some absolute. He who
refuses as absurd to treat that which is phenomenally relative
as an absolute must posit an absolute which limits this relative.
That is why Kant admits the reality of unknowable " things in

themselves." This means that the affirmation of the form as a phenomenon invites us to affirm a non-phenomenal reality (survival of realism in Kant) although the phenomenal form by no means qualifies this reality in itself, and does not represent any ontological essence (Kantian agnosticism).

We have mentioned elsewhere (*Cahier IV*) the discussions which the notion of things in themselves had evoked already during Kant's lifetime. It seems to us that he was right when he claimed that this notion was logically implied in the affirmation of the phenomenon. But were his opponents on this point wrong when they considered the Kantian Thing-in-itself unthinkable and incoherent?

Nevertheless, the author of the *Critique* was right when he concluded from the affirmation of the phenomenon to the necessary reality of the Thing-in-itself. We believe that this paradox may be dissolved as follows: despite his shrewdness for spotting the weak points in an argument, Kant, owing to some remnant of the rationalistic illusion, was positing a conclusion which was materially valid without noticing the real middle term of his inference. There is a total lack of proportion between its antecedent and its consequent, as formulated by him, that is, between the phenomena and the Thing-in-itself. How could we with purely formal and static representations, with phenomena and with the sole help of the analytic principle understood in a merely normative meaning, discover, without recourse to any other source of information, a necessary *beyond* of these phenomena, nay an absolute *beyond,* opposed to the subject as a reality in itself? It would seem that simple analysis, applied to the phenomena, should yield phenomena, nothing else. In the Kantian demonstration a link is missing. What is this link which Kant overlooked?

Kant defines the Thing-in-itself as an absolute reality which limits the phenomena. Now in order to know a limit as limit one must, if deprived of the immediate intuition of the domain extending beyond this limit, encounter this side of it a dynamic principle which virtually surmounts it. The Kantian reasoning would have made its point on one condition: that the phenomenon should reveal its own limitation by standing in the way of an objectivating impulse, striving beyond it; by undergoing the exigency of an affirmation which exceeds it; in brief, by opposing itself to a tendency which would carry the subject, through the phenomena, towards an ulterior term which is no longer phenomenal. But if Kant had conceived the affirmation of the phenomena in this way, he would have conceived the transcendental subject *dynamically* and would have laid the foundation of a well defined metaphysics.

Kant never clearly formulated in his own mind this dynamic conception, although he uses it, without acknowledging it, when he admits the strict relativity of the phenomenon and when he argues from it as from a relativity with respect to some *objective* beyond. He skirts transcendental metaphysics without ever penetrating into it. Even while adding to the phenomenal form a relation to the absolute and projecting it against the undetermined background of reality in itself, he merely applies globally to the phenomenal objects in general the extrinsic, metacritical, precategorical pressure of an absolute but amorphous Reason which cannot make up its mind to affirm something which is purely relative. For Kant the particular form of every phenomenal object implies no corresponding noumenal actuality. It does not stand out, in immediate evidence, as the superficial but typical outline of a subsisting reality. Strictly speaking, it is only connected with the Thing-in-itself through some dark and necessary compulsion of Reason. The connection of the phenomena with the Thing-in-itself is attributed to them from without, globally, through some logical decree. It is not exercised and recognized implicitly in every phenomenon.

On the other hand, the objective evidence of the scholastics supposes that subject and object stand in *real* communion across the particular phenomenon, not through a simple similitude of forms, but through this immediate dynamic grasp which constitutes the foundation of the logical truth of our direct judgments.

Such is the thesis which we have explained and defended in our pages. It cannot be rejected by those who wish to avoid both rationalistic ontologism and Kantian agnosticism. For if it is true that the form, considered precisively as form, gives us by itself alone neither directly nor indirectly the existential act; if it is true that the conceptual representation of the act is still " formal," and that, moreover, the analytic relations, in the strict sense, are also formal relations, there is only one way out in order to safeguard the objective evidence of reality: to establish this evidence not merely on a formal representation but on a relation which we might perhaps call " extra-representative." In other words, to admit the existence in us of an immediate (implicit or explicit) awareness of a communication of object to subject, through the very line of act. A scholastic would say: the awareness of a vital participation of the subject to the object.

Such a participation becomes possible for us only through the intermediary of a material receptive faculty, a sensibility, where the subject's and the object's actuality meet in one and the same spot. But the coincidence in a concrete form is not enough yet to constitute the evidence of an *object*. The active community of subject and object must be translated in consciousness, not only according to the outline of the sensible form, but according to the actual continuity which connects the two aspects, the subjective and objective aspect of this form.

But the consciousness of the object's actuality in the very activity of the subject is, of course, possible only in a self-transparent faculty. Sensibility, an intrinsically material faculty, which is unable to reflect on its own act, causes us to experience concretely the sense object, but does not reveal its ontological actuality. Although the objective elements of this revelation are introduced into the subject by the sensation, it cannot be read by the senses. It might be read only by an immaterial faculty which would, implicitly or explicitly, know that it is limited (determined, specified) in its own activity by the very object inherent in the sense. . . .

If it is to provide us directly, although without ontological intuition, with the evidence not only of the form but of the absolute reality of the object, the intellectual operation must be *constructive, synthetic*.

XXXIX. SYNTHESIS AND CONSCIOUSNESS

The senses put us immediately in touch with reality, but do not make us know it as reality. The senses reach reality, immediately but materially.

The intellect reaches reality as such, but only in the object of sense. Moreover, we know that the intelligence can grasp reality as *act* only through its own dynamic continuity with it. What is the nature of this dynamic continuity?

To be sure, the intellect does not simply assume the function of a form of which sense reality should be the immediate matter. For in that case it would sink to the level of a higher sensibility and the whole problem of objectivation would again arise. Hence it will exert not an exclusively formal causality, but a real activity with respect to the immanent sense object which will be for it only a " quasi-matter " or a *materia circa quam*.

But an activity exerted on, through or upon the sensible representation confers upon it something which is not the exclusive possession of concrete sensibility, something which is synthesized with the purely sensible diversity. Hence the product which results, in consciousness, from this collaboration of intellect and sensibility is really an *immanent construction,* made with the sense data and with some principle of intellectual origin: abstractive *a priori*, form of universality or whatever it may be.

This whole state of affairs, as it emerges into consciousness, should explain *objective* evidence.

Somebody might object that it is needless to continue this investigation. We are in a blind alley. If the immanent term of the intellectual operation, the intelligible in act, derives from a synthesis, if the subject has constructed it by contributing something of its own to it, how should the resemblance with the outside object subsist in it? Does constructivity not do away with objectivity?

This might be the case if the immanent term of intellection (the mental word, the universal in act) were faithfully to represent the outside object. But nobody holds this except a few, possibly extant, defenders of an old-fashioned indifferentistic ultra-realism. Almost all philosophers, including most Platonizing ones, distinguish to some extent " the way things are in the mind " from the " way things are in reality." And St. Thomas, who emphasizes this distinction, affirms squarely that the proper object of our abstractive understanding can be a " universal in act " or even an " intelligible in act " only within the immanence of thought—while the outside object is only universal and intelligible " in potency."

Let us not confuse *immanent object* and *known object*. Of course the two of them are intimately connected, but one is not the other. Their properties partially diverge. For instance, in a discursive intelligence the immanent object (that which is cognoscible in act) is formally known only through reflection. It constitutes the proximate condition (*id quo*), not the primary object (*id quod*) of knowledge. The immanent object (not its *id quod*) is called by Aristotle and St. Thomas, and also by Kant, synthetic and constructed. It belongs to the vital, preconscious, sensitivo-rational, assimilating stage of intellection. The life of an assimilating intelligence is necessarily a synthesis of acquired elements (assimilation, *ratio formalis veri*), although consciousness as such (knowledge, as an effect of truth), which follows upon the assimilation, is an intuition and an analysis.

What element, in this vital communion of object and subject, as it emerges in the defining light of consciousness, becomes objectively evident for us? What will, strictly speaking, be the *known object,* that *which is known*?

We have answered this question in detail before. . . . If by *known object* we mean the totality of objective knowledge, implicit and explicit, which the knowing subject may gather through or in the synthesis which happens in him, the range of this known or knowable object would extend far beyond the external, particular object, which gave rise to the synthetic process and becomes its first conscious term. If, on the other hand, we mean by known object this primary term itself (the object which is explicitly apprehended in the direct act of knowledge), then we must say that this known object, this *id quod,* is nothing but the object concretely presented by the senses, but grasped already from a higher point of view, *objectively* posited and perceived through a *universal*, which consciousness at first does not distinguish from the sense representation in which it is individualized.

Hence direct intellection provides clear consciousness only with a *physical object* corresponding to the material content of the immanent intelligible. As we start reflecting, the *metaphysical object* emerges under the transcendental aspects of being, truth, goodness; next, formally, as "universal *in re.*" It is only here that the difficulty arises which we mentioned above of reconciling constructivity and objectivity, the immanent mode of the concept and its external meaning. During the direct stage of intellection, the subject's intervention consisted only in rendering the physical object "actually" cognoscible, in a vital, universalizing immediation, which added no distinctively perceptible element to the qualitative content of sensibility. From now on, under the light of reflection, which re-examines it in an act that considers also the subjective operation, the object of knowledge will successively reveal the very peculiarities it acquired when it became immanent to the subject.

Do these peculiarities have an objective meaning?

As we said above, the gradual awareness of the intelligible attributes of the immanent object is also, by way of an immediate *logical* repercussion, the manifestation of as many corresponding metempirical features in the outside object. Whatever actuality the latter acquires when assimilated to the subjective faculty necessarily reveals in it a corresponding aptitude or potency. That which the immanent object is *in act,* the outside object is ontologically *in potency.* Thus, the immanent object is perceived formally, under reflection, as a limitation of the active subject, as true in act, or intelligible in act, or desirable in act, or again as universal in act, according to this or that exogenous qualitative diversity. It follows that the directly apprehended outside object, which gives rise to the revelatory reflection, can only be conceived as limiting *being,* or as "something" in itself; next, as *true* in potency, as *intelligible* in potency, *desirable* in potency; finally, as *universal* in potency according to such and such qualitative features.

What more should we expect, unless we demand an intellectual intuition? The whole of metaphysics, which is elaborated by reflecting upon direct physical knowledge, yields us nothing which is not logically contained either in these different levels of "potentiality" of the outside object or in the correlative and proportional hierarchy of the subjective actuations.

In this way, by constructing the immanent object, the subject himself becomes, as it were, within the order of intelligibility the "test" of the physical object which served as the "given."

We have here a real experimentation of the intelligible given through the senses, a probing of the raw materials, through an application of the exigencies of thought. To the extent in which these materials react to the natural postulations of the intelligence, their concrete and contingent existence, which is at first affirmed by the sole fact of their penetrating within the subjective becoming, enters ever more deeply into a logical chain of necessary relations. The metaphysical quintessence of external reality rises slowly to the surface owing to its affinities with the intelligible actuality of the subject.

Of course, the intelligible " potency " of the sense object, which is the measure of its metaphysical reality, is revealed by immediate correlation only to the precise extent in which it meets and completes the virtual act (first act) of the intellective subject. And this correlation manifests only ontological features inherent in the object. Should we wish to proceed thence until the last, transcendental metaphysical conditions, we would have to use a less direct dialectics. Two equally possible ways would open up before us, the way of the subject and the way of the object—the way of the logical implications of an immaterial act which is not wholly act, since it continues to actuate itself through some assimilating genesis, and the way of the logical presuppositions of a potency of intelligibility, which is not mere potency, since it provides us by itself with a qualitative " datum." But the analytic axioms about the priority of act force us to affirm that no act invades a potency and that no potency yields to an act but through the motion, whether progressive or privative, of a proportioned act. By means of this principle we shall be able to connect the essence of the subject as subject and that of the sense object to the supreme, infinitely simple actuality of the first Cause, while moving back along the two parallel and complementary lines of creative emanation : the line of the *intelligence* (the subject as transcendental subject) and the line of the *intelligible* object (the object as in potency of intelligibility).

XL. SUBJECTIVE OR OBJECTIVE NECESSITY

Part Two of our work contains the elements of a third epistemological demonstration, which is more direct, but of a more restricted scope. Although still essentially metaphysical, it comes nearer to the strictly transcendental way of reasoning.

Its main lines are clearly drawn in this frequently quoted text of St. Thomas, where he mentions, as in an afterthought, the stages of a rational justification of our objective knowledge.

[Truth] is in the intellect as a consequence of the act of the intellect and as known by the intellect. Truth follows the operation of the intellect inasmuch as it belongs to the intellect to judge about a thing as it is. And truth is known by the intellect in view of the fact that the intellect reflects upon its own act—not merely as knowing its own act, but as knowing the proportion of its act to the thing. Now, this proportion cannot be known without knowing the nature of the act; and the nature of the act cannot be known without knowing the nature of the active principle, that is, the intellect itself, to whose nature it belongs to be conformed to things. Consequently, it is because the intellect reflects upon itself that it knows truth (*Ver.*, I, 9, c).

Hence, in order to become reflectively aware of the already implicitly possessed truth of its objective content, the intelligence must find, in its direct act, a " proportion to the thing," a something which refers it to reality in itself. But this can be known only if we know the nature and the internal finality of this particular act, and the nature of this act can only become manifest to us through the nature of the active principle from which it derives, that is, from the nature or the internal finality of the intellect itself, " made to be conformed to things."

Therefore, according to St. Thomas, the objective value of knowledge would be formally revealed to the subject through the analysis *of its own* a priori *exigencies*, acting upon a present datum, that is, ultimately, through the objective exigencies of the necessary *affirmation*.

We may wonder whether this " evidence of truth " which is already *exercised* and *felt* in direct knowledge and afterwards imposes itself through rational self-reflection, to the *explicit* acceptance of the subject, carries the assurance of a *subjective* or of an *objective* necessity.

Should we be entitled to presuppose a metaphysics of finality, our conclusion would at once assume an objective value. It seems to us that such is the point of view which corresponds to the literal meaning of this passage of St. Thomas. But if we wish to consider this way of reasoning in itself, outside of every metaphysical presupposition, what does it strictly demonstrate, not about the necessary belief of the knowing subject, but about the *known object*? It is strange enough that such a question may be raised at all. Might we not state at once that the mere reflective analysis of the cognitive act would never show in it anything more than subjective exigencies? But in epistemology we are looking for a conclusion which is objectively justified before theoretical reason. Hence our demonstration should share the very necessity of the principle of contradiction—else it should not be objective—while nevertheless not being merely analytical, since, in the present case, analysis alone remains powerless. Hence we are facing a very special type of objective demonstration. A moment of examination will allow us to make interesting comparisons.

Let us first notice that St. Thomas' text does not offer us a demonstration of " truth " in the abstract, but the rational justification which *a knowing subject* (any knowing subject) may acquire of the objective value of *his* knowledge. In these well determined conditions, the reasoning *from the subject* and *in the subject* becomes analytic, if we supply a minor, not mentioned by St. Thomas in the lines we have quoted, although it is quite familiar to his way of thinking. Let us render it explicit.

Strictly speaking, the subject who undertakes the critique of his own thought might still, without *logical* contradiction, escape a subjective secondary and partial exigency of this thought, provided the very act of refusal or abstention should not depend on conditions which impose this limited necessity. Such would be the case with a subjective necessity which refers only to the affirmation of a category of objects. But when the subjective necessity is absolutely *primitive and universal,* when it extends to *all* objective thought, it becomes impossible for the intellectual faculty to deny this necessity or to call it into doubt without nevertheless affirming it in that which is logically implicit in the very act of doubting or of denying. Hence if the basic condition of *any* attitude *whatsoever* of the intellect (in an undetermined subject) really resides in the absolute objective reference, according to some formal coincidence, this general objective reference will constitute a condition of the possibility of the doubting or denying attitude (always reducible to an affirmation) as well as of the directly affirmative attitude. To deny the object or to call it into doubt would entail in the subject an obvious incoherence, a rejection of the first principle.

Whether or not it is possible to demonstrate the impossibility *in itself* of the proposition "there is no objective truth," one thing is certain: *no subject* can assert it without contradicting himself. Hence the objective necessity, enveloped in the universal exigencies of affirmation, differs from a blindly undergone subjective constraint; it is a "necessary fact" which, although not containing its own demonstration *propter quid,* allows it to control its necessity with the touchstone of the first principle.

Let us admit it, however: the logical contradiction, which we invoke here as a sanction against any rejection of the absolute exigencies of the affirmation, is not directly a formal contradiction between conceptual terms (a contradiction in the terms), but a contradiction between that which is *implicit and explicit* in a judgment. Besides, a mere logical contradiction "in the terms," independently of any more or less concealed positing, affirming or presupposing, would be unable to yield us (possible or actual) reality on the rebound. He who tries to demonstrate the absolute necessity of being merely and exclusively by analyzing concepts—even through a logical analysis of the idea of nothingness—would commit the typical error of the ontological argument or of the Cartesian rationalistic postulate.

It is true that reflection, which forces the implicit to become explicit, will allow the knowing subject to compare thereafter, on the same level, the two opposed terms and to notice their obvious incompatibility. But even so, of what nature exactly is the contradiction which will emerge and, correspondingly, the evidence which imposes itself? This question is important, since the critique operates precisely on this level of reflection, not on the level of spontaneous evidences.

Let us come back to the alleged judgment, "there is no truth." Since this judgment, by implicitly affirming the truth which it denies, destroys itself, its contradictory must be true: "there exists logical truth"—provided, at least, that the alternative " truth or non-truth " makes sense. What is it which in the proposition " truth is " (where " is " means, of course, not the representation of existence, but its affirmation) is immediately evident to us? The intrinsic and immediate relation of its terms: *Truth is*? But this would obviously involve us in the ontological paralogism, since we should claim to discover, in the mere concept of " truth " the absolute affirmation of existence. Yet this proposition " truth exists " is undoubtedly evident. St. Thomas says: " That truth exists, in general, is self-evident " (*S.T.*, 1, 2, ad 3). In what sense? In order to perceive directly the objective bond of *truth* and to *exist*, we would have to be God, endowed with the essential intuition both of intelligence and of being. In fact, what our discursive faculty clearly sees is not this bond in itself, but that *this bond must be affirmed under penalty of contradiction*. Our evidence is not the essential evidence of the *thing*, but the logical evidence of the *judgment* in which the thing is expressed.

This indirect character of the evidence applies to every properly metaphysical object. We are merely transcribing here St. Thomas and his classic commentators. They say that in the empirical (sense) domain, our knowledge reaches immediately the concrete actuality of the material objects. In the metempirical domain, ontological reality is no longer for us an evident *fact*, but a concluded *necessity*. Ferrarensis lays down this distinction in connection with the statement " God is " (*Comment in S.c.G.*, I, 12): we may know the reality of a thing according to the very actuality of the *esse* of this thing (" Socrates is "), or only through the truth of the statement made about this thing, or, as St. Thomas puts it, according to " the *esse* which means the intellect's composition " (*S.c.G.*, 1, c).

This second, indirect manner of knowing *esse* opens for our discursive intelligences the only way of approach to the reality not only of God, but of the metaphysical objects in general (metempirical objects or metempirical attributes of the sense objects). The evidence of these objects, with respect both to their actual and their possible existence, is revealed to us only in the evident necessity of affirming them within a judgment, that is, ultimately, through the impossibility of assuming a logically coherent objective attitude outside such an affirmation.

Should we be surprised that our metaphysical knowledge —which is reflective knowledge—implies no other objective evidence than the evident logical necessity of *affirming* the metempirical object? That the metaphysical demonstration in its totality, when going back to its principles, is always *indirect,* never *wholly* apodictical, that is, never deduced analytically from an essential intuition?

We are fully aware that we are touching here the cornerstone of critical realism (Aristotelian realism of essence and existence) insofar as it differs from all Platonic ontologisms. But we may safely proceed, since the doctrine we are developing comes straight from the Stagirite and has been taken over, with full clarity, by St. Thomas, in his *Commentary on the Metaphysics of Aristotle.* Both of them teach that every metaphysical demonstration reduces the particular proposition it wishes to demonstrate to the necessity of the *first principle,* thus first of all the principle of contradiction (and, we might add, all the transcendental principles of unity, truth, finality, whose evidence is the very evidence of the principle of being). Consequently, the value of the metaphysical demonstration will entirely depend on that of these first principles.

What is their value?

Of course, their objective evidence should be immediate and natural to the mind: " Such a knowledge of the principles exists in us naturally " (*In III Metaphysics,* lect. 5). It rules all our direct and reflective knowledge: the first principles " demonstrate," but they are not " demonstrated." . . . We might hold on to this as to a primary, unavoidable light, whose essence remains mysterious and whose origin is unknown. It is a primordial evidence, not an ontological intuition, for it still is the evidence of a relation between terms, of a synthesis.

Can the metaphysician, nevertheless, justify to some extent, before reflective reason, the objective, universal and metempirical necessity of the first principles? He will try to do so with profit, either in order to solve the " methodical doubt " which we have mentioned above, or to convince the sophists of their error. He should, of course, not think of a demonstration of these principles considered in themselves. "There exists simply no demonstration of these principles" (Aristotle, *Metaphysics*, X, 5, K 1062 a, 2-3). What he may do is to refute victoriously *ad hominem* every velleity to call them into doubt. He will build some kind of *ad hominem* proof, through a reduction to the absurd. "The philosopher does not consider principles of this kind in such a way as to make them known by defining them or by demonstrating them in an absolute sense, but by refutation, that is, by arguing disputatively against those who deny them" (*In III Metaphysics*, lect. 5).

What is, in speculative philosophy, the meaning of this indirect proof, *in subjecto*? It is extremely important and in such a case *ad hominem* arguing assumes the value of a demonstration, when the *homo* in question is nothing less than every discursive intelligence. Aristotle reveals his innermost thought in Book III of his *Metaphysics*: "He who destroys reason, upholds reason" (1006 a, 26).

That whose evidence the sophist rejects is neither this nor that; it is reason itself, considered in the primordial law of affirmation, which binds it to its *logos*, to its internal or external "word." What the sophist tries to do is but a vain effort. For the very object which the scorner of the first principles explicitly denies is implicitly affirmed by him. He restores through his activity what he destroys through his words. The unshakable realism of his deeper affirmation wrecks in advance the shallow nihilism of his statements.

Hence we must recognize at the root of the metaphysical demonstration, as shoring up the first principles in the immanence of our understanding, a natural factor: a primordial exigency, a postulation of nature, a transcendental act of affirmation (whatever we may call it) which, without being an intuition of essences, forces us nevertheless, under penalty of logical annihilation, to apply categorically the formal laws of being to every content of consciousness. Should somebody try to avoid this necessity, which the scholastic identify with the divine motion which constitutes the "first act" of our intelligence, he would not only offend against an absolute theoretical "imperative"; he would also establish in himself the most senseless speculative lie, which he can uphold only while at the same time denying it. He would keep up the impossible divorce between the life of the mind and the internal locution, the *mental word* in which it is expressed. St. Thomas remarks (probably in order to quiet the misgivings of the logicians unable to demonstrate the indemonstrable) that, although this divorce might be put in words or even imagined, it could never be accepted by our thought.

While trying to build up a demonstration of " truth " which would be less comprehensive but more direct than the totality of metaphysics, we have come back to the critical *preambulum* of all ancient realism, to that elementary justification of the absolute assent which was the foundation of the first philosophy of Aristotle. We insinuated above that this preliminary justifica-tion contained the gist of an authentic transcendental reasoning, thus satisfying the exigencies of modern critique. Let the reader himself decide whether we had a right to bring these two historical extremes together.

The necessity of objectively affirming all the contents of consciousness according to the first principles of being took shape in Aristotle's *ad hominem* proof, as the logical impos-sibility of every attitude other than this affirmation. Since the nature of the thinking subject remains essentially affirming, even in doubt and negation, such doubt and negation, when referring to the absolute value of being, put the judgment's *implicit* and *explicit* elements in conflict with each other.

Let us localize even more carefully the terms between which the contradiction arose. Is it between the judgment itself, con-sidered as a psychological reality, and the psychological subject considered as a real essence (or at least as a spiritual power inherent in this essence)? This is obviously not the case. Although all these metaphysical expressions designate the reali-ties at stake, they do not designate them according to the formal aspect which gives rise to the conflict in consciousness.

Let us then drop the ontological qualification which encum-bers the Aristotelian terminology and see what remains. Only this. On the one hand, an objective content of thought (an explicit negative or dubitative judgment); on the other hand, the function of judging itself which actually gives this content its unity in our thought and its objective meaning (logical function of the judgment, that is, necessarily, a *positing* according to some synthesis). The thinking subject intervenes in this internal conflict only as a function of judging, as an objectivating function of the (negative or dubitative) content of consciousness. Is it also a well defined ontological subject? A critical philosopher would reply: Possibly. But he would add at once: Let us not mix up the problems. Let us restrict ourselves to the precisive consideration of the function of judging, grasped at the indivisible moment when it embraces its content.

We may for the time being accept this limitation of our point of view. For it is within these limits that the contradiction from which we argue formally occurs—a contradiction between the absolute nature of our *positing of being* or our *affirmation,* which is the necessary backbone of every judgment, and the negative or dubitative *content* which emerges into consciousness. We did not need any other elements in order to discover the conflict and to draw from it its logical consequences. The ontological determinations of the terms we employed did not concern the *consequence itself,* that is, the formal concatenation of our way of reasoning. They were legitimately present in it, but concomitantly, " materially." We should have reached the same conclusion if we had said: in every judgment which denies or calls into doubt truth as such, or the first principle, or being in general, the primordial or absolute (" transcendental ") function of affirmation destroys the very content posited by it. Hence these judgments are logically impossible.

While thus more strictly delimiting, through abstraction, the terms between which immediately and inevitably arises the logical contradiction, we have simply transposed our reasoning from the metaphysical to the transcendental level, in which the subject is defined only by his determining function in the object. Even more exactly: from the *ad hominem* reasoning of Aristotle we have disengaged the tenuous thread of a transcendental *deduction,* in which the contingent existence of the subject no longer is featured, so that the only elements left to face each other are the judgment as necessitating *function* and the judgment as necessitated *content.*

In the critical philosophies the transcendental deduction of an

a priori condition (*a priori* form, category, or anything metempirical) consists in demonstrating analytically that this *a priori*
condition is a condition of the possibility of every object in
consciousness, hence that to give up this condition would be
tantamount to denying the very possibility of objective thought.

The reader is invited to compare with this critical deduction either the " reduction to the absurd " by means of which
Aristotle vindicates against the sophists the objective value of
the first principle or (if he prefers a more developed demonstration) the reasoning of St. Thomas which we quoted above (*Ver.,*
I, 9, c). We recall the great lines of the latter proof : the mind
knows its own truth, either inchoatively or implicitly, or in a
fully reflective and rational manner (which is the very purpose
of the transcendental deduction) only to the extent in which it
discovers the necessary " proportion " of its acts to reality, that
is, to the extent in which it discovers in these very acts (in the
objects as immanent) a natural exigency of objective reference
(an objectivating *a priori,* an objective transcendental function)
an exigency which is itself based upon the radical and universal
law of intelligence " to whose nature it belongs to be conformed
to things " (we might translate : based on the " transcendental
act of apperception " or on " the transcendental act of judging,
of affirming "). Somewhat as if we should say : I acquire a
critical knowledge of the truth of my representations when, by
means of a strict line of reasoning, I have connected them with
the essentially assimilating (hence affirming) tendency of the
intellect as to an intrinsic condition of the possibility of
absolutely every objective representation.

Between the logical form of this kind of reasoning reduced to
its essential elements and the logical form of the transcendental
deduction, there exists, despite the difference in horizon and
material content, a resemblance which might very well be an
identity.

If the preliminary justification of ancient realism was really
the preview of a " transcendental deduction," we remain faithful
to the purest realistic tradition when we conclude that properly
objective evidence, in the order of metaphysical knowledge,
derives at the same time from two logical sources : from a
normative, strictly *analytical* necessity and from a pure, radical

necessity of affirming, which we beg leave to call—since the term exists—a *transcendental* necessity. The analytical necessity weaves for our mind a hypothetical network of formal alternatives: being or non-being. But it is the transcendental necessity of the affirmation which forces us to apply them to a content and resolves them in advance in favor of the Real.

We deem it superfluous to insist on the extreme importance which this primordial transcendental necessity possesses for the critical justification of metaphysics.

In the third part, Maréchal endeavors " to condense the whole of the Thomistic theory of knowledge into a few concise propositions, systematically arranged under points of view which are familiar to modern philosophy."

Maréchal insists that this is not his own system of epistemology. If he had to write such a system, he would use the same basic ideas, but he would organize them in a much simpler way. The manner in which he actually presents his ideas he describes as follows :

XLI. THE THOMISTIC CRITIQUE OF KNOWLEDGE TRANSPOSED INTO THE "TRANSCENDENTAL" MODE

[The sequence] intends mainly to make easier a comparison between Thomism and the philosophies inspired by Kant. That is why we deemed it preferable not to give up completely the sequence of points of view suggested by the history of the systems as presented in the previous *Cahiers*. This is the only reason for the threefold division of this chapter. The three paragraphs which follow represent not subordinated stages of one single demonstration, but three successive approaches to a solution which, from the critical point of view, is complete and decisive only in the third attempt.

The author summarizes his threefold approach:

a) First, and without deciding anything about the ontological value of the objects, we shall, by means of a reflexive *analysis*, uncover the elements and the relations contained in the " object as such." We shall then set out to examine the logical value of the results of this inventory.

b) The examination of the analytic elements of the object as such will induce us to conclude first to the absolute value of the necessary object of affirmation, as a *practical postulate*. Although this value of the affirmed object is absolute, it is, by its very nature, only indirect and subjective, since it is based on the *a priori* necessity of a voluntary attitude of the active subject. Kant's philosophy does not go beyond this conclusion; the Kantian metaphysics of the " postulates " is a moral dogmatism.

c) Hence, if we wish to proceed beyond Kant, we shall also have to establish the absolute objective value of the affirmed object, by deducing the ontological (" noumenal ") affirmation as a theoretical or speculative necessity. We shall have to show that the practical and extrinsic necessity of a " transcendent order," admitted by Kant, is based itself upon an absolute necessity, which takes hold of every immanent object from within and as soon as it is constituted in consciousness. But the critical philosophers admit that a necessary and " constitutive " condition of every immanent object shares the theoretical necessary value of the objects which it sets up. Denying this condition would be tantamount to denying the very possibility of objects in the mind, that is, to denying the primary datum of every critique: thought in act. Hence, should this condition logically imply the affirmation of a transcendent object, such an affirmation would be endowed not only with the practical necessity of a " postulate," but with the theoretical necessity of a speculative evidence, at least of an indirect (" analogical ") speculative evidence.

In this way our final demonstration would become what Kant, if he had deemed it possible, at all, would have called the " transcendental deduction " of the ontological affirmation.

Maréchal proceeds then to present the threefold approach to this transcendental deduction in a series of statements. After each statement, he refers to the sections of Cahier V *where this statement has been demonstrated. Some of the statements are followed by longer comments or explanations.*

In the following pages, we shall offer a translation of all these statements, references to previously translated sections that may help the reader understand the statements, and some of the more important comments or explanations.

Analysis of the Object as Such

First proposition. The content of consciousness becomes an object, that is, demands the attribute of logical truth, only within a judgment or, more precisely, within a judicative affirmation. In other words: the objective apperception of the object is the formal effect of an affirmation (pp. 149-153).

Second proposition. Since the object as object exists for us only as a product of the judicative affirmation, it follows that the power of objectivation extends in us beyond the power of formally representing; our power of affirming is not restricted to the objects which we can represent according to their proper form (pp. 139-149).

Third proposition. The object, insofar as it is the product of the affirmation, comprises necessarily: a) a sense datum (pp. 115-125); b) a concretive synthesis (static and categorial); c) an objective synthesis (dynamic and transcategorial) (pp. 149-161).

Fourth proposition. The constitutive conditions of the object, as revealed by reflection and analysis (see 3), entails a certain number of presuppositions concerning the nature of the knowing subject and of the known object. They are: a) the relativity of the sense datum and the quantitative nature of the faculty which receives it; b) in the faculty of concretive synthesis itself, the absence of every internal quantitative determination (immateriality), but also the extrinsic dependence on a quantitative or material condition; c) in the objective synthesis (of the affirmation) the absolute positing of the relation of analogy, that is, in logical order: 1) the (implicit) absolute positing of the infinite Being as the upper, unique and necessary term of every relation of analogy; 2) the absolute positing of the datum or of the content of the representation, as the lower, multiple and contingent term of the relation of analogy. In other words, the necessary existence of God and the essential contingency of the things which are directly represented (pp. 115-153).

> *Next comes the* voluntaristic *stage of the critical proof of realism. It corresponds to Kant's admission of an* absolute *affirmation of the noumenal object as a postulate of* practical reason.

Noumenal Reality as Practical Necessity

The *a priori* necessity of voluntary action implies the necessity of an absolute objective affirmation which logically precedes every particular action. In this way, the existence of a noumenal reality assumes the value of a practical postulate.

> *Maréchal remarks that, in the practical domain, the* absolute *affirmation accrues to the object only after it has already been constituted as object, at least as phenomenal object. It is not a necessary condition of the object as such, but only of the morally acting subject as such.*
>
> *This practical and subjective necessity will become a theoretical and objective necessity only if:*

The introduction of the object into the absolute order of ends, instead of resulting only from elicit volitions, which suppose that the object is already constituted in consciousness, should take place in the very genesis of the object as object, within the implicit and still undifferentiated dynamism whence derive both speculation and action.

> *He tries to show that such is really the case in the third section of his deduction.*

Noumenal Reality as Speculative Necessity

First proposition. Human intelligence is discursive. Both immediate self-reflection and the structural analysis of the judgment discover, in our cognitive activity, a dynamic progression, a movement from potency to act (pp. 149-153; 162-198).

Second proposition. Every movement strives towards an ultimate End, according to a law or specifying form, which imprints upon every stage of the movement the dynamic mark of the ultimate End.

Since the objection is frequently made that this statement is a metaphysical one that cannot be used without begging the question, in a vindication of metaphysics, we translate here an important passage in which Maréchal explains:

This proposition derives from the mere analysis of the notion of *movement,* at least if we understand the movement *in the dynamic sense* and not as a pure temporal series of immobilities.

We insist on the strictly rational, and even properly analytical character of the above proposition. He who denies it interprets movement not as a synthetic function, as a complementary unity of actuality and potentiality, but as a strict identity of act and potency. In this case act as act is potency and, on the other hand, potency as potency is act, which is a flagrant contradiction.

Let us consider movement defined in a very general way as the passage from potency to act. Whether this passage is successive or instantaneous (it does not matter here), the function exercised in this very passage is either *wholly indifferent* with respect to its term, that is, it neither precontains nor demands the latter, or it is connected to this term because it *precontains* or *demands* it.

In the former case, the so-called term is not the term of an active movement, but something which comes wholly from elsewhere, an absolute beginning (this is no longer our hypothesis; see the first proposition). If, without paying attention to the meaning of words, one would nevertheless call it the term of a movement, it would have to be conceived (to the extent to which it is supposed to proceed from the movement) as the terminal exercise of an undetermined function which is exercised in a determined way according to its very indeterminacy. In other words, we would have a function which would be at once and in the selfsame respect in act and in potency.

In the second case, the function exercised in and through the movement is a function which is predetermined with respect to its term because it either precontains the latter formally and in act (but in this case there would no longer be any movement, unless we should claim that act as act is potency), or precontains it only as an exigency, a tendency or a desire. Hence within the movement there exists, between the function as *exercising itself* and the function *which is exercised* (or the proximate term of the exercise of the function) only one logically possible connection, namely the *antecedent proportion of a tendency to the term of a tendency* or to an *end*. And if every element of the movement is orientated towards an end, it is easy to show that the movement as a whole and in the totality of its conditions is striving towards an *ultimate end* (which is *not necessarily* a last moment *in time* of the movement itself).

If becoming or movement is essentially dynamic, we are forced by the inflexible rules of analytic logic to posit that every *becoming*, every movement which would not be a mere passive displacement, strives of itself towards some terminal rest or ultimate end, and that it strives towards it according to a well defined form (or law) which determines the tendency with respect to the end. Hence this form of a tendency really represents, at every stage of the movement, the tendency's well defined and lasting orientation towards the last end. And this specifying form is *a priori*, since the impulsion towards the last end had to be a condition previous to the very first stirring of the subject in motion. As soon as one admits the dynamism of the movement, one admits that the first stage of the movement is intelligible only through the very motion of the obscurely perceived last end.

Third proposition. The specifying form which directs *a priori* our intellectual dynamism (in scholastic terms: the adequate formal object) can only be conceived as the universal and unlimited form of being. Likewise, the " ultimate objective end " (*finis cujus* of St. Thomas), which would put the movement of our intelligence at rest, tolerates no limiting determination and must therefore be identified with the absolute Being, that is, with the " unlimited " in the domain of Act (pp. 144-177).

Fourth proposition. A discursive (non-intuitive) knowing power, which has to strive towards its end through a succession of passages from potency to act, can do this only by assimilating an outside datum. Therefore, the activity of our intelligence supposes the cooperation of a sensibility (pp. 125-143).

Fifth proposition. Since our intellectual operation is an active becoming, every act by which it assimilates new determinations, with the help of the senses, must have a double aspect: a) the aspect of an acquisition: the new determination is introduced under the *a priori* form of the intellectual becoming (in scholastic terms, under the formal object of the intellect); b) the aspect of a dynamic starting point: the determination can be assimilated only according to its dynamic relation to the ultimate End, that is, as an eventual end, as a possible means (pp. 162-198).

Sixth proposition. a) The assimilation of the datum, considered statically as a subjective acquisition, does not yet contain, for consciousness, the element of an immanent opposition of an object to a subject. b) On the other hand, the dynamic relation of the datum to the absolute End of the intellect contains—implicitly—the elements of such an opposition, hence constitutes the object as object in consciousness and connects it with the ontological order (pp. 177-198).

Seventh proposition. The intellectual assimilation of the data, inseparably joined to their introduction into the absolute order of finality, is nothing but the affirmation, the " transcendental act " or the " objective form " of the judgment. Therefore, the affirmation has a metaphysical value (pp. 149-153).

Eighth proposition. If the relation of the data to the ultimate End of the intellect is an *a priori* intrinsically "constitutive" condition of every object in our thought, the analogical knowledge of the absolute Being, as the upper and ineffable term of this relation, enters " implicitly " into our immediate consciousness of every object as object. But the fact of necessarily belonging to the necessary object of thought is the supreme speculative criterion of validity demanded by the critical philosophies. We may therefore conclude that, according to the principles of these philosophies, the affirmation of the transcendent Being, as ultimate End (and correlatively as first Cause), and likewise the absolute ontological value which derives from it for the contingent data themselves, are necessary not only in the objectivo-practical domain, but first and foremost in the objectivo-theoretical domain of reason.

If it has been established that the motion of the absolute Being, as ultimate end, controls in us every intellectual assimilation of the data of experience, we become aware of a possible metaphysical interpretation of that supreme logical and functional condition of the objective apperceptions, which, in the idealistic philosophies derived from Kantianism, receives the name of " transcendental consciousness," or " synthetic act of transcendental consciousness," or " transcendental act of the judgment," or simply " transcendental act," and so on. These various expressions designate the primitive transcendental subject, the *transcendental Ego,* considered as necessary principle of objective consciousness.

In post-Kantian idealistic monism, the transcendental Ego coincides subjectively and objectively with the absolute principle postulated by reason at the origin of all things. This Ego may posit itself absolutely as pure Ought which strives towards self-consciousness (Fichte). It may posit itself absolutely as the fundamental identity of the two opposed " becomings " of nature and of the spirit (Schelling). Or, finally, it may posit itself as absolute Idea, forever building itself, from bottom to top, through logical syntheses always completed and forever starting anew (Hegel).

Under considerable differences we discover a common trait of these great systems of idealism : we mean the logical impossibility for its absolute principle—the transcendental Ego— of reaching consciousness (hence of positing itself as an Ego) without creating in itself diverse contents, which it opposes to itself as *object* and which it recovers, as it were, as *consciousness of an object.*

The threefold speculative moment—Position, Opposition, Synthesis—of our imperfect Ego is transferred without any modification into the divine Absolute, as a primordial rational necessity. Rightly so, since the Absolute was identified with a *transcendental Ego.* For, by its very definition, the " transcendental " *refers* essentially *to the object.* It is the intellectual *light,* which is useless if there is nothing to illuminate, a light which is only darkness if it meets no screen which reflects it. Or again, the transcendental is reason's *a priori,* an *a priori* which is superfluous and even inconceivable without a content to which it applies. There exists a mutual and necessary relation between the notions of transcendental subject and conscious object. Thus the transcendental Absolute was logically and morally necessitated to posit an object.

There is a misleading element in this pantheistic error. The transcendental Ego, that is, the *a priori* of our objective knowledge, undoubtedly possesses some of the properties of an absolute. To put beside it, as Kant does, another independent absolute, that of the Thing-in-itself, might well be utterly meaningless. Moreover, how can a critical philosophy consider its task finished before it has overcome the dualism of intellect and being?

We have already remarked that, on this point, Kant's position is difficult to defend, or, at least, that it would become defensible only if he further developed his critique. The thesis of the idealistic pantheists is true, insofar as, putting the Spirit, the only Absolute, at the origin of all things, they refuse to radically oppose the Real and the Idea. But these philosophers go further: they set up, as the absolutely first principle, not the Spirit in its perfect actuality, but the Spirit or the Ego defined by the supreme *transcendental* function. By what right? In final analysis, they rely on the following presupposition: that a transcendental Ego which is absolute and infinite as *objective function* (as determination of possible objects), must likewise be absolute and infinite as *subject in itself* (as self-positing). They do not think that a transcendental Ego, which is *objectively* absolute and infinite, might be *subjectively* contingent and finite.

But this assumption is by no means necessary. Why should a finite intellect not be objectively infinite, that is, infinite as a capacity of objects? It is true that this blending of finite and infinite would be contradictory for every hypothesis but one— which Kant does not seem to have considered seriously, although he comes near to it in the *Critique of Judgment*. This hypothesis supposes that finite and infinite are reconciled through the natural finality, through the basic tendency of the intellective power. A tendency which is necessarily contingent as existence and finite as a subjective essence (*tamquam res quaedam*) may, on the other hand, be infinite in its objective capacity and absolute in the necessity it imposes upon the becoming orientated by it. The objective capacity and necessity of a tendency are measured only by the range and the necessity of its ultimate end, while the existence and subjective essence of it depend on conditions which are necessarily limiting and contingent. The first of these conditions, as may be demonstrated, is the reception of a *natural motion* proportioned to the ultimate end.

Although the transcendental act of judging, when considered as an objective function, is the ultimate exigency and the logical presupposition of the Absolute, although this exigency and this presupposition really constitute the absolute beginning in the order of the rational priority of our acts of objective knowledge, it follows by no means that the same transcendental act, considered as a " positing of self " or as subject, purely and simply coincides with the Absolute.

Yet this identification, which is erroneously made in the pantheistic systems, amounts merely to the exaggeration and deformation of a truth which Kant was unable to use in his critique of theoretical reason, because he put too much of an opposition between finality and speculation. We mean that a transcendental Ego, which is contingent and limited as a subject, cannot by *itself alone* constitute the adequate principle of an absolute objective necessity. Thus the absolute character of the objective function logically supposes similar absolute features, if not in the subject himself, who exercises this function, at least on the subject's side, in the subject's line.

This rational exigency of an authentic *subjective* absolute, as a condition of the objective absolute, can be satisfied in only two ways: by idealistic pantheism, with its antinomies and powerlessness, hidden beneath an amazing dialectical virtuosity, and by finalistic intellectualism, as exposed above. In this in-tellectualism, the absolute Spirit is the beginning and the end of everything, but *through transcendence.* As for the transcendental subject in its necessary reciprocal relation with the object, it is not an absolute, but only a function of absolute (*une fonction d'absolu*). As such it can be nothing but the very motion, both dynamic and formal, of the absolute Spirit in the innermost center of the finite intellect. The " transcendental act " derives from a transcendent Act as from its primary source.

Ninth proposition. A critique of knowledge cannot lead us beyond the conclusions set down in the eighth proposition. Once we have established—as we have done above—that an attitude of abstention or of negation before the ontological reality of the objects of thought would do away with the very possibility of objective thought, every further critical problem becomes not only fictitious, but unthinkable and contradictory.

Every hypercritical effort is self-destructive. It would suppose that the " statements " which the spirit cannot not *affirm* under pain of falling at once into logical contradiction, might still, absolutely speaking, be *false,* because their necessity derives from the natural constitution of our understanding, a constitution which is subjective and perhaps fallacious. Our most rigorously defined evidences would not undoubtedly be immune from illusion. Although their necessity *in the knowing subject* is admittedly based upon the first analytical principle, this might not be the case for their absolute necessity *in the object.*

In final analysis this subtle objection is an echo of the sophists and brings up a pseudo-problem. We can formulate it exactly to the extent that we may indifferently put any kind of " words " near each other, but logically it denies itself. No subject can, without contradiction, conceive as logically possible a hypothesis which would contain the negation of the very act by which he conceives it—or even more precisely: which would be *the negation of the very law according to which it is objectively conceived. . . .*

At the root of this objection . . . lies a false conception of the nature and the possibilities of our human knowledge. Why is the objector not satisfied with objective evidence, defined as above? Because he wishes to reach, instead of the undeniable, objective but indirect evidence of the *affirmation,* the objective direct evidence of the *ontological intuition.* He would like to see clearly not only *that* the two terms of a judgment must be united in the identity of the same *suppositum,* but *why and how* this identity is necessary in itself. He believes that he can know things rationally only by *directly penetrating into their essence.* He transforms the *natural desire* of a saturating intuition into a *logical exigency* which he wishes to impose upon every objective certitude. If this chimerical wish of knowing in a purely intuitive way were fulfilled, there would be no more need for a critique of knowledge. Thus, strangely enough, a hypercritique leading into absolute relativism turns into the worst metaphysical dogmatism. It posits arbitrarily as an unsatisfied methodological exigency what ontologism, in an equally arbitrary way, posited as a necessary mode of our understanding.

Ultimately, absolute relativism is nothing but disappointed inverse rationalism.

At this terminal point of the critique, the immediate "evidence" which accompanied the possession of the truth in the direct judgments takes on, before our reflection, a precise and handy criteriological definition, which connects it with the most fundamental theoretical necessity, that of the *first principle*. . . .

The "first principle," the principle of identity—and likewise the principle of contradiction, its negative formula—must now appear like the stable axis around which evolves every critique, whether metaphysical or transcendental. It is through the very application of the first principle that a glimmer of the absolute insinuates itself into our raw data of consciousness and raises them to the dignity of objective knowledge. It is important to note why the first principle can exert this important function.

It is not only the first foundation of the analytical judgments, but also at the same time the *a priori* synthesis par excellence, the synthesis which controls all other syntheses, because it coincides with the very life of the intellect, as faculty of being. This requires a few words of explanation.

First, it seems evident that a principle of identity, which is strictly tautological in its form, that is, which states nothing new in its predicate, but signifies only the equivalent reduplication of the "same" ("that which is = that which is") could at the utmost serve as a rule for utilizing or a norm for discovering given elements. It would add nothing to the previously acquired knowledge of elements. Such was approximately Hume's point of view.

But we cannot stop there. As soon as we endow the first principle with the mode of necessity ("that, which is, *necessarily* is that which is"), its predicate clearly extends beyond its subject. The subject expresses "that which is" only in the manner of a raw datum, of a fact about which we do not know yet whether it is contingent or necessary. Through its coherence with the copula the predicate affirms that there is in this fact something more than a brute fact, a necessity. On account of this the judgment is already extensive, synthetic.

Let us examine more closely the logical structure of the predicate. Even if we abstract from its necessity, is it, in itself, a mere repetition (*duplicatum*) of the subject? In the authentic formula of the principle of identity, " that which is, is," we notice easily that it is not. Moreover, the seemingly tautological expressions of this principle lead us to the same conclusion. When we say, " being is being," or " that which is, is that which is," the explicitated meaning of these propositions can only be the following: " being is that which has the form (*rationem*) of being," or " that which is, is that which has the *quality* (or the *form*) expressed in the words: that which is." All these judgments express, through the affirmative copula, the necessary unity of a hypothetical supposit—being as a raw datum—and of being as " intelligible." It is as if we were saying: " As soon as something is given in the manner of a supposit (that is, as existing, or connected to some existence, hence in the line of *esse*), to the same extent and under the same aspect this something is given as necessarily defined by a *form* (that is as a mode of being, hence in the line of *essence*). Hence the principle of identity expresses, in the most general possible terms, the necessary synthesis of the *quod* and the *quo* (of *that which* and *the way in which*), of existence and essence. In last analysis, it means that every being, as being, is " intelligible."

Maréchal explains then why the first principle is sometimes formulated with a mention of time, " that which is cannot at the same time not be." This derives from the " concretive synthesis," from our human manner of " representation," which is always connected with the senses, hence with matter and time.

But let us overlook this concretive duality, which the principle of identity derives from the material imperfection of our concepts. Even according to its purely rational signification it presents, as shown above, a logical structure which is clearly synthetic, since it affirms the necessary unity of every being with its intelligible essence. How can it then be absolutely necessary? Of itself no synthesis is ever necessary. Since diversity as diversity cannot be the principle of its own justification, the necessity of a synthesis must derive from the very necessity of a unity in which the diversity of the synthetic terms has disappeared. But in the principle of identity we possess already the most universal possible type of synthetic unity: *position* as " esse " and *determination* as " essence." Or again : being as *Reality* and being as *Idea*. This unity remains a duality and does not justify itself. What higher unity, by imposing implicitly its absolutely primordial necessity, might logically justify a synthesis which is so universal? Only one unity remains, the perfect unity where *Esse* and essence would coincide, where Reality and Idea would be wholly identified, the unity of the pure Act of being.

But this sovereign unity can no longer be expressed in concepts or through judgments, since concepts and judgments always contain at least the synthetic unity of the principle of identity itself. Thus the unity which justifies the logical necessity of the latter must needs be rejected outside our thought, in a subsisting Absolute. This undeniable conclusion puts epistemology before a decisive dilemma, the only one, in truth, which is logically possible. Either we accept the primitive evidence of the first principle, and we implicitly posit the absolutely Real who is also the absolute Idea. Or we reject the primitive evidence of the first principle, and with the ancient sophists we try in vain to deny thought itself by means of our thought . . . in which case, however, our impotent negativism cannot be refuted.

Therefore, the evidence of the first principle is truly the light of our intelligence, but only through the natural communication of the absolute and transcendent Unity. The latter is imprinted in our intellect as an inexorably compelling and wholly unconditional exigency of unity, an exigency which controls our primordial " syntheses " and makes us refer all their eventual contents to the absolute Reality. We do not believe that what the moderns call the " transcendental act of judgment " really designates in our intelligence in act anything but this natural grip of the Absolute, which they consider abstractively, under its purely functional aspect.

Besides, the epistemological problem raised by the first principle does not arise *first* in the abstract terms in which we have considered it above. The first principle is given to us in its application to some matter. We perceive the objective necessities of our thought only as they affect the very objects of our direct knowledge. In our distinct consciousness " this is " comes before " whatever is, is." It would be a dangerous fiction to imagine the first principle as a self-sufficient logical entity which may, in isolation, serve as a starting point for the epistemological construction. We recognize here the error of some Augustinian philosophers, who claimed that they could demonstrate the existence of God through the sole " necessary truths," independently of all logical support from the objects. Their error consisted not so much in the way they reasoned from the " necessary truths " than in the illusion which made them consider these truths objectively present to the mind by themselves and not through the *logical* mediation of the objects of experience.

MÉLANGES JOSEPH MARÉCHAL

In November 1928 Father Maréchal was invited to deliver a series of lectures at the Institut Supérieur de Philosophie of the University of Louvain. They were afterwards published in Revue néoscolastique de Philosophie (*31, 1929, pp. 27–52, 121–147 and 309–342*) *and reprinted in* Mélanges Joseph Maréchal, *the* Festschrift *published by his friends and admirers after his death in 1950, since he had rejected their plan of offering him such a tribute on the occasion of his Golden Jubilee as a Jesuit (1943). Following are a few extracts from these important lectures.*

XLII. ABSTRACTION OR INTUITION

Should we spend much time defining the formal object of metaphysics? This is a familiar theme for the scholastics. According to Aristotle's definition, taken over by St. Thomas, the object of metaphysics is being as being, *ens in quantum ens* (*In IV Metaphysics,* 1.1); not being under this or that difference, but being considered in that total universality, which excludes no particular being, perfectly universal being, hence also, since the logical properties of universality and necessity are correlative, being which is unconditionally necessary, in one word, the absolute of being.

Philosophers generally agree that the two notes of absolute universality and necessity, when affecting an objective content of thought, indicate the metaphysical value of this content. Concerning this nominal designation, no basic difference separates philosophers who, in other respects, stand as far apart as St. Thomas and Kant, Wolff and Hegel, Spinoza and Spencer, and so on. Hence we can enter into a dialogue with all of them, realists or idealists, metaphysicians or agnostics, since, right now, it does not matter whether the metaphysical foundation of reality should be called thought or being, idea or thing. By definition every object will be called metaphysical, which will display the absolute properties of universality and necessity. . . .

Hence, if possible at all, metaphysics does not tolerate being divided into two more or less connected segments: an abstractive (or inductive) metaphysics and a transcendent metaphysics. Transcendent metaphysics is the hidden soul of abstractive metaphysics. That is why the causal argument, by means of which, starting from the objects of experience, we reach the transcendent God, should in fact consist in an explicitation of the internal necessity of these objects, and not in some kind of suprastructure, whether obligatory or optional. . . .

It is undeniable that physical experience must remain the mooring mast of our metaphysics. But we cannot resign ourselves to develop a down-to-earth, cut-rate metaphysics, under the illusory pretext that the lower ontological levels, being more accessible to us, may be defended in isolation. In reality, all the levels of metaphysics are solidary and the real contest takes place at the top. A truncated metaphysics may deceive some people for a while, but its equilibrium is shaky, for it is shored by cheap stanchions, which will sooner or later be eroded and hollowed by the ceaseless work of the critique.

Hence, when I speak of metaphysics, I always mean an objective, noumenal science, which excludes from its formal object the contingent and the particular as such. Among its material objects it admits contingent and particular objects, but only *insofar as* they are endowed with universality and necessity, based upon the totally unconditioned Absolute. We do not have to examine here whether this Absolute should be immanent or transcendent, since we are trying only to cross a threshold, not to explore the dwelling which lies beyond it. Yet the answer to our question may indirectly solve this new problem. . . .

Here then is the hypothesis which forces itself upon our attention. The object of sense experience—let us call it the *physical object*—would, as soon as it enters our consciousness, contain a metempirical element, which is intimately associated with a strictly empirical element. Human science would not have to construct, on the more or less organized foundation of sense representations, an ontological interpretation of them. Our objective knowledge would start with an experience which is blended with metaphysics. Every sense perception which reaches the focus of consciousness would already be an intellectual apperception *sub ratione entis* (in the light of being), an ontological apperception.

This hypothesis is attractive and might impose itself by a process of elimination. But if we examine it more closely, it looks hard to understand and to define. It will discourage the good will of many philosophers. Does it not claim to blend water with fire?

We enter into the heart of our topic. It is no longer possible to escape the antinomy which we foresaw from the start. Before any formal application of the axioms of our reason, our objective knowledge, even of the most elementary kind, should contain two radically opposed principles. In what way will it do so?

Are they simply juxtaposed, parallel, symmetrical? What then is their coordinating principle? If their harmony is more intimate, less extrinsic, so to speak, the difficulty is even greater. What mental acrobatics are required to conceive of an immediate synthesis, almost of a compenetration, of the necessary and the contingent, the universal and the particular, the absolute and the relative?

Yet this is the option before which our problem, when we think it through to the end, will place us: within our primary apprehension of the object we must admit either some unexplainable parallelism between a purely empirical intuition and a metaphysical apperception—which would then, however we may characterize it, constitute an authentic intellectual intuition —or, on the other hand, the intimate and paradoxical synthesis of an empirical datum with a metasensible *a priori,* which would have lost the character of an intellectual intuition, while yet remaining a function aiming at the absolute (*une fonction d'absolu*).

Either term of the alternative is defended by some of the scholastics who admit the composite nature of the initial object of human knowledge and keep the word "abstraction." In the two following lectures I hope to tell you, with the modesty which befits such a thorny topic, why, in my opinion, the first term of the alternative (the parallel juxtaposition of an intuition and an abstraction in the same primitive object) provides us not with a solution to the problem but rather with a dogmatic

way out, which looks like a faraway prolongation of Platon-
ism. . . . Despite its advantages, which may be quite attractive,
our efforts will rather turn to an exploration of the second
term of the alternative (the synthesis of a non-intuitive *a priori*
with the pure datum). In this direction the only available road
starts from the Lyceum rather than from the Academy. It may
look uneven, bristling with new problems, it may shamefully
seem to reopen the question of the threshold. But, as a com-
pensation, it will lead us further than the other road. . . .

What would this straight Aristotelianism look like? We may
now define it, by contrasting it not only with all forms of open
intuitionism, but also with every doctrine in which the Platonic
principle would remain latent.

St. Thomas says, " Some, in investigating the truth about the
nature of things, have started from intelligible principles (*ex
rationibus intelligibilibus*), and this was typical of the Platonists.
Others have started from the objects of sense experience, and
this is typical of Aristotle's philosophy " (*Q. Disp. de Spir. Creat.*,
3, c). To start from intelligible principles (*ex rationibus intelligibilibus*) means to endow the intellectual subject with at least
virtual inborn ideas, or to suppose that the primordial objects
of our understanding are already, in some respect, in themselves " actually intelligible."

On the other hand, an authentic Aristotelian theory of abstraction will have to :

1) Remove from the rational subject every *a priori* representation, every *a priori* which represents objects, that is, every
kind of inborn ideas, whether formally or virtually inborn.

2) Deny the presence in the natural primitive object of our
intelligence, before the latter enters in act, of every intelligibility
in act; in other words : of every property belonging to a " pure
idea." Thus it is evident that the first natural objects of our
intelligence can only be the material objects of our sense experience.

3) Attribute nevertheless to our intelligence some " non-repre-
sentational " *a priori,* as the basis of the intelligible necessity of
the abstractions operated on the sense objects. Without such an
a priori the Aristotelian theory of knowledge would be reduced

to the level of a phenomenalistic empiricism, which is unable
to serve as the basis of a metaphysics.

Let us admit that a cognitive *a priori,* which would not even
be a virtual inborn idea, amazes and shocks us as an undecipher-
able enigma. Yet we will have to decipher it, if we do not wish
to retrace our steps, that is, to become full-fledged disciples of
Plato, after perhaps a short apprenticeship in the school of Duns
Scotus. . . .

It seems to me that we are now sufficiently aware of the
conditions imposed upon an Aristotelian theory of abstraction,
at least if we expect it not only to spin out of a formal network
covering experience, but to introduce us, through objective evidence, into the metaphysics of the transcendent. I summarize
them under four headings: we possess no *a priori* ideas in act
—there is no " intelligible in act " in the proper, primary and
immediate object of our intelligence—yet there are in us *a priori*
conditions which are capable of actualizing the potential intelligibility of the object, that is, of making of it an intelligible
object; and these conditions are such that their functioning in
objective knowledge logically implies the affirmation of the
noumenal absolute.

It does not seem easy to synthesize these four conditions. The
secret of Thomistic Aristotelianism consists precisely in this
synthesis.

Scholastic philosophy holds that, when our intellect apprehends an object, we have, on the one hand, an " intelligence
in first act " and, on the other hand, a concrete object, which
is " intelligible in potency " presented under the guise of a phantasm, of a sense image.

Intellection takes place when the intellect passes to its second
act, when the intelligible in potency becomes intelligible in act,
and when this happens in such a way that the intellect in act
and the intelligible in act coincide in the unity of an immanent
operation. *Intellectus in actu et intelligibile in actu sunt idem.*
The intellect in act and the intelligible in act are the same thing.

We shall successively examine the various elements implied in
this classical and necessary state of the question.

The intelligence at first is in potency of intelligible determinations; yet not in pure potency but in " first act," as is the case

for a faculty which, in its very passivity, remains nevertheless a principle of activity. Since it is a first act, in real potency of intelligible objects from outside, it is not indifferent with respect to these intelligibles. By nature it is made for them, tending towards them. Let us say that it is a radical tendency to possess them. St. Thomas places a "natural appetite" within every faculty, even the speculative ones. Hence we may speak of an intellectual dynamism. There is nothing more shocking in this than in calling the intellect an "operative power," a "*potentia praedicamentalis*": does *potentia* not correspond to the Greek *dúnamis,* an expression which does not originally mean a "pure undetermined passivity"?

As soon as intelligible contents are presented to the intellect in tension, the second act, the intellection, will spring forth like a spark: the natural tendency, all set in the first act, will enter into exercise, through an at least partial actuation of its "potentiality." Far from being only a passive reflection of the outside, intellection possesses the most decisive features of an expanding activity, although this activity is, at first, more an assimilating than a productive activity.

But every agent acts for an end and primarily for its ultimate end. *Finis est primum in ordine intentionis,* the end is the first thing in the order of intention. We know the proper end of a faculty from the formal object of this faculty; and the total formal object of the intellect, being as being, extends beyond every conceivable limit. It follows that the ultimate end of the intellectual activity must likewise, as objective end, equal the intelligible fullness of being, whose possession would, in the strict sense, constitute the supreme perfection, the subjective last end of the intellect.

Finally, since an activity grasps its particular objects only in virtue of its tendency towards the ultimate end, the intellect will grasp the partial intelligibles only in virtue of its tendency towards the possession of the perfect Intelligible. This assimilating dynamism of our intelligence is an integral part of Thomistic psychology. I do not believe that any Thomist will question this.

Before the intellect in first act stands the sense object, the intelligible in potency. What do we mean by this?

According to the scholastics the form is the principle of intelligibility. When the form is in act as pure form, it constitutes an idea, an actual intelligible, objectively proportioned to some intelligence. On the other hand, matter extinguishes intelligibility, because it prevents the form from being in act according to its pure formal unity. Hence material things either in themselves, or in the sense images which represent them, possess no actual intelligibility, but only some potential intelligibility, that is, a more or less proximate disposition for meeting an act of intelligibility which completes them.

St. Thomas teaches that the object which is in proximate potency of intelligibility, the object represented in the phantasm, is rendered actual (*factum in actu*) by the intellect itself, considered as principle of intelligible actuation, in short, by the agent intellect.

Wherein does this actuation consist?

Thomistic and semi-Thomistic authors generally distinguish two stages in the intelligible actuation of the phantasm:

Under the (preconscious) motion of the agent intellect, the phantasm is illuminated and raised to a higher level of efficiency. If I understand this correctly, the phantasm would, as instrumental cause (and only in this respect, for it is not physically modified), acquire a certain proportion to the possible intellect, which it must impress. The phantasm, so these authors put it, becomes *intelligible in act in the causal sense.*

Next, the combined influence of the agent intellect as a principal cause and of the subordinated phantasm produces in the potential intelligence, in the possible intellect, the impressed *species,* the idea, a real intelligible in act—the intelligible in act in the formal sense—shaped after the phantasm and exactly filling the latter's potency for intelligibility. This is the final actuation within the possible intellect, to which the Angelic Doctor alludes when, in an elliptical and often repeated formula, he assigns as function to the agent intellect, "to actuate intelligibles in potency," and to turn them into real ideas, *de non intelligibilibus in actu facere intelligibilia in actu.*

If we consider in itself the intelligible actuation contributed by the agent intellect, it seems to me that we may summarize the

authentically Thomistic data which refer to our topic under the
four following headings:

In its origin the active function of the agent intellect is nothing
but the natural communication of the " divine light " to our
intelligence under the form of the " first principles." The active
power of the agent intellect derives from the transcendent absolute of the divine intelligence the first principles, that is, being
and its transcendental properties. This is the minimum which
our intelligence does not receive from without, but from its
own natural stock. Yet our intelligence is not intuitive in the
way in which the ontologists understand it, it does not possess
an inborn idea, not even a virtually inborn idea of the trans-
cendentals. St. Thomas states it categorically: the knowledge of
the first principles and their habitual possession through formed
concepts *derives* from the abstraction performed by the agent
intellect on sense objects.

But what is left, in this event, as the agent intellect's own
fund, and how can we still say that it possesses the first principles? Let us listen to St. Thomas: " The agent intellect must
pre-exist to the habitual knowledge of the principles (*habitui
principiorum*) *as its cause* " (*Q. Disp. de Anima*, 5, c).

The answer may not seem very illuminating. Before it operates, a cause is not entirely indifferent to the determinations
brought about by it; it contains at least something of the specifications of its effect. Hence the agent intellect must somehow formally precontain the " first intelligible principles." This is more
than once asserted by St. Thomas; for instance, when speaking
of the first principle, he attributes to it this rather strange
property that " it comes from without to somebody who possesses it already by nature." This means that being and its
primary properties are represented in us *a priori,* in some manner which does not, however, imply either an inborn idea or an
intuition in the strict sense.

When we consider it in its actual exercise, we see how the
agent intellect actively subordinates the phantasm to itself
in the way in which a principal cause grasps its tool. The phantasm's instrumental causality consists merely in providing a
specification to the efficiency of the agent intellect. Such a cooperation becomes inconceivable if we think of the cooperating

elements as distinct entities. But if we think of them as merely the partial functions of one single radical activity, we see how, through it, the agent intellect imprints upon the possible intellect a formal determination molded after the qualitative features of the phantasm. *Intellectus possibilis patitur ex lumine intellectus agentis,* the possible intellect is passive with respect to the light of the agent intellect (*S.T.,* II^a-II^ae, 171, 2, ad 1). Of the formal network borrowed from the concrete phenomena in the image, the intellectual *a priori* makes a consistent " quiddity," a *quod quid est.*

In its last stage the actuation contributed to the possible intellect by the agent intellect is nothing but the *species intelligibilis* (the impressed *species*), a real idea, received in the intellectual potency. But let us not forget that the potency of the possible intellect, an immaterial power, is the potency of a " first act " tending naturally towards an end. Hence the receiving of the intelligible *species* is not a mere " passivity." It is an active assimilation which constitutes a stage in an infinite becoming. We say " infinite," because this stage is crossed under the motion of an ultimate end which cannot be inferior to the absolute Truth.

Once all the conditions of the objective assimilation have been realized, intellection will essentially consist in the luminous awareness of the acquired riches, in that " cognition " which St. Thomas considers an immediate formal effect of the lived truth, that is, of the very assimilation of the outside form.

It is a remarkable fact—and one which, although well known, is often overlooked—that, according to St. Thomas, this intellectual apperception occurs through the production of an internal structure, of a " word " which is either a judgment (*compositio aut divisio*) or a definition (*definitio*) that is, once more, a judgment, at least a virtual one. It seems to me that the production of the judicative word must coincide with the analytic[1] consciousness of the lived relation of truth, which has already been brought about in the potential intellect by the very assimilation itself, that is, by the active reception of the impressed *species.* If we understand it in this way, the mental word is by

---

[1] Apprehension is synthetic, " consciousness " is analytic.

no means a useless superfluity, but the explicit and conscious expression of the synthetic moment which came before it. In this synthesis the outside object, through the intermediary of the phantasm, contributed its share, as much as the intellective subject.

Finally, it is an essential feature of our direct intellections that they appear as immediately objective, that is, that they refer at once to an " in itself " distinct from the knowing power. This psychological feature seems, in St. Thomas' doctrine, to stand in close relation to the judicative structure of the mental word. What do we mean by objective knowledge? We no longer naïvely imagine that the intelligence opens up before its outside objects like a window before a landscape. Our intelligence knows through strict immanence. To know objectively means to know a relation of truth terminating in the object. And this, for the scholastics, is the same as to " judge." We understand then why the mental word must be a " judgment."

Such is, in its luminous simplicity, the gist of the Thomistic doctrine of intellectual abstraction.

Fr. Maréchal first published this article in 1927 in the Revue néoscolastique de Philosophie.

XLIII. ON INTELLECTUAL DYNAMISM

During the golden age of medieval realism the philosophers, who tried to build a metaphysics of knowledge, attempted mainly to explain how an outside object could according to its form become immanent to cognitive faculties. Once this intussusception had been realized, it seemed quite natural that, through it, the subject should be immediately aware of the object as an outside object. Nowadays we look at the problem from the other side, or rather, our interest focuses elsewhere. We wish above all to know how it is possible that the formal determinations which emerge in the luminous zone of consciousness make us know, at once, not their own subjective reality, but that of the " things in themselves " which they " specify."

We would like to consider this question very briefly, without display of erudition, and in the very terms in which it is set down in Thomistic rational psychology.

Let us assume that the theory of the agent intellect is correct. It logically connects the first steps of the sense object, as it enters the sanctuary of the subject and becomes the specifying form (*species*) of the intellectual faculty. Our investigation takes as its starting point the "impressed *species*" inhering in the possible intellect.

Here is the point which we wish to elucidate: How does the impressed *species* provide the subject, whom it informs, with the knowledge of an object opposed to it? How can we explain that, in the self-awareness of the subject, equipped with the *species*, the content of the latter refers at once to the extrinsic term of a relation of logical truth? For, undeniably, we have here a relation of logical truth. The intellectual knowledge of an object as object is identically the awareness of the opposition of subject and object according to a formal determination common to both: *adaequatio intellectus et rei*. The problem of objectivation and the problem of the knowledge of the true (*verum*) are one and the same problem. . . . How can we, starting from the impressed *species* inhering in the possible intellect, explain the immediate knowledge of the object as object?

Since knowledge "in second act" or "consciousness," the inner light of act, is indifferent with respect to the objectivity or the subjectivity of the immanent content which it illuminates, it is the very nature of this content previous to the act of knowledge, which should explain the presence in the subject and the actual cognoscibility of the relation of objectivity or of "logical truth." But in this respect the only possible factors are the two principles which essentially take part in the immanent operation of the possible intellect: the natural dynamism of the intellect, as "active principle," and the impressed *species* as formal principle. Hence the possible types of explanation come down to the following:

1) The impressed *species* alone, without any kind of intellectual dynamism, explains the objectivation. Since by its very nature it is relative to the object, a mere "likeness-idea," it

enters into consciousness only as the manifestation of " something else," as " the form of the other."

2) The *species* remains the sufficient condition of the objectivation. But apart from this, the natural dynamism of the intellect (considered *ut res quaedam,* as some kind of reality in nature, that is, as an assimilating agent, striving towards a last end) develops, on its side, some opposition of subject and object, which might constitute the basis of some kind of objectivation in the practical order, while the *species* is the basis of the objectivation in the speculative order.

3) The relativity of the *species,* and the intellectual dynamism, *taken together,* constitute the necessary and sufficient cause of the objectivation in the speculative order.

4) The intellectual dynamism performs this function by itself alone, while the *species* has, in the subject, only the role of a specifying form.

Of these four possible solutions, the third one, which requires, for the objectivation as such, not only the parallelism, but the strict and complementary unity of the *species* and the intellectual dynamism, is the only one which satisfies the exigencies of the question . . .

First, nothing can shed more light upon our solution than a right conception of the intellect's dynamism. To this effect we should get rid of the false assumption which would wholly separate the speculative order of knowledge from the practical order of ends. This assumption is false, because, when carried to their perfection, these two orders coincide. What end does our action intend? We are speaking here only of the ends which consist in the possession of some good. It is true that possessing some good may simply mean that we own this good, that we can keep it within the reach of our faculties. But this case touches our topic only indirectly. Only the immanent possession interests the question which we are examining. Moreover, external possession is always ultimately ordered to the realization of some immanent perfection.

When the agent, which strives towards an end, is material, its internal dynamism does not necessarily carry it beyond the formal integrity of its own nature. In every material agent, the distance between the actual imperfection of the form restricted

by matter and the specific perfection of this form gives rise
to a natural tendency and determines its range. But wherever
a finite form is, like the intellective soul, in act as form and
not simply as form of some matter, another dynamism arises,
which obeys a higher law based on the " immaterial potency "
of the form. Let us remember that the form as such is nothing
but the immediate limitation of *esse* (to be), the limitation of *act*
as such. In virtue of the principle of the infinite virtuality of
the act, the distance between the formal limitation and the
absolute fullness of *esse*, between the degree and the maximum,
must determine, in the finite form or essence, the range of an
inner drive, of an urge towards infinite self-transcendence. But
for the immaterial form, which is already perfect as a natural
form, there is only one way of self-transcending and of striving
for the perfection of being: the " objective " way, through intentional enrichment, through assimilation of intelligibles.
Hence, on its higher level, human finality no longer intends the
acquisition of " natural " but of intelligible perfections. Since
the spiritual agent cannot, without contradiction, intend in himself any other purpose than speculative possession, the last
end of the will turns out to be identical, not parallel, with that
of the intellect. Does St. Thomas not go so far as to state that
the entire finality of creation is ordered to the speculative good,
to the *truth:* " Therefore truth must be the last end of the whole
universe " (*S.c.G.,* I, 1)?

Hence the active finality of the intelligence is, in a very real
sense, a finality. Yet the term intended by it is as really a speculative state.

Let us examine more closely the last end of the intelligence.
It consists, according to St. Thomas, in the " true," not merely
in the formal rectitude of every equation established between the
intellect and the object, but in the fullness of the true considered
in its content. In other words, it is being considered intelligibly,
in all its possible fullness and perfection. This last saturating
end has to be an " intellectual intuition of being." St. Thomas
further notes that, by reaching its supreme intuition, the intellect
would reach the transcendent principle which moves it towards
all its partial and successive operations. " It is clear that the last
beatitude or happiness of man consists in his noblest operation,

which is to understand, and whose ultimate perfection must consist in this, that our intellect *enters into union with its active principle*" (*Q. Disp. de Anima*, 5, c).

This shows the extraordinary amplitude of intellectual finality. The very law of its imperfect exercise obliges us to admit, at the origin of this active finality, a first principle whose impelling power cannot be less than that of pure *esse*. And it is also *esse*, pure actuality, the absolute as wholly " in itself," which it wishes to embrace in an immediate intuition. This is, of course, an intentional, not a physical, possession, but one where the idea of being, carried by an insatiable desire, would reach such a degree of perfection that it could no longer be distinguished from the reality of being.

Thus, we discover far off at the origin and at the end of the inborn love which animates the succession of the stages of knowledge something which is, par excellence, the " Real in itself."

But every particular volition is inspired by the natural volition of the last end. Hence no activity of our intellect, no intellectual assimilation is possible but in virtue of the deep yearning whose saturating end would be the intuition of the absolute Real. Thus the reception of the impressed *species* in the possible intellect takes on the necessary meaning of a partial anticipation of the final intuitive possession. In other words, the reception of the *species* must share in that which, for the intellective subject, constitutes the attractive value of the intuition of being. But there would be no such sharing if the *species* were not in some way a manifestation of real being, if it did not yield (however imperfectly) some *being*. For, in that case, there would be a total disproportion between a secondary subordinated end and the last end; the reception of the *species* would constitute a metaphysical impossibility. From its very start the whole apprehensive activity of the intellect is carried out under the sign of the *true*, that is, in function of being in itself.

Of course, the particular acts of the intellect grasp being only in an imperfect way. They are imperfect, first, from the point of view of extension, since the partial acts of the intellect represent the beings not simply as beings, but always as *this* or *that* being, without ever exhausting the formal capacity of thought through the sum of their diversity. Exactly as when " lower terms " subsumed under a universal, are, despite their multitude, surpassed by the infinite capacity of the universal. Next, these particular apprehensions of being are imperfect not only from the point of view of their formal diversity, but also in the intensive line of being as such. Whatever the intellect apprehends this side of its last intuition is necessarily compared with an implicitly willed *maximum* which is nothing but the actual fullness of *esse*. Every finite determination must be assimilated as an *intensive degree* of being.

. . . We may conclude: to know *objectively* is to assume, with respect to a content of consciousness, the attitudes described above. To know the *objectivity* of knowledge is to be aware of these attitudes insofar as they express a definite relation of subject and object. In a spiritual subject, who knows himself in his operations, objective knowledge is always to some extent, at least vaguely, a reflexive knowledge of the very mode of objectivity, that is, of the " logical truth."

The three moments—we might call them retrospective, actual and prospective—which we have distinguished in every undivided stage of the assimilation, blend with the *species* which is *species* only because it corresponds to their dynamism. In fact, the actual consciousness which we have of the *species*, according to the dynamic implications which refer it to the object, is expressed in the " mental word " which is formally or equivalently a judgment. This word always presents a formal content, that of the *species* under a complex structure (*definitio*, or *compositio et divisio, enuntiatio*) which reveals an objectivating dynamism, that of the assimilating subject. The affirmation—without which the two structural modes of the " word," the " definition " and the " enunciation," would be impossible— is nothing but the awareness of the " absolute positing " (that is, of the referring to the perfect intelligible), which is implied in every intentional apprehension of outside forms.

Thus we understand the seemingly so divergent properties which the Thomists ascribe to the mental word. As an " internal locution " it is objectively present to the mind while yet in no way standing in the way of the outside object meant by it. It is the immediate " formal sign " (*quo* or *in quo*: " by means of which " or " in which ") of the object. No need of any inference from it to the object. This paradox, which puzzles many moderns, conceals an elementary and profound truth: there is no problem concerning the passage from the mental word (or from the conscious representation) to the known object, because as soon as there is a mental word, and for the same reason, there is a known object. There simply is no passing from one to the other.

Of course, this volatilization of a false problem supposes that we have demonstrated that the objective meaning possessed by the mental word, far from being added to it through some secondary operation of the intellect, is born with it and originates from its constitutive law. It is easy to see that the dynamic interpretation proposed above fulfills this condition. We even submit that it is the only one which does.